Who We Are

BLACKS

DATE DUE

Demco

Who We Are

BLACKS

2nd EDITION

BY THE NEW STRATEGIST EDITORS

New Strategist Publications, Inc.

Ithaca, New York

New Strategist Publications, Inc.
P.O. Box 242, Ithaca, New York 14851
800/848-0842; 607/273-0913
www.newstrategist.com

ISBN 978-1-935775-33-1 (hardcover)
ISBN 1-935775-34-8 (paper)

Printed in the United States of America

Table of Contents

List of Tables

Chapter 3. Health

Chapter 4. Housing

Chapter 7. Living Arrangements

Chapter 8. Population

Chapter 9. Spending

List of Illustrations

Introduction

The 2010 census surprised us: The population of the United States turned out to be even more diverse than the Census Bureau had anticipated. Fully 36 percent of the nation's residents are Asian, African American, Hispanic, or another minority. The count of minorities was 3 million people greater and 1 percentage point bigger than the Census Bureau had estimated.

The 2010 census counted 42 million blacks in the United States—or one in seven Americans. Blacks have made tremendous strides in education and earning power over the past few decades and become decidedly middle class. Two other minority groups are also central to the U.S. culture and economy: Hispanics are the largest minority and growing rapidly. Asians are highly educated and more affluent than non-Hispanic whites. Only by understanding each of these increasingly important segments of the population can policymakers and businesses hope to tailor their programs and products to the wants and needs of the more than 308 million Americans.

The second edition of *Who We Are: Blacks* provides a comprehensive look at the characteristics of this fast growing and politically powerful minority. In addition to detailed 2010 census counts of the numbers of blacks nationally and by state and metropolitan area, *Who We Are: Blacks* includes the latest socioeconomic data on the black population. It has detailed spending data for black households and the latest update on black household wealth—including the impact of the Great Recession on black net worth, assets, and debt. Results from the American Time Use Survey can also be found here, profiling black time use and comparing it with the averages. Attitudinal data from the General Social Survey compare and contrast black attitudes with those of Asians, Hispanics, and whites on a whole range of issues.

Understanding the demographics and lifestyles of racial and ethnic groups is of vital importance to researchers and policymakers. *Who We Are: Blacks* provides the key to understanding both the similarities and differences between blacks and other Americans. Regardless of race or ethnic origin, there is no doubt Americans are more alike than different, and *Who We Are: Blacks* documents our many similarities. But there are also important differences among racial and ethnic groups that, if not taken into account, can derail public policy efforts and business strategies. The living arrangements of blacks differ from those of the average American, for example, and those differences affect not only lifestyles but also consumer behavior. The substantial educational, employment, and economic gains made by blacks over the past few decades and documented in these pages, are contrary to popular perception and media portrayals, but these realities are of utmost importance to policymakers and business leaders.

Racial classification

The 2010 census used the same racial definitions that were first introduced in the 2000 census, which transformed racial classification in the United States. The 2000 census allowed Americans, for the first time in modern history, to identify with more than one racial group. This made the analysis of racial and ethnic diversity more complex, but also more rewarding.

To understand the federal government's racial classification system, you need to understand three terms: race alone, race in combination, and race alone or in combination. The "race alone" population consists of people who identify themselves as being of only one race. The "race in combination" population consists of people who identify themselves as being of more than one race, such as black and white. The "race, alone or in combination" population includes both those who identify themselves as being of one race and those who identify themselves as being of more than one race. For example, the "black, alone or in combination" population includes those who say they are black alone and those who say they are black and white and those who say they are black, white, and Asian, and so on.

While the new classification system is a goldmine for researchers, the numbers do not add up. This may frustrate some, but it provides a more accurate picture of each racial group than the old classification scheme did, which required the multiracial to align with only one race. Under the current methodology, however, tables that show the "race alone" population exclude the multiracial. Tables that show the "race in combination" population count some people more than once. To make matters even more complex, Hispanics are considered an ethnic group rather than a race and can be black, white, or Asian. Keep these factors in mind as you peruse the numbers.

Whenever possible, the tables in *Who We Are: Blacks* show the "race alone or in combination" populations. We prefer this classification because it includes everyone who identifies with a particular racial group and does not exclude the multiracial. In some instances, the "race alone or in combination" population figures are not available. In these cases, the "race alone" population is shown. The racial classification used is noted at the bottom of each table, if the information is available. Note that some data sources do not define their racial classifications.

How to use this book

Who We Are: Blacks is designed for easy use. It is divided into 11 chapters arranged alphabetically: Attitudes, Education, Health, Housing, Income, Labor Force, Living Arrangements, Population, Spending, Time Use, and Wealth. Descriptive text and charts accompany most of the tables, highlighting the important trends.

Most of the tables in *Who We Are: Blacks* are based on data collected by the federal government, in particular the Census Bureau, the Bureau of Labor Statistics, the National Center for Education Statistics, the National Center for Health Statistics, and the Federal

Reserve Board. The federal government continues to be the best source of up-to-date, reliable information on the changing characteristics of Americans.

Several government databases are of particular importance to *Who We Are: Blacks*. One is the 2010 census, the findings of which are included here if they were available at the time of publication. Another important source is the Census Bureau's Current Population Survey. The CPS is a nationally representative survey of the civilian noninstitutional population aged 15 or older. The Census Bureau takes the CPS monthly, collecting information from 50,000 households on employment and unemployment. Each year, the March survey includes a demographic supplement that is the source of most national data on the characteristics of Americans, such as their educational attainment, living arrangements, and incomes. CPS data appear in many tables of this book.

The American Community Survey is another important source of data for *Who We Are: Blacks*. The ACS is an ongoing nationwide survey of 250,000 households per month, providing detailed demographic data at the community level. Designed to replace the census long-form questionnaire, the ACS includes more than 60 questions that formerly appeared on the long form, such as queries about language spoken at home, income, and education. ACS data are available for the nation, regions, states, counties, metropolitan areas, and smaller geographic units.

The Consumer Expenditure Survey is the data source for the Spending chapter. Sponsored by the Bureau of Labor Statistics, the CEX is an ongoing study of the day-to-day spending of American households. The data collected by the survey are used to update prices for the Consumer Price Index. The CEX includes an interview survey and a diary survey administered to two separate, nationally representative samples. The average spending figures shown in the Spending chapter of this book are the integrated data from both the diary and interview components of the survey. For the interview survey, about 7,500 consumer units are interviewed on a rotating panel basis each quarter for five consecutive quarters. For the diary survey, another 7,500 consumer units keep weekly diaries of spending for two consecutive weeks.

The Bureau of Labor Statistics' American Time Use Survey (ATUS) is the source of data for the Time Use chapter. Through telephone interviews with a nationally representative sample of noninstitutionalized Americans aged 15 or older, ATUS collects information in minute detail about what survey respondents did during the previous 24 hours—or diary day. Time use data allow social scientists to better understand our economy and lifestyle and how policy decisions affect our lives.

The data in the Wealth chapter come from the Survey of Consumer Finances, a triennial survey taken by the Federal Reserve Board. The SCF collects data on the assets, debt, and net worth of American households. In a unique effort, the Federal Reserve Board funded a follow-up of its 2007 survey and re-interviewed participants in 2009 to collect information on the impact of the Great Recession on household wealth. Those findings are presented here.

Note that the SCF provides wealth data for only two racial and ethnic groups: "non-Hispanic whites" and "non-whites and Hispanics." There are no wealth data for Asians.

To compare and contrast the attitudes of blacks with those of Asians, Hispanics, and whites, New Strategist extracted custom data from the nationally representative General Social Survey of the University of Chicago's National Opinion Research Center. NORC conducts the biennial GSS through face-to-face interviews with an independently drawn, representative sample of 3,000 to 4,000 noninstitutionalized people aged 18 or older in the United States. The GSS is the best source of data on American attitudes available today.

The outsourcing of trend analysis

Most of the tables in *Who We Are: Blacks* are based on data collected by the federal government, which continues to be the best, if not the only, source of up-to-date, reliable information on the changing characteristics of Americans. For those who need to know the trends, there is no better source than the government's massive demographic and socioeconomic databases. But searching, downloading, and analyzing information from these databases can be time consuming. Essentially, the government has outsourced the job of uncovering the trends to bloggers, market researchers, students, and library visitors, many of whom may feel overwhelmed by computer screens filled with numbers. In short, it has become more time consuming than ever to track the trends.

In *Who We Are: Blacks*, New Strategist has done the work for you. Although the government collected most of the data presented here, each table in *Who We Are: Blacks* was handcrafted by New Strategist's demographers. Our editors have spent hundreds of hours scouring government web sites, extracting numbers, creating tables that reveal trends, and producing indexes, percent distributions, and other calculations that provide context. *Who We Are: Blacks* has the numbers and the stories behind them. Thumbing through its pages, you can gain more insight into the dynamics of the black population than you could by spending all afternoon surfing databases on the Internet. By having *Who We Are: Blacks* on your computer (with links to the Excel version of each table) or on your bookshelf, you can get the answers to your questions faster than you can online—no calculator required. Researchers who want to go further can use the source listed at the bottom of each table to explore the original data. The book contains a comprehensive table list to help readers locate the information they need. For a more detailed search, use the index at the back of the book. Also in the back of the book is the glossary, which defines most of the terms commonly used in the tables and text.

Who We Are: Blacks gives you the opportunity to discover and become familiar with the large and rapidly growing black population and its many unique characteristics. Armed with such knowledge, you will be closer to understanding what the future holds for our vast and complex nation.

Executive Summary

What You Need to Know about Blacks

The United States is no longer about to be transformed into a multicultural melting pot. It already has been transformed. In 2010, 36 percent of the population—more than 100 million people—were black, Hispanic, Asian, or another minority. Keeping track of the changing racial and ethnic makeup of the nation requires more than hearsay and hunches. It requires more than cursory attention to media reports—which are usually wrong. To seize the opportunity, you need to know the facts about the country's growing minority populations. Whether you are a marketer, retailer, manufacturer, politician, policymaker, or social service provider, the nation's Asians, blacks, and Hispanics are a growing share of your customers and constituents.

Unfortunately, many Americans know little about the racial and ethnic make-up of the population. The public often wildly overestimates the size of minority groups while at the same time underestimating or even ignoring their powerful influence. In these difficult times, getting it wrong can mean the difference between profit and loss, winning and losing, successful programs and failures. To keep you informed, the summary charts below highlight the most important facts you need to know about the nation's black or African American population. More details are available in the chapters that follow. Use these charts as a starting point for generating product ideas, developing marketing insights, and creating innovative policies.

1. Blacks are the second-largest minority in the United States.

The 2010 census counted 42 million blacks and 50 million Hispanics in the United States. Because the Asian, black, and Hispanic populations are growing faster than the non-Hispanic white population, the non-Hispanic white share of the population is shrinking. The nation's minorities now account for more than one-third of Americans. (For more information, see the population chapter.)

Fourteen percent of Americans are black

(percent of population by race and Hispanic origin, 2010)

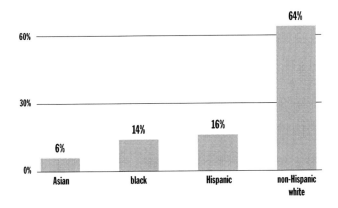

2. More than half of blacks live in the South

The 55 percent majority of blacks live in the South, where they account for 20 percent of the region's population. A substantial 13 percent of the residents of the Northeast are black, as are 11 percent of Midwesterners. In the West, only 6 percent of the population is black.

Only 10 percent of blacks live in the West

(percent distribution of the black population by region, 2010)

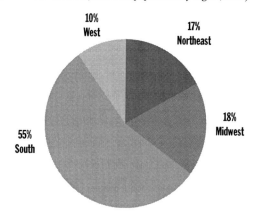

3. Blacks are a large share of some state populations

Blacks account for more than one in four residents of six states, all in the South. In ten metropolitan areas, blacks account for more than 40 percent of the population. Seven metropolitan areas are home to more than 1 million blacks: Atlanta, Chicago, Houston, Miami, New York, Philadelphia, and Washington, D.C. (For more information, see the population chapter.)

Nearly one-third of Georgia's population is black

(black share of population in the states in which blacks account for at least 25 percent of residents, 2010)

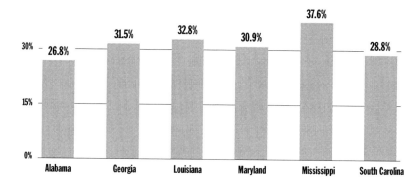

4. Blacks believe in the American Dream

Seventy-six percent of blacks agree with the statement, "The way things are in America, people like me and my family have a good chance of improving our standard of living." Blacks are as likely as Hispanics to believe in the American Dream, and they are more likely to believe than Asians (69 percent) or whites (53 percent). (For more information, see the attitudes chapter.)

Blacks are optimistic about opportunities in the United States

(percent of people aged 18 or older who agree with the statement, "The way things are in America, people like me and my family have a good change of improving our standard of living," by race and Hispanic origin, 2010)

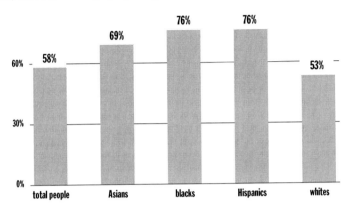

5. Black couples have relatively high incomes

Black household incomes are below average largely because married couples—the most affluent household type—head relatively few black households. Female-headed families—one of the poorest household types—are almost as numerous as married couples among black households (28 versus 29 percent, respectively), pulling down black household income statistics. (For more information, see the income chapter.)

The median income of black couples is well above average

(median income of total and black households by household type, 2009)

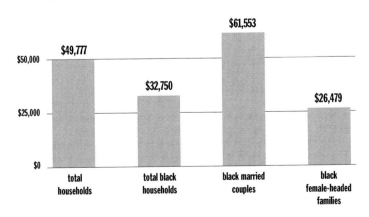

6. Black incomes are rising

Although the incomes of black households have fallen recently because of the Great Recession (a decline experienced by every racial and ethnic group), the big picture shows that black incomes have been growing faster than average. Between 1990 and 2009, the median household income of blacks grew 10 percent, after adjusting for inflation—more than twice as fast as the median income of all households during those years. The median income of black men also grew rapidly between 1990 and 2009, in contrast to a decline in the median income of all men. Behind the rising incomes of blacks is their growing educational attainment. (For more information, see the income chapter.)

Black household incomes are growing faster than average

(percent change in median income of total and black households, 1990 to 2009; in 2009 dollars)

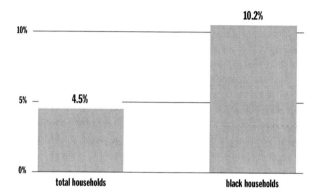

The incomes of black men are also growing faster than average

(percent change in median income of total and black men who work full-time, 1990 to 2009; in 2009 dollars)

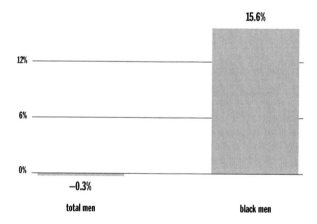

7. Most blacks are not poor

The 74 percent majority of blacks are not poor. Although the poverty rate of blacks is higher than average, it is lower than it used to be as blacks have made gains in education and employment. The black poverty rate fell from 31.9 percent in 1990 to 25.9 percent in 2009. Among black married couples, only 8.6 percent are poor. (For more information, see the income chapter.)

The black poverty rate has declined

(percent of blacks with incomes below poverty level, 1990 and 2009)

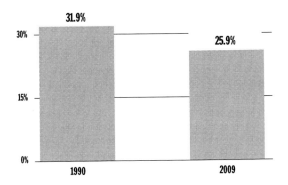

8. Most black children are born out of wedlock

Black women gave birth to 623,029 babies in 2008, and 72 percent of those children were born out-of-wedlock. This high rate of out-of-wedlock childbearing creates female-headed families. (For more information, see the health chapter.)

More than 70 percent of black babies are born to single mothers

(percent of total and black babies born out of wedlock, 2008)

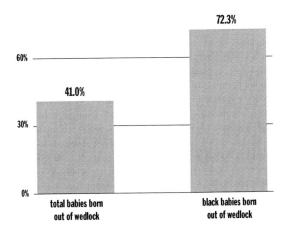

9. Black households spend more on many products

Black household spending is below average because so many households are female-headed families. On many individual items, blacks spend more than the average household. They spend 10 percent more than average on residential telephone service, for example, and 33 percent more on footwear. (For more information, see the spending chapter.)

Black households spend about $35,000 a year

(average annual spending of total and black households, 2009)

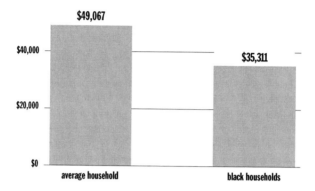

10. Blacks spend more time in religious activities

Nothing distinguishes black time use from average time use as much as their involvement in religious activities. On an average day, blacks spend nearly twice as much time as the average person participating in religious activities. (For more information, see the time use chapter.)

More than one in eight blacks participate in religious activities on an average day

(percent of total people and blacks aged 15 or older who participated in religious activities as a primary activity on an average day, 2009)

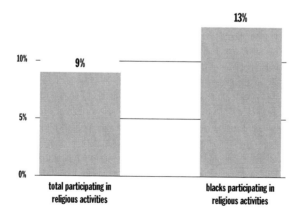

1

Attitudes

■ More blacks think life is exciting (49 percent) than think it is only routine (41 percent).

■ Only 13 percent of blacks say most people can be trusted. Blacks and Hispanics are far less trusting than Asians or whites.

■ Blacks are more likely than Asians, Hispanics, or whites to think their family income is below average. Forty-seven percent said their income was below average in 2010.

■ Only 17 percent of blacks are satisfied with their personal financial situation, less than the proportion among Asians (26 percent) or whites (25 percent) but greater than the share among Hispanics (11 percent).

■ Fifty-eight percent of blacks say their standard of living is at least somewhat better than their parents' was at the same age.

■ Blacks are less likely than any other racial or ethnic group to believe in evolution, with only 42 percent agreeing that humans developed from earlier species of animals. Fifty-six percent of blacks believe the Bible is the actual word of God.

■ Most blacks do not support same-sex marriage. Only 36 percent agree that gays and lesbians should have the right to marry.

■ Asians, blacks, and Hispanics favor the Democratic party. Seventy-two percent of blacks identify themselves as Democrats, while only 12 percent say they are Republicans.

Most People Say They Are Pretty Happy

But few trust others.

By race and Hispanic origin, the 52 to 64 percent majority of each racial and ethnic group feels pretty happy. But a substantial 20 to 21 percent of Asians, blacks, and Hispanics admit that they are not too happy, far above the 12 percent of whites who feel that way.

Most husbands and wives say they are very happily married. The proportion is above 50 percent for blacks, Hispanics, and whites. Among Asians, however, the figure is slightly below the 50 percent mark.

The share of Americans who say life is exciting (52 percent) substantially tops the percentage saying it is pretty routine (43 percent). The majority of Asians, Hispanics, and whites think life is exciting. Among blacks, the figure is slightly below 50 percent. Nine percent of blacks say life is dull.

Few believe most people can be trusted. Only 32 percent of the total public agrees that most people can be trusted. Blacks and Hispanics are far less trusting than Asians or whites.

■ The low levels of trust among blacks and Hispanics is a problem for marketers who need to convince potential customers of the value of their products or services.

Blacks and Hispanics are less trusting

(percent of people aged 18 or older who think most people can be trusted, by race and Hispanic origin, 2010)

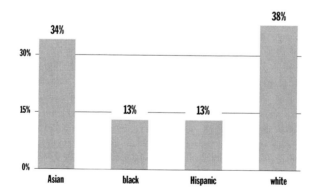

Table 1.1 General Happiness, 2010

"Taken all together, how would you say things are these days—
would you say that you are very happy, pretty happy, or not too happy?"

(percent of people aged 18 or older responding by race and Hispanic origin, 2010)

	very happy	pretty happy	not too happy
Total people	**28.8%**	**57.0%**	**14.2%**
Asian	14.8	64.1	21.1
Black	24.6	55.3	20.1
Hispanic	27.9	52.4	19.7
White	30.8	57.0	12.2

Note: Hispanics may be of any race.
Source: Survey Documentation and Analysis, Computer-assisted Survey Methods Program, University of California, Berkeley, General Social Surveys, 1972–2010 Cumulative Data Files, Internet site http://sda.berkeley.edu/cgi-bin32/hsda?harcsda+gss10; calculations by New Strategist

Table 1.2 Happiness of Marriage, 2010

"Taking all things together, how would you describe your marriage?"

(percent of married people aged 18 or older responding by race and Hispanic origin, 2010)

	very happy	pretty happy	not too happy
Total people	**63.0%**	**34.3%**	**2.6%**
Asian	49.8	47.6	2.5
Black	54.7	41.9	3.4
Hispanic	50.5	47.2	2.3
White	64.9	32.6	2.5

Note: Hispanics may be of any race.
Source: Survey Documentation and Analysis, Computer-assisted Survey Methods Program, University of California, Berkeley, General Social Surveys, 1972–2010 Cumulative Data Files, Internet site http://sda.berkeley.edu/cgi-bin32/hsda?harcsda+gss10; calculations by New Strategist

Table 1.3 Life Exciting or Dull, 2010

"In general, do you find life exciting, pretty routine, or dull?"

(percent of people aged 18 or older responding by race and Hispanic origin, 2010)

	exciting	pretty routine	dull
Total people	**52.1%**	**43.3%**	**4.6%**
Asian	51.4	45.2	3.4
Black	49.5	41.4	9.1
Hispanic	51.9	45.1	3.1
White	52.5	43.8	3.7

Note: Hispanics may be of any race.
Source: Survey Documentation and Analysis, Computer-assisted Survey Methods Program, University of California, Berkeley, General Social Surveys, 1972–2010 Cumulative Data Files, Internet site http://sda.berkeley.edu/cgi-bin32/hsda?harcsda+gss10; calculations by New Strategist

Table 1.4 Trust in Others, 2010

"Generally speaking, would you say that most people can be trusted or that you can't be too careful in life?"

(percent of people aged 18 or older responding by race and Hispanic origin, 2010)

	can trust	cannot trust	depends
Total people	**32.2%**	**62.5%**	**5.3%**
Asian	34.3	55.5	10.2
Black	12.7	81.2	6.0
Hispanic	13.5	84.9	1.6
White	37.6	57.3	5.1

Note: Hispanics may be of any race.
Source: Survey Documentation and Analysis, Computer-assisted Survey Methods Program, University of California, Berkeley, General Social Surveys, 1972–2010 Cumulative Data Files, Internet site http://sda.berkeley.edu/cgi-bin32/hsda?harcsda+gss10; calculations by New Strategist

Most Think Hard Work Leads to Success

Many Asians, blacks, and Hispanics doubt that private enterprise can solve U.S. problems.

How do people get ahead? Nearly 70 percent of Americans say it is through hard work, and another one-fifth cite a combination of hard work and luck. By race and Hispanic origin, the majority of blacks, Hispanics, and whites believe hard work is the answer. Among Asians, only 43 percent feel this way. A larger 44 percent of Asians believe it is a combination of hard work and luck that leads to success.

There are large differences in the lifetime geographic mobility of Americans by race and Hispanic origin. In 2010, nearly half of Asians and Hispanics said they had lived outside their current state of residence at age 16. Many probably lived outside the United States when they were teenagers. Among blacks and whites, only 30 to 34 percent say they lived outside their current state of residence at age 16. Half of blacks are in the same city they lived in at age 16.

Forty-five percent of the public thinks private enterprise will solve our problems. Among Asians, blacks, and Hispanics, the figure is much smaller. Just 24 percent of blacks think private enterprise will come to our rescue. The figure is 35 percent among Asians and 38 percent among Hispanics. In contrast, nearly half (49 percent) of whites see private enterprise as the answer. The 62 percent majority of blacks agree that we worry too much about the environment and too little about the economy. Nearly half of Hispanics agree. Among Asians and whites, the figures are a smaller 35 and 39 percent, respectively.

■ Anxiety about the economy is making many people question their stance on environmental issues.

Blacks doubt that private enterprise will solve our problems

(percent of people aged 18 or older who agree that private enterprise will solve U.S. problems, by race and Hispanic origin, 2010)

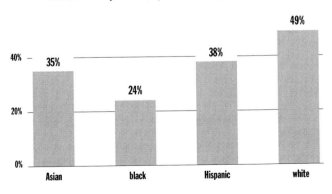

Table 1.5 How People Get Ahead, 2010

"Some people say that people get ahead by their own hard work; others say that lucky breaks or help from other people are more important. Which do you think is most important?"

(percent of people aged 18 or older responding by race and Hispanic origin, 2010)

	hard work	both equally	luck
Total people	**69.6%**	**20.4%**	**10.0%**
Asian	42.6	44.1	13.3
Black	64.8	21.0	14.2
Hispanic	84.0	9.3	6.7
White	71.5	19.8	8.7

Note: Hispanics may be of any race.
Source: Survey Documentation and Analysis, Computer-assisted Survey Methods Program, University of California, Berkeley, General Social Surveys, 1972–2010 Cumulative Data Files, Internet site http://sda.berkeley.edu/cgi-bin32/hsda?harcsda+gss10; calculations by New Strategist

---

Table 1.6 Geographic Mobility since Age 16, 2010

"When you were 16 years old, were you living in this same (city/town/county)?"

(percent of people aged 18 or older responding by race and Hispanic origin, 2010)

	same city	same state different city	outside state
Total people	**39.4%**	**25.7%**	**34.9%**
Asian	35.2	16.8	48.0
Black	50.4	19.7	29.9
Hispanic	34.6	15.7	49.7
White	37.6	28.0	34.4

Note: Hispanics may be of any race.
Source: Survey Documentation and Analysis, Computer-assisted Survey Methods Program, University of California, Berkeley, General Social Surveys, 1972–2010 Cumulative Data Files, Internet site http://sda.berkeley.edu/cgi-bin32/hsda?harcsda+gss10; calculations by New Strategist

Table 1.7 Private Enterprise Will Solve Problems, 2010

"Private enterprise will solve U.S. problems. Do you agree or disagree?"

(percent of people aged 18 or older responding by race and Hispanic origin, 2010)

	strongly agree	agree	neither agree nor disagree	disagree	strongly disagree
Total people	**14.4%**	**30.2%**	**27.5%**	**22.8%**	**5.1%**
Asian	13.4	21.7	25.1	36.9	2.9
Black	8.2	15.4	24.7	40.3	11.3
Hispanic	8.4	29.3	35.8	20.0	6.4
White	15.8	33.6	27.8	18.9	3.9

Note: Hispanics may be of any race.
Source: Survey Documentation and Analysis, Computer-assisted Survey Methods Program, University of California, Berkeley, General Social Surveys, 1972–2010 Cumulative Data Files, Internet site http://sda.berkeley.edu/cgi-bin32/hsda?harcsda+gss10; calculations by New Strategist

Table 1.8 Environment versus Economy, 2010

"We worry too much about the environment, too little about the economy. Do you agree or disagree?"

(percent of people aged 18 or older responding by race and Hispanic origin, 2010)

	strongly agree	agree	neither agree nor disagree	disagree	strongly disagree
Total people	**10.2%**	**32.3%**	**18.1%**	**31.7%**	**7.7%**
Asian	11.8	23.1	30.4	29.5	5.3
Black	21.3	40.4	11.4	23.5	3.3
Hispanic	8.6	40.3	20.6	23.8	6.7
White	8.0	30.6	18.9	33.7	8.9

Note: Hispanics may be of any race.
Source: Survey Documentation and Analysis, Computer-assisted Survey Methods Program, University of California, Berkeley, General Social Surveys, 1972–2010 Cumulative Data Files, Internet site http://sda.berkeley.edu/cgi-bin32/hsda?harcsda+gss10; calculations by New Strategist

Blacks and Hispanics Call Themselves Working Class

Asians and whites are most likely to identify themselves as middle class.

Among all Americans in 2010, only 42 percent identified themselves as middle class while a larger 47 percent said they were working class. Hispanics are least likely to put themselves in the middle class (25 percent) and most likely to identify as working class (66 percent). Among blacks, the 55 percent majority says they are working class and 28 percent call themselves middle class. Asians are more likely than whites to call themselves middle class (49 percent versus 46 percent).

Thirty-six percent of Americans say their family income is below average. By race and Hispanic origin, blacks and Hispanics are most likely to say their income is below average (47 and 46 percent, respectively). Asians are most likely to say their family income is above average (29 percent).

Only 23 percent of the public is satisfied with their present financial situation. The figure is smallest among Hispanics (11 percent) and largest among Asians and whites (26 and 25 percent, respectively). Blacks are most likely to say they are not at all satisfied with their finances, 44 percent feeling that way.

■ Asians are most satisfied with their finances because their incomes are higher than those of blacks, Hispanics, or whites.

Hispanics are least likely to say they are satisfied with their financial situation

(percent of people aged 18 or older who are satisfied with their present financial situation, by race and Hispanic origin, 2010)

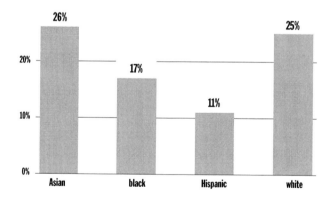

Table 1.9 Social Class Membership, 2010

"If you were asked to use one of four names for your social class,
which would you say you belong in: the lower class, the
working class, the middle class, or the upper class?"

(percent of people aged 18 or older responding by race and Hispanic origin, 2010)

	lower	working	middle	upper
Total people	**8.2%**	**46.8%**	**42.4%**	**2.5%**
Asian	7.2	42.5	48.9	1.3
Black	14.2	55.1	28.1	2.6
Hispanic	9.0	65.5	25.3	0.2
White	7.0	44.0	46.4	2.6

Note: Hispanics may be of any race.
Source: Survey Documentation and Analysis, Computer-assisted Survey Methods Program, University of California, Berkeley, General Social Surveys, 1972–2010 Cumulative Data Files, Internet site http://sda.berkeley.edu/cgi-bin32/ hsda?harcsda+gss10; calculations by New Strategist

Table 1.10 Family Income Relative to Others, 2010

"Compared with American families in general, would you say
your family income is far below average, below average,
average, above average, or far above average?"

(percent of people aged 18 or older responding by race and Hispanic origin, 2010)

	far below average	below average	average	above average	far above average
Total people	**6.8%**	**28.8%**	**43.5%**	**18.4%**	**2.5%**
Asian	2.6	22.7	45.6	25.5	3.7
Black	10.9	36.0	45.3	7.6	0.2
Hispanic	7.9	37.9	47.4	5.3	1.5
White	6.0	26.8	42.8	21.5	2.9

Note: Hispanics may be of any race.
Source: Survey Documentation and Analysis, Computer-assisted Survey Methods Program, University of California, Berkeley, General Social Surveys, 1972–2010 Cumulative Data Files, Internet site http://sda.berkeley.edu/cgi-bin32/ hsda?harcsda+gss10; calculations by New Strategist

Table 1.11 Satisfaction with Financial Situation, 2010

"We are interested in how people are getting along financially these days. So far as you and your family are concerned, would you say that you are pretty well satisfied with your present financial situation, more or less satisfied, or not satisfied at all?"

(percent of people aged 18 or older responding by race and Hispanic origin, 2010)

	satisfied	more or less satisfied	not at all satisfied
Total people	**23.3%**	**45.2%**	**31.5%**
Asian	26.2	49.9	23.8
Black	17.0	38.9	44.1
Hispanic	11.0	57.2	31.8
White	25.4	45.5	29.1

Note: Hispanics may be of any race.
Source: Survey Documentation and Analysis, Computer-assisted Survey Methods Program, University of California, Berkeley, General Social Surveys, 1972–2010 Cumulative Data Files, Internet site http://sda.berkeley.edu/cgi-bin32/ hsda?harcsda+gss10; calculations by New Strategist

Many Think Their Standard of Living Is Falling

Fewer Americans believe they are better off than their parents.

When comparing their own standard of living now with that of their parents when they were the same age, 59 percent of respondents say they are better off. The figure was a higher 67 percent 10 years ago. Asians and Hispanics are more likely than blacks or whites to say they are doing better than their parents.

When asked whether they think they have a good chance of improving their present standard of living, only 58 percent of Americans agree. A decade earlier, fully 77 percent felt optimistic. By race and Hispanic origin, whites are least likely to feel like they will be able to get ahead. Only 53 percent of whites think they have a good chance of improving their standard of living.

Fifty-nine percent of parents believe their children will have a better standard of living when they reach their age. The share was a larger 69 percent 10 years earlier. Hispanics are most likely to think things will improve for their children, 81 percent feeling that way.

■ Americans who have the least are most likely to believe that things will get better.

Most think their children will be better off

(percent of parents who think their children's standard of living will be better than theirs is today, by race and Hispanic origin, 2010)

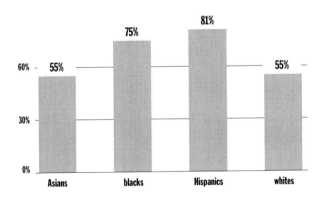

Table 1.12 Parents' Standard of Living, 2010

"Compared to your parents when they were the age you are now, do you think your own standard of living now is much better, somewhat better, about the same, somewhat worse, or much worse than theirs was?"

(percent of people aged 18 or older responding by race and Hispanic origin, 2010)

	much better	somewhat better	about the same	somewhat worse	much worse
Total people	29.2%	29.7%	24.8%	12.1%	4.2%
Asian	60.0	18.4	14.0	7.6	0.0
Black	29.8	28.6	25.6	8.9	7.1
Hispanic	35.4	37.7	14.5	7.0	5.4
White	27.3	30.1	26.2	12.8	3.6

Note: Hispanics may be of any race.
Source: Survey Documentation and Analysis, Computer-assisted Survey Methods Program, University of California, Berkeley, General Social Surveys, 1972–2010 Cumulative Data Files, Internet site http://sda.berkeley.edu/cgi-bin32/hsda?harcsda+gss10; calculations by New Strategist

Table 1.13 Standard of Living Will Improve, 2010

"The way things are in America, people like me and my family have a good chance of improving our standard of living. Do you agree or disagree?"

(percent of people aged 18 or older responding by race and Hispanic origin, 2010)

	strongly agree	agree	neither	disagree	strongly disagree
Total people	13.1%	44.9%	16.2%	21.6%	4.2%
Asian	18.6	50.6	18.4	10.4	2.0
Black	25.6	50.5	9.9	11.6	2.4
Hispanic	20.0	56.3	11.7	9.4	2.6
White	9.5	43.6	17.3	24.9	4.7

Note: Hispanics may be of any race.
Source: Survey Documentation and Analysis, Computer-assisted Survey Methods Program, University of California, Berkeley, General Social Surveys, 1972–2010 Cumulative Data Files, Internet site http://sda.berkeley.edu/cgi-bin32/hsda?harcsda+gss10; calculations by New Strategist

Table 1.14 Children's Standard of Living, 2010

"When your children are at the age you are now, do you think their standard of living will be much better, somewhat better, about the same, somewhat worse, or much worse than yours is now?"

(percent of people aged 18 or older with children responding by race and Hispanic origin, 2010)

	much better	somewhat better	about the same	somewhat worse	much worse
Total people	**27.4%**	**32.0%**	**20.6%**	**15.0%**	**5.1%**
Asian	15.9	39.3	31.1	11.4	2.1
Black	44.3	31.1	12.6	7.7	4.4
Hispanic	48.1	32.5	10.4	7.6	1.4
White	21.7	32.9	22.8	17.2	5.5

Note: Hispanics may be of any race.
Source: Survey Documentation and Analysis, Computer-assisted Survey Methods Program, University of California, Berkeley, General Social Surveys, 1972–2010 Cumulative Data Files, Internet site http://sda.berkeley.edu/cgi-bin32/hsda?harcsda+gss10; calculations by New Strategist

The Two-Child Family Is Most Popular

Most Asians and whites say two children are ideal.

Among all Americans, the 48 percent plurality thinks two is the ideal number of children. Among Asians and whites, the figures are even higher. Fifty-six percent of Asians and 51 percent of whites think two children is the ideal number. A smaller 46 percent of Hispanics think two are ideal. Among blacks, only 34 percent think two are ideal. Slightly more than half of blacks say three or more children are ideal.

The great majority of the public believes children should get a good, hard spanking when they misbehave. By race and Hispanic origin, the figure ranges from 80 percent among blacks to 61 percent among Asians.

Traditional sex roles—defined as the man being the breadwinner and the woman caring for the home—are spurned by most Americans today. In 2010, only 35 percent of the public thought traditional sex roles were best. Asians are least likely to favor traditional sex roles, with only 21 percent saying they are best. Regardless of race or Hispanic origin, few think work harms a mother's relationship with her children.

Forty-seven percent of all Americans think the federal government should help people pay their medical bills. A larger 55 to 69 percent majority of Asians, blacks, and Hispanics think the government should help. In contrast, only 42 percent of whites support government involvement.

■ Few Asians, blacks, Hispanics, or whites regard one child as ideal.

Whites are least likely to think the government should help with medical bills

(percent of people aged 18 or older who agree that the government should help people pay for their doctor and hospital bills, by race and Hispanic origin, 2010)

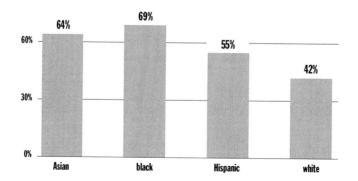

Table 1.15 Ideal Number of Children, 2010

"What do you think is the ideal number of children for a family to have?"

(percent of people aged 18 or older responding by race and Hispanic origin, 2010)

	none	one	two	three	four or more	as many as want
Total people	**0.3%**	**2.5%**	**48.4%**	**26.3%**	**12.0%**	**10.5%**
Asian	0.0	1.9	56.7	32.0	9.4	0.0
Black	0.2	1.8	33.8	23.4	27.0	13.8
Hispanic	0.0	0.8	46.4	30.8	16.7	5.3
White	0.4	2.9	51.5	25.8	8.5	10.9

Note: Hispanics may be of any race.
Source: Survey Documentation and Analysis, Computer-assisted Survey Methods Program, University of California, Berkeley, General Social Surveys, 1972–2010 Cumulative Data Files, Internet site http://sda.berkeley.edu/cgi-bin32/hsda?harcsda+gss10; calculations by New Strategist

Table 1.16 Spanking Children, 2010

"Do you strongly agree, agree, disagree, or strongly disagree that it is sometimes necessary to discipline a child with a good, hard spanking?"

(percent of people aged 18 or older responding by race and Hispanic origin, 2010)

	strongly agree	agree	disagree	strongly disagree
Total people	**23.6%**	**45.4%**	**23.5%**	**7.5%**
Asian	27.6	33.1	31.0	8.3
Black	35.4	44.2	16.3	4.0
Hispanic	22.7	42.2	27.7	7.4
White	21.1	47.0	23.9	8.0

Note: Hispanics may be of any race.
Source: Survey Documentation and Analysis, Computer-assisted Survey Methods Program, University of California, Berkeley, General Social Surveys, 1972–2010 Cumulative Data Files, Internet site http://sda.berkeley.edu/cgi-bin32/hsda?harcsda+gss10; calculations by New Strategist

Table 1.17 Better for Man to Work, Woman to Tend Home, 2010

"Do you strongly agree, agree, disagree, or strongly disagree with
the statement: It is much better for everyone involved if the man is the achiever
outside the home and the woman takes care of the home and family?"

(percent of people aged 18 or older responding by race and Hispanic origin, 2010)

	strongly agree	agree	disagree	strongly disagree
Total people	**6.8%**	**28.6%**	**43.5%**	**21.2%**
Asian	2.8	18.4	60.5	18.4
Black	7.2	28.8	44.0	20.0
Hispanic	8.9	29.9	43.5	17.7
White	7.0	28.1	42.5	22.4

Note: Hispanics may be of any race.
*Source: Survey Documentation and Analysis, Computer-assisted Survey Methods Program, University of California,
Berkeley, General Social Surveys, 1972–2010 Cumulative Data Files, Internet site http://sda.berkeley.edu/cgi-bin32/*

Table 1.18 Working Mother's Relationship with Children, 2010

"Do you strongly agree, agree, disagree, or strongly disagree with
the statement: A working mother can establish just as warm and secure
a relationship with her children as a mother who does not work?"

(percent of people aged 18 or older responding by race and Hispanic origin, 2010)

	strongly agree	agree	disagree	strongly disagree
Total people	**28.8%**	**45.9%**	**20.1%**	**5.1%**
Asian	36.4	32.0	24.2	7.4
Black	28.3	47.7	15.2	8.8
Hispanic	27.3	44.3	23.5	4.9
White	29.0	46.3	20.6	4.1

Note: Hispanics may be of any race.
*Source: Survey Documentation and Analysis, Computer-assisted Survey Methods Program, University of California,
Berkeley, General Social Surveys, 1972–2010 Cumulative Data Files, Internet site http://sda.berkeley.edu/cgi-bin32/
hsda?harcsda+gss10; calculations by New Strategist*

Table 1.19 Should Government Help the Sick, 2010

"Some people think that it is the responsibility of the government in Washington to see to it that people have help in paying for doctors and hospital bills; they are at point 1. Others think that these matters are not the responsibility of the federal government and that people should take care of these things themselves; they are at point 5. Where would you place yourself on this scale?"

(percent of people aged 18 or older responding by race and Hispanic origin, 2010)

	government should help 1	2	agree with both 3	4	people should help themselves 5
Total people	**30.5%**	**16.4%**	**31.9%**	**11.1%**	**10.1%**
Asian	38.6	25.1	25.0	9.2	2.1
Black	53.1	15.7	26.9	1.9	2.4
Hispanic	38.6	16.6	36.1	5.3	3.4
White	24.7	16.9	32.9	13.1	12.5

Note: Hispanics may be of any race.
Source: Survey Documentation and Analysis, Computer-assisted Survey Methods Program, University of California, Berkeley, General Social Surveys, 1972–2010 Cumulative Data Files, Internet site http://sda.berkeley.edu/cgi-bin32/hsda?harcsda+gss10; calculations by New Stategist

Religion Is Important to Most Americans

The majority of blacks, Hispanics, and whites say they are at least moderately religious.

Asked whether science makes our way of life change too fast, the 52 to 53 percent majority of blacks and whites disagree. But most Asians and Hispanics agree that science is making things change too fast.

Most Asians, Hispanics, and whites believe in evolution, with Asians especially likely to believe (82 percent). Among blacks, only 42 percent believe human beings developed from earlier species of animals.

Fifty-eight percent of all Americans identify themselves as at least moderately religious. Religiosity is especially high among blacks (68 percent) and Hispanics (63 percent). In contrast, only 33 percent of Asians say they are at least moderately religious.

Religious preference varies widely by race and Hispanic origin. Blacks are most likely to identify themselves as Protestant (65 percent). Hispanics are most likely to be Catholic (63 percent). Asians are most likely to identify themselves as Buddhists (18 percent) or to say they have no religious preference (36 percent). Blacks are the only race/Hispanic origin group in which the majority believes the Bible is the actual word of God (56 percent).

■ Asians are the only ones in which the majority approves of the Supreme Court ruling banning Bible reading in public schools.

Religious preference varies greatly by race and Hispanic origin

(percent of people aged 18 or older by selected religious preference, by race and Hispanic origin, 2010)

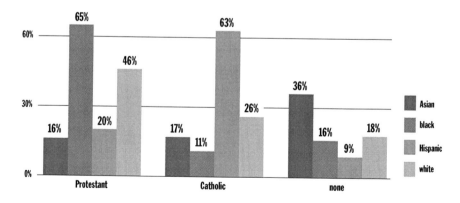

Table 1.20 **Attitude toward Science, 2010**

"Do you strongly agree, agree, disagree, or strongly disagree with
the statement: Science makes our way of life change too fast?"

(percent of people aged 18 or older responding by race and Hispanic origin, 2010)

	strongly agree	agree	disagree	strongly disagree
Total people	**7.2%**	**41.5%**	**43.2%**	**8.1%**
Asian	23.5	38.6	23.5	14.4
Black	10.5	36.5	44.7	8.3
Hispanic	7.7	58.1	29.2	5.1
White	5.8	41.7	44.7	7.8

Note: Hispanics may be of any race.
Source: Survey Documentation and Analysis, Computer-assisted Survey Methods Program, University of California, Berkeley, General Social Surveys, 1972–2010 Cumulative Data Files, Internet site http://sda.berkeley.edu/cgi-bin32/hsda?harcsda+gss10; calculations by New Strategist

Table 1.21 **Attitude toward Evolution, 2010**

"True or false: Human beings, as we know them today,
developed from earlier species of animals?"

(percent of people aged 18 or older responding by race and Hispanic origin, 2010)

	true	false
Total people	**55.7%**	**44.3%**
Asian	82.1	17.9
Black	42.5	57.5
Hispanic	61.5	38.5
White	57.0	43.0

Note: Hispanics may be of any race.
Source: Survey Documentation and Analysis, Computer-assisted Survey Methods Program, University of California, Berkeley, General Social Surveys, 1972–2010 Cumulative Data Files, Internet site http://sda.berkeley.edu/cgi-bin32/hsda?harcsda+gss10; calculations by New Strategist

Table 1.22 Religious Preference, 2010

"What is your religious preference?"

(percent of people aged 18 or older responding by race and Hispanic origin, 2010)

	Protestant	Catholic	Jewish	Buddhism	Hinduism	Moslem/Islam	other	none
Total people	**46.7%**	**25.2%**	**1.6%**	**0.9%**	**0.2%**	**0.6%**	**6.8%**	**18.0%**
Asian	15.9	17.2	3.6	18.2	4.0	2.6	2.7	35.8
Black	64.9	10.7	0.2	0.3	0.0	2.1	6.1	15.7
Hispanic	20.3	63.1	0.4	0.0	0.0	0.0	7.0	9.2
White	46.4	25.9	1.9	0.4	0.0	0.3	7.0	18.1

Note: Hispanics may be of any race.
Source: Survey Documentation and Analysis, Computer-assisted Survey Methods Program, University of California, Berkeley, General Social Surveys, 1972–2010 Cumulative Data Files, Internet site http://sda.berkeley.edu/cgi-bin32/ hsda?harcsda+gss10; calculations by New Strategist

---

Table 1.23 Degree of Religiosity, 2010

"To what extent do you consider yourself a religious person?"

(percent of people aged 18 or older responding by race and Hispanic origin, 2010)

	very religious	moderately religious	slightly religious	not religious
Total people	**16.8%**	**41.6%**	**23.6%**	**18.1%**
Asian	12.5	20.1	46.5	20.9
Black	28.5	39.3	16.8	15.5
Hispanic	11.5	51.8	26.3	10.3
White	14.6	42.5	23.9	19.0

Note: Hispanics may be of any race.
Source: Survey Documentation and Analysis, Computer-assisted Survey Methods Program, University of California, Berkeley, General Social Surveys, 1972–2010 Cumulative Data Files, Internet site http://sda.berkeley.edu/cgi-bin32/ hsda?harcsda+gss10; calculations by New Strategist

Table 1.24 Belief in the Bible, 2010

"Which of these statements comes closest to describing your feelings about the Bible? 1) The Bible is the actual word of God and is to be taken literally, word for word; 2) The Bible is the inspired word of God but not everything in it should be taken literally, word for word; 3) The Bible is an ancient book of fables, legends, history, and moral precepts recorded by men."

(percent of people aged 18 or older responding by race and Hispanic origin, 2010)

	word of God	inspired word	book of fables	other
Total people	**34.1%**	**43.6%**	**20.6%**	**1.7%**
Asian	12.5	35.2	49.6	2.7
Black	55.8	29.7	12.8	1.7
Hispanic	41.9	40.6	16.9	0.6
White	29.8	47.6	21.0	1.7

Note: Hispanics may be of any race.
Source: Survey Documentation and Analysis, Computer-assisted Survey Methods Program, University of California, Berkeley, General Social Surveys, 1972–2010 Cumulative Data Files, Internet site http://sda.berkeley.edu/cgi-bin32/hsda?harcsda+gss10; calculations by New Strategist

Table 1.25 Bible in the Public Schools, 2010

"The United States Supreme Court has ruled that no state or local government may require the reading of the Lord's Prayer or Bible verses in public schools. What are your views on this? Do you approve or disapprove of the court ruling?"

(percent of people aged 18 or older responding by race and Hispanic origin, 2010)

	approve	disapprove
Total people	**44.1%**	**55.9%**
Asian	59.8	40.2
Black	38.3	61.7
Hispanic	43.6	56.4
White	44.9	55.1

Note: Hispanics may be of any race.
Source: Survey Documentation and Analysis, Computer-assisted Survey Methods Program, University of California, Berkeley, General Social Surveys, 1972–2010 Cumulative Data Files, Internet site http://sda.berkeley.edu/cgi-bin32/hsda?harcsda+gss10; calculations by New Strategist

Most Asians Support Same-Sex Marriage

Hispanics and blacks are least supportive.

Fifty-three percent of Americans believe premarital sex is not wrong at all. Among Asians, the 66 percent majority feels this way. A smaller 54 percent of whites agree. Blacks and Hispanics are more conservative. Less than half of blacks and Hispanics think premarital sex is not wrong at all.

When it comes to sexual relations between adults of the same sex, 43 percent of all Americans say homosexuality is not wrong at all. Asians are much more accepting than the average person, with 60 percent saying homosexual relations are not wrong at all. Only 25 percent of blacks and 30 percent of Hispanics agree.

On the issue of whether gays and lesbians should have the right to marry, 47 percent of the public thinks they should. Support is greatest among Asians (71 percent). Only 34 percent of Hispanics and 37 percent of blacks believe same-sex marriage should be legal.

■ American attitudes toward sexuality have been changing as younger, more tolerant generations replace older generations with less tolerance.

Only about one-third of Hispanics support same-sex marriage

(percent of people aged 18 or older who agree with the statement, "Homosexual couples should have the right to marry one another," by race and Hispanic origin, 2010)

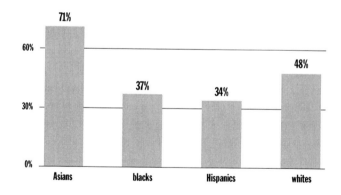

Table 1.26 Premarital Sex, 2010

"If a man and woman have sex relations before marriage,
do you think it is always wrong, almost always wrong,
wrong only sometimes, or not wrong at all?"

(percent of people aged 18 or older responding by race and Hispanic origin, 2010)

	always wrong	almost always wrong	sometimes wrong	not wrong at all
Total people	**21.3%**	**7.8%**	**17.8%**	**53.1%**
Asian	5.5	6.8	21.2	66.4
Black	28.2	11.1	11.3	49.4
Hispanic	23.9	4.6	23.1	48.5
White	20.9	7.3	18.3	53.5

Note: Hispanics may be of any race.
Source: Survey Documentation and Analysis, Computer-assisted Survey Methods Program, University of California, Berkeley, General Social Surveys, 1972–2010 Cumulative Data Files, Internet site http://sda.berkeley.edu/cgi-bin32/hsda?harcsda+gss10; calculations by New Strategist

Table 1.27 Homosexual Relations, 2010

"What about sexual relations between two adults of the same sex?"

(percent of people aged 18 or older responding by race and Hispanic origin, 2010)

	always wrong	almost always wrong	sometimes wrong	not wrong at all
Total people	**45.7%**	**3.7%**	**7.9%**	**42.7%**
Asian	20.1	4.8	15.5	59.6
Black	66.6	3.7	4.3	25.5
Hispanic	59.1	4.3	6.3	30.3
White	42.8	3.7	7.8	45.7

Note: Hispanics may be of any race.
Source: Survey Documentation and Analysis, Computer-assisted Survey Methods Program, University of California, Berkeley, General Social Surveys, 1972–2010 Cumulative Data Files, Internet site http://sda.berkeley.edu/cgi-bin32/hsda?harcsda+gss10; calculations by New Strategist

Table 1.28 Gay Marriage, 2010

"Do you agree or disagree? Homosexual couples
should have the right to marry one another."

(percent of people aged 18 or older responding by race and Hispanic origin, 2010)

	strongly agree	agree	neither agree nor disagree	disagree	strongly disagree
Total people	**21.1%**	**25.4%**	**12.8%**	**15.6%**	**25.1%**
Asian	21.1	49.6	3.4	16.9	8.9
Black	13.4	23.2	13.9	22.5	26.9
Hispanic	11.4	23.0	26.6	16.6	22.3
White	23.6	24.4	11.4	14.3	26.4

Note: Hispanics may be of any race.
Source: Survey Documentation and Analysis, Computer-assisted Survey Methods Program, University of California, Berkeley, General Social Surveys, 1972–2010 Cumulative Data Files, Internet site http://sda.berkeley.edu/cgi-bin32/ hsda?harcsda+gss10; calculations by New Strategist

Television News Is Most Important

Asians, blacks, and Hispanics are particularly dependent on TV for news.

Asians, blacks, and Hispanics are much more likely than whites to get most of their news from television. Sixty percent of Asians, 69 percent of blacks, and 71 percent of Hispanics depend primarily on television for news. In contrast, only 44 percent of whites say television is number one. Asians and whites are much more likely than blacks or Hispanics to get their news from the Internet. Whites are more likely than other groups to get their news from newspapers.

When asked about their political leanings, liberals outnumber conservatives among Asians, blacks, and Hispanics. In particular, Asians are much more liberal (40 percent) than conservative (26 percent). In contrast, whites are more conservative (36 percent) than liberal (27 percent). Political party identification is even more tilted than political leanings. The majority of Asians, blacks, and Hispanics identify themselves as Democrats (near to strong). Blacks are particularly likely to be Democrats (72 percent). In contrast, whites are about evenly split between Democrats (40 percent) and Republicans (39 percent).

■ Democrats could win more elections if Asians and Hispanics were more likely to vote.

Democrats are heavily favored by Asians, blacks, and Hispanics

(percent of people aged 18 or older who identify themselves as near to strong Democrats or Republicans, by race and Hispanic origin, 2010)

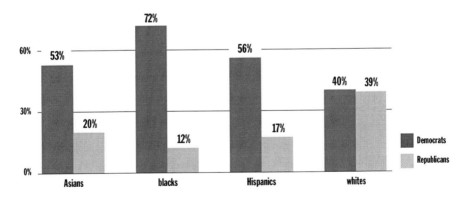

Table 1.29 Main Source of Information about Events in the News, 2010

"We are interested in how people get information about events in the news. Where do you get most of your information about current news events?"

(percent of people aged 18 or older responding by race and Hispanic origin, 2010)

	television	Internet	newspapers	radio	family, friends, or colleagues	books, other printed	government agencies	magazines
Total people	**49.1%**	**21.6%**	**17.7%**	**7.7%**	**2.2%**	**0.8%**	**0.6%**	**0.3%**
Asian	60.0	25.0	10.0	5.0	0.0	0.0	0.0	0.0
Black	68.7	6.0	13.4	0.0	7.1	0.0	4.8	0.0
Hispanic	71.2	14.8	7.0	0.0	7.0	0.0	0.0	0.0
White	44.0	24.2	19.4	9.7	1.4	0.8	0.0	0.4

Note: Hispanics may be of any race.
Source: Survey Documentation and Analysis, Computer-assisted Survey Methods Program, University of California, Berkeley, General Social Surveys, 1972–2010 Cumulative Data Files, Internet site http://sda.berkeley.edu/cgi-bin32/hsda?harcsda+gss10; calculations by New Strategist

Table 1.30 Political Leanings, 2010

"We hear a lot of talk these days about liberals and conservatives. On a seven-point scale from extremely liberal (1) to extremely conservative (7), where would you place yourself?"

(percent of people aged 18 or older responding by race and Hispanic origin, 2010)

	1 extremely liberal	2 liberal	3 slightly liberal	4 moderate	5 slightly conservative	6 conservative	7 extremely conservative
Total people	**3.8%**	**12.9%**	**11.9%**	**37.6%**	**12.8%**	**16.6%**	**4.4%**
Asian	1.4	22.5	16.5	33.9	14.8	5.9	5.0
Black	7.1	16.7	10.3	38.4	8.3	13.6	5.6
Hispanic	2.8	10.2	18.4	44.4	11.5	9.3	3.3
White	3.2	11.6	11.8	37.3	13.7	18.3	4.0

Note: Hispanics may be of any race.
Source: Survey Documentation and Analysis, Computer-assisted Survey Methods Program, University of California, Berkeley, General Social Surveys, 1972–2010 Cumulative Data Files, Internet site http://sda.berkeley.edu/cgi-bin32/hsda?harcsda+gss10; calculations by New Strategist

Table 1.31 Political Party Affiliation, 2010

"Generally speaking, do you usually think of yourself as a Republican, Democrat, independent, or what?"

(percent of people aged 18 or older responding by race and Hispanic origin, 2010)

	strong Democrat	not strong Democrat	independent, near Democrat	independent	independent, near Republican	not strong Republican	strong Republican	other party
Total people	**16.5%**	**15.7%**	**13.5%**	**18.8%**	**10.0%**	**13.4%**	**9.6%**	**2.6%**
Asian	16.3	19.3	17.0	21.9	6.6	10.3	3.2	5.3
Black	40.0	19.1	13.3	14.0	4.2	7.0	1.1	1.3
Hispanic	13.0	22.7	19.9	26.0	6.7	8.0	2.0	1.8
White	12.2	14.9	12.5	18.6	11.8	15.1	12.2	2.7

Note: Hispanics may be of any race.
Source: Survey Documentation and Analysis, Computer-assisted Survey Methods Program, University of California, Berkeley, General Social Surveys, 1972–2010 Cumulative Data Files, Internet site http://sda.berkeley.edu/cgi-bin32/hsda?harcsda+gss10; calculations by New Strategist

Most Support Right to Die, Gun Permits

Blacks are against capital punishment, while others support it.

Americans have long been in support of the death penalty for convicted murderers. In 2010, 68 percent of the public was in favor of the death penalty. Blacks are the only demographic segment in which the majority (52 percent) opposes the death penalty. Sixty-five percent of Asians, 53 percent of Hispanics, and 73 percent of whites favor the death penalty for people convicted of murder.

Most Americans favor requiring a permit for gun ownership. In 2010, fully 74 percent favored requiring a permit before buying a gun. By race and Hispanic origin, support ranges from a low of 71 percent among whites to a high of 94 percent among Asians.

Among racial and ethnic groups, Hispanics are least likely to support abortion. Only 26 percent think abortion should be allowed for any reason. Nevertheless, the great majority of Hispanics support abortion if a woman's health is endangered, if she has been raped, or if there is a serious defect in the baby. Asians are most supportive of abortion rights, with 60 percent saying women should be able to obtain a legal abortion for any reason.

More than two-thirds of Americans support the right of the terminally ill to die with a doctor's assistance. Support ranges from a low of 54 percent among blacks to a high of 92 percent among Asians.

■ Although a growing number of states are outlawing the death penalty, the public continues to overwhelmingly support it.

Asians support abortion rights for any reason

(percent of people aged 18 or older who responded "yes" to the question, "Should a woman be able to obtain a legal abortion for any reason?" by race and Hispanic origin, 2010)

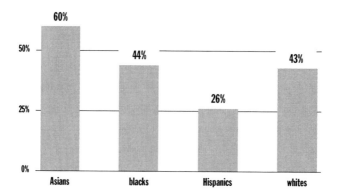

Table 1.32 Favor or Oppose Death Penalty for Murder, 2010

"Do you favor or oppose the death penalty for persons convicted of murder?"

(percent of people aged 18 or older responding by race and Hispanic origin, 2010)

	favor	oppose
Total people	**67.8%**	**32.2%**
Asian	64.5	35.5
Black	47.8	52.2
Hispanic	53.2	46.8
White	72.9	27.1

Note: Hispanics may be of any race.
Source: Survey Documentation and Analysis, Computer-assisted Survey Methods Program, University of California, Berkeley, General Social Surveys, 1972–2010 Cumulative Data Files, Internet site http://sda.berkeley.edu/cgi-bin32/hsda?harcsda+gss10; calculations by New Strategist

Table 1.33 Favor or Oppose Gun Permits, 2010

"Would you favor or oppose a law which would require a person
to obtain a police permit before he or she could buy a gun?"

(percent of people aged 18 or older responding by race and Hispanic origin, 2010)

	favor	oppose
Total people	**74.3%**	**25.7%**
Asian	93.8	6.2
Black	83.5	16.5
Hispanic	83.1	16.9
White	71.3	28.7

Note: Hispanics may be of any race.
Source: Survey Documentation and Analysis, Computer-assisted Survey Methods Program, University of California, Berkeley, General Social Surveys, 1972–2010 Cumulative Data Files, Internet site http://sda.berkeley.edu/cgi-bin32/hsda?harcsda+gss10; calculations by New Strategist

Table 1.34 Support for Legal Abortion by Reason, 2010

"Please tell me whether or not you think it should be possible for a pregnant woman to obtain a legal abortion if the woman wants it."

(percent of people aged 18 or older responding yes by race and Hispanic origin, 2010)

	her health is seriously endangered	pregnancy is the result of rape	there is a serious defect in the baby	she cannot afford more children	she is married, but does not want more childen	she is single and does not want to marry the man	for any reason
Total people	**86.4%**	**79.1%**	**73.9%**	**44.9%**	**47.7%**	**41.9%**	**42.9%**
Asian	92.5	85.0	81.2	67.3	73.7	58.7	60.0
Black	83.9	79.9	69.8	48.6	50.7	41.8	43.9
Hispanic	75.4	62.8	63.7	31.1	37.3	24.3	25.8
White	87.2	79.7	75.1	44.2	46.7	42.6	43.3

Note: Hispanics may be of any race.
Source: Survey Documentation and Analysis, Computer-assisted Survey Methods Program, University of California, Berkeley, General Social Surveys, 1972–2010 Cumulative Data Files, Internet site http://sda.berkeley.edu/cgi-bin32/hsda?harcsda+gss10; calculations by New Strategist

Table 1.35 Allow Patients with Incurable Disease to Die, 2010

"When a person has a disease that cannot be cured, do you think doctors should be allowed by law to end the patient's life by some painless means if the patient and his family request it?"

(percent of people aged 18 or older responding by race and Hispanic origin, 2010)

	yes	no
Total people	**68.4%**	**31.6%**
Asian	92.4	7.6
Black	54.3	45.7
Hispanic	61.2	38.8
White	71.3	28.7

Note: Hispanics may be of any race.
Source: Survey Documentation and Analysis, Computer-assisted Survey Methods Program, University of California, Berkeley, General Social Surveys, 1972–2010 Cumulative Data Files, Internet site http://sda.berkeley.edu/cgi-bin32/hsda?harcsda+gss10; calculations by New Strategist

2

Education

■ More than 84 percent of blacks are high school graduates, a share not far below the 87 percent of all Americans with a high school diploma.

■ Of the nation's 77 million students, 17 percent are black. Blacks account for at least one-third of public elementary and secondary students in seven states.

■ The college enrollment rate of blacks is nearly equal to the average rate. In 2009, nearly 70 percent of black high school graduates enrolled in college within 12 months of getting their high school diploma.

■ Among the nation's 20 million college students, 14 percent are black.

■ Blacks earned 10 percent of bachelor's degrees awarded in 2008–09. They earned 11 percent of master's degrees, and 13 percent of associate's degrees.

Black Educational Attainment Is Only Slightly below Average

Blacks are almost as likely as the average American to be high school graduates.

More than 84 percent of blacks aged 25 or older are high school graduates, not far below the 87 percent of all Americans with a high school diploma. Blacks still lag in college experience, however. Twenty percent of blacks have a bachelor's degree compared with 30 percent for the population as a whole. Nearly half the black population has at least some college education.

The educational attainment of blacks varies greatly by age. Among blacks under age 65, more than 80 percent have graduated from high school. Among those aged 65 or older, the proportion is just 65 percent. Most blacks under age 55 have college experience, 31 to 34 percent have at least an associate's degree, and more than one in five has a bachelor's degree. The greater opportunity available to younger blacks is clearly evident in these statistics.

■ If college were more affordable, a larger proportion of blacks would be college graduates.

Black educational attainment is not far below average

(percent of total people and blacks aged 25 or older by educational attainment, 2010)

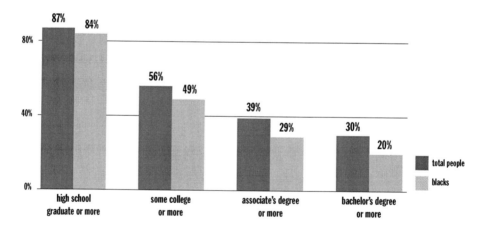

Table 2.1 Educational Attainment of Total People and Blacks, 2010

(number and percent distribution of total people and blacks aged 25 or older by educational attainment, black share of total, and black percent distribution indexed to total, 2010; numbers in thousands)

		blacks	
	total	number	share of total
Total people	**199,928**	**23,702**	**11.9%**
Not a high school graduate	25,711	3,741	14.6
High school graduate only	62,456	8,279	13.3
Some college, no degree	33,662	4,723	14.0
Associate's degree	18,259	2,243	12.3
Bachelor's degree	38,784	3,169	8.2
Master's degree	15,203	1,233	8.1
Professional degree	3,074	187	6.1
Doctoral degree	2,779	126	4.5
High school graduate or more	174,217	19,960	11.5
Some college or more	111,761	11,681	10.5
Associate's degree or more	78,099	6,958	8.9
Bachelor's degree or more	59,840	4,715	7.9

	total	total	index, black to total
PERCENT DISTRIBUTION			
Total people	**100.0%**	**100.0%**	–
Not a high school graduate	12.9	15.8	123
High school graduate only	31.2	34.9	112
Some college, no degree	16.8	19.9	118
Associate's degree	9.1	9.5	104
Bachelor's degree	19.4	13.4	69
Master's degree	7.6	5.2	68
Professional degree	1.5	0.8	51
Doctoral degree	1.4	0.5	38
High school graduate or more	87.1	84.2	97
Some college or more	55.9	49.3	88
Associate's degree or more	39.1	29.4	75
Bachelor's degree or more	29.9	19.9	66

Note: Blacks are those who identify themselves as being of the race alone or as being of the race in combination with other races. The index is calculated by dividing the black percentage by the total percentage and multiplying by 100. "–" means not applicable.
Source: Bureau of the Census, 2010 Current Population Survey Annual Social and Economic Supplement, Detailed Tables, Internet site http://www.census.gov/hhes/www/cpstables/032010/perinc/toc.htm; calculations by New Strategist

Table 2.2 Educational Attainment of Blacks by Age, 2010

(number and percent distribution of blacks aged 25 or older by educational attainment and age, 2010; numbers in thousands)

	total	25 to 34	35 to 44	45 to 54	55 to 64	65 or older
Total blacks	**23,702**	**5,800**	**5,250**	**5,464**	**3,782**	**3,405**
Not a high school graduate	3,741	683	560	686	625	1,188
High school graduate only	8,279	1,942	1,846	2,038	1,350	1,103
Some college, no degree	4,723	1,400	1,078	1,037	748	460
Associate's degree	2,243	565	579	586	351	162
Bachelor's degree	3,169	904	855	748	402	259
Master's degree	1,233	224	276	306	247	180
Professional degree	187	52	41	36	33	25
Doctoral degree	126	30	15	28	26	27
High school graduate or more	19,960	5,117	4,690	4,779	3,157	2,216
Some college or more	11,681	3,175	2,844	2,741	1,807	1,113
Associate's degree or more	6,958	1,775	1,766	1,704	1,059	653
Bachelor's degree or more	4,715	1,210	1,187	1,118	708	491
PERCENT DISTRIBUTION						
Total blacks	**100.0%**	**100.0%**	**100.0%**	**100.0%**	**100.0%**	**100.0%**
Not a high school graduate	15.8	11.8	10.7	12.6	16.5	34.9
High school graduate only	34.9	33.5	35.2	37.3	35.7	32.4
Some college, no degree	19.9	24.1	20.5	19.0	19.8	13.5
Associate's degree	9.5	9.7	11.0	10.7	9.3	4.8
Bachelor's degree	13.4	15.6	16.3	13.7	10.6	7.6
Master's degree	5.2	3.9	5.3	5.6	6.5	5.3
Professional degree	0.8	0.9	0.8	0.7	0.9	0.7
Doctoral degree	0.5	0.5	0.3	0.5	0.7	0.8
High school graduate or more	84.2	88.2	89.3	87.5	83.5	65.1
Some college or more	49.3	54.7	54.2	50.2	47.8	32.7
Associate's degree or more	29.4	30.6	33.6	31.2	28.0	19.2
Bachelor's degree or more	19.9	20.9	22.6	20.5	18.7	14.4

Note: Blacks are those who identify themselves as being of the race alone or as being of the race in combination with other races.
Source: Bureau of the Census, 2010 Current Population Survey Annual Social and Economic Supplement, Detailed Tables, Internet site http://www.census.gov/hhes/www/cpstables/032010/perinc/toc.htm; calculations by New Strategist

Table 2.3 Educational Attainment of Black Men by Age, 2010

(number and percent distribution of black men aged 25 or older by educational attainment and age, 2010; numbers in thousands)

	total	25 to 34	35 to 44	45 to 54	55 to 64	65 or older
Total black men	**10,542**	**2,705**	**2,349**	**2,475**	**1,673**	**1,339**
Not a high school graduate	1,738	389	206	362	289	491
High school graduate only	4,079	1,033	993	1,027	599	427
Some college, no degree	2,020	653	440	438	317	172
Associate's degree	835	203	223	200	152	57
Bachelor's degree	1,264	334	358	284	189	98
Master's degree	468	68	108	127	97	68
Professional degree	78	14	15	19	17	12
Doctoral degree	60	10	5	17	14	14
High school graduate or more	8,804	2,315	2,142	2,112	1,385	848
Some college or more	4,725	1,282	1,149	1,085	786	421
Associate's degree or more	2,705	629	709	647	469	249
Bachelor's degree or more	1,870	426	486	447	317	192
PERCENT DISTRIBUTION						
Total black men	**100.0%**	**100.0%**	**100.0%**	**100.0%**	**100.0%**	**100.0%**
Not a high school graduate	16.5	14.4	8.8	14.6	17.3	36.7
High school graduate only	38.7	38.2	42.3	41.5	35.8	31.9
Some college, no degree	19.2	24.1	18.7	17.7	18.9	12.8
Associate's degree	7.9	7.5	9.5	8.1	9.1	4.3
Bachelor's degree	12.0	12.3	15.2	11.5	11.3	7.3
Master's degree	4.4	2.5	4.6	5.1	5.8	5.1
Professional degree	0.7	0.5	0.6	0.8	1.0	0.9
Doctoral degree	0.6	0.4	0.2	0.7	0.8	1.0
High school graduate or more	83.5	85.6	91.2	85.3	82.8	63.3
Some college or more	44.8	47.4	48.9	43.8	47.0	31.4
Associate's degree or more	25.7	23.3	30.2	26.1	28.0	18.6
Bachelor's degree or more	17.7	15.7	20.7	18.1	18.9	14.3

Note: Blacks are those who identify themselves as being of the race alone or as being of the race in combination with other races.
Source: Bureau of the Census, 2010 Current Population Survey Annual Social and Economic Supplement, Detailed Tables, Internet site http://www.census.gov/hhes/www/cpstables/032010/perinc/toc.htm; calculations by New Strategist

Table 2.4 Educational Attainment of Black Women by Age, 2010

(number and percent distribution of black women aged 25 or older by educational attainment and age, 2010; numbers in thousands)

	total	25 to 34	35 to 44	45 to 54	55 to 64	65 or older
Total black women	**13,160**	**3,095**	**2,902**	**2,989**	**2,109**	**2,066**
Not a high school graduate	2,003	293	354	323	337	697
High school graduate only	4,200	909	853	1,011	751	676
Some college, no degree	2,703	746	638	599	431	288
Associate's degree	1,408	362	356	385	199	106
Bachelor's degree	1,905	570	497	464	214	161
Master's degree	765	156	168	179	150	112
Professional degree	109	38	26	17	15	13
Doctoral degree	66	21	10	11	12	13
High school graduate or more	11,156	2,802	2,548	2,666	1,772	1,369
Some college or more	6,956	1,893	1,695	1,655	1,021	693
Associate's degree or more	4,253	1,147	1,057	1,056	590	405
Bachelor's degree or more	2,845	785	701	671	391	299
PERCENT DISTRIBUTION						
Total black women	**100.0%**	**100.0%**	**100.0%**	**100.0%**	**100.0%**	**100.0%**
Not a high school graduate	15.2	9.5	12.2	10.8	16.0	33.7
High school graduate only	31.9	29.4	29.4	33.8	35.6	32.7
Some college, no degree	20.5	24.1	22.0	20.0	20.4	13.9
Associate's degree	10.7	11.7	12.3	12.9	9.4	5.1
Bachelor's degree	14.5	18.4	17.1	15.5	10.1	7.8
Master's degree	5.8	5.0	5.8	6.0	7.1	5.4
Professional degree	0.8	1.2	0.9	0.6	0.7	0.6
Doctoral degree	0.5	0.7	0.3	0.4	0.6	0.6
High school graduate or more	84.8	90.5	87.8	89.2	84.0	66.3
Some college or more	52.9	61.2	58.4	55.4	48.4	33.5
Associate's degree or more	32.3	37.1	36.4	35.3	28.0	19.6
Bachelor's degree or more	21.6	25.4	24.2	22.4	18.5	14.5

Note: Blacks are those who identify themselves as being of the race alone or as being of the race in combination with other races.
Source: Bureau of the Census, 2010 Current Population Survey Annual Social and Economic Supplement, Detailed Tables, Internet site http://www.census.gov/hhes/www/cpstables/032010/perinc/toc.htm; calculations by New Strategist

Blacks Represent a Large Share of the Nation's Students

Blacks account for at least one-third of public elementary and secondary students in seven states.

Of the nation's 77 million students, nearly 13 million—or 17 percent—are black. More than 90 percent of blacks are in school from ages 5 to 6 through ages 16 to 17. At ages 18 to 19, nearly two-thirds of blacks are still in school. The proportion drops below the 50 percent mark among blacks aged 20 or older.

In seven states, blacks account for at least one-third of public elementary and secondary students: Alabama, Delaware, Georgia, Louisiana, Maryland, Mississippi, and South Carolina. The number of black high school graduates is projected to decline 10 percent over the next decade, according to projections by the National Center for Education Statistics, falling from 451,000 in 2009–10 to 405,000 in 2019–20. Nationally, the number of high school graduates is projected to decline by 1 percent.

■ The black share of the student population does not vary much by age.

More than 3 million blacks aged 18 or older are in school

(number of black students aged 18 or older, by sex, 2009)

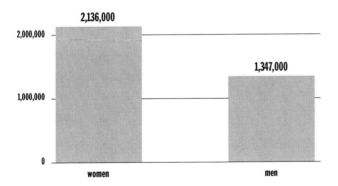

Table 2.5 Total and Black School Enrollment by Age, 2009

(total number of people aged 3 or older enrolled in school, number of blacks enrolled, and black share of total, by age, October 2009; numbers in thousands)

		black	
	total	number	share of total
Total aged 3 or older	**77,288**	**12,825**	**16.6%**
Aged 3 to 4	4,475	869	19.4
Aged 5 to 6	7,783	1,219	15.7
Aged 7 to 9	11,921	1,953	16.4
Aged 10 to 13	15,688	2,629	16.8
Aged 14 to 15	7,789	1,289	16.5
Aged 16 to 17	7,939	1,382	17.4
Aged 18 to 19	5,935	939	15.8
Aged 20 to 21	4,163	561	13.5
Aged 22 to 24	3,818	602	15.8
Aged 25 to 29	2,819	434	15.4
Aged 30 to 34	1,576	292	18.5
Aged 35 to 44	1,927	386	20.0
Aged 45 to 54	1,064	186	17.5
Aged 55 or older	393	85	21.6

Note: Blacks are those who identify themselves as being of the race alone or as being of the race in combination with other races.
Source: Bureau of the Census, School Enrollment—Social and Economic Characteristics of Students: October 2009, Internet site http://www.census.gov/population/www/socdemo/school/cps2009.html

Table 2.6 School Enrollment of Blacks by Age and Sex, 2009

(number and percent of blacks aged 3 or older enrolled in school, by age and sex, October 2009; numbers in thousands)

	total		female		male	
	number	percent	number	percent	number	percent
Total blacks enrolled	**12,825**	**33.5%**	**6,796**	**33.0%**	**6,029**	**34.0%**
Aged 3 to 4	869	57.1	446	56.9	423	57.4
Aged 5 to 6	1,219	93.8	578	93.9	640	93.8
Aged 7 to 9	1,953	97.4	981	97.6	972	97.2
Aged 10 to 13	2,629	98.6	1,308	98.9	1,321	98.3
Aged 14 to 15	1,289	97.7	661	99.4	628	95.9
Aged 16 to 17	1,382	94.4	686	93.1	696	95.6
Aged 18 to 19	939	64.7	512	68.9	427	60.4
Aged 20 to 21	561	44.2	286	46.1	274	42.3
Aged 22 to 24	602	31.6	382	36.5	219	25.7
Aged 25 to 29	434	14.7	274	17.5	160	11.5
Aged 30 to 34	292	11.1	196	13.5	96	8.1
Aged 35 to 44	386	7.3	303	10.3	83	3.5
Aged 45 to 54	186	3.4	138	4.6	48	2.0
Aged 55 or older	85	1.2	45	1.1	40	1.3

Note: Blacks are those who identify themselves as being of the race alone or as being of the race in combination with other races.
Source: Bureau of the Census, School Enrollment—Social and Economic Characteristics of Students: October 2009, Internet site http://www.census.gov/population/www/socdemo/school/cps2009.html

Table 2.7 Black Enrollment in the Nation's Public Elementary and Secondary Schools by State, 1998 and 2008

(percentage of students enrolled in public elementary and secondary schools who are black, by state, 1998 and 2008; percentage point change, 1998–2008)

	2008	1998	percentage point change
Total enrolled	**17.0%**	**17.0%**	**0.0**
Alabama	35.3	36.2	−0.9
Alaska	3.5	4.6	−1.1
Arizona	5.8	4.5	1.3
Arkansas	22.4	23.5	−1.0
California	7.3	8.7	−1.4
Colorado	6.0	5.6	0.3
Connecticut	13.9	13.6	0.3
Delaware	33.2	30.4	2.9
Dist. of Columbia	81.5	85.9	−4.3
Florida	24.0	25.5	−1.4
Georgia	39.0	38.1	0.9
Hawaii	2.3	2.4	−0.1
Idaho	1.3	0.7	0.6
Illinois	20.0	21.4	−1.4
Indiana	12.8	11.4	1.4
Iowa	5.8	3.6	2.2
Kansas	8.8	8.6	0.2
Kentucky	11.0	10.4	0.6
Louisiana	46.1	47.1	−1.0
Maine	2.7	1.0	1.8
Maryland	38.0	36.6	1.4
Massachusetts	8.2	8.6	−0.4
Michigan	20.2	19.5	0.6
Minnesota	9.6	5.8	3.7
Mississippi	50.5	51.0	−0.5
Missouri	17.8	17.1	0.7
Montana	1.0	0.5	0.5
Nebraska	8.1	6.3	1.7
Nevada	11.2	9.9	1.4
New Hampshire	2.1	1.0	1.1
New Jersey	17.1	18.1	−1.0
New Mexico	2.6	2.3	0.3
New York	19.3	20.4	−1.1
North Carolina	31.2	31.2	0.0
North Dakota	2.2	1.0	1.3
Ohio	16.9	15.8	1.0
Oklahoma	10.9	10.7	0.2
Oregon	3.1	2.7	0.4
Pennsylvania	15.8	14.6	1.1

	2008	1998	percentage point change
Rhode Island	9.0%	7.6%	1.4
South Carolina	38.8	42.0	−3.2
South Dakota	2.5	1.0	1.4
Tennessee	24.6	20.9	3.7
Texas	14.2	14.4	−0.2
Utah	1.4	0.8	0.6
Vermont	1.7	0.9	0.8
Virginia	26.4	27.2	−0.8
Washington	5.7	5.1	0.6
West Virginia	5.4	4.2	1.2
Wisconsin	10.5	9.8	0.7
Wyoming	1.6	1.0	0.5

Source: National Center for Education Statistics, Digest of Education Statistics: 2010, Table 43, Internet site http://nces .ed.gov/programs/digest/d10/

Table 2.8 Projections of Total and Black Public High School Graduates, 2009–10 to 2019–20

(projected number of total people and blacks graduating from public high schools, 2009–10 to 2019–20; percent change 2009–10 to 2019–20; numbers in thousands)

	total graduates	black graduates	
		number	share of total
2009–10	2,991	451	15.1%
2010–11	2,937	444	15.1
2011–12	2,906	432	14.9
2012–13	2,891	419	14.5
2013–14	2,868	405	14.1
2014–15	2,872	406	14.1
2015–16	2,906	411	14.1
2016–17	2,933	412	14.0
2017–18	2,989	418	14.0
2018–19	2,985	411	13.8
2019–20	2,953	405	13.7
Percent change			
2009–10 to 2019–20	–1.3%	–10.1%	–

Note: "–" means not applicable.
Source: National Center for Education Statistics, Projections of Education Statistics to 2019, Internet site http://nces.ed.gov/programs/projections/projections2019/tables.asp; calculations by New Strategist

The Black College Enrollment Rate Is at a Record High

The college enrollment rate of blacks is nearly equal to the average rate.

Most black students who graduate from high school enroll in college within 12 months of getting their diploma. In 2009, the black college enrollment rate was 69.5 percent—nearly equal to the 70.1 percent average rate. The black rate surged between 2008 and 2009, and it remains to be seen whether the gain will be temporary or lasting.

The number of blacks in college has nearly tripled since 1976, rising from 1 million to nearly 3 million. Among the nation's 20 million college students, 14 percent are black. Fifty-two percent of black college students are enrolled in four-year colleges, 32 percent are in two-year schools, and 17 percent attend graduate school.

■ Scholarship aid is critical to boosting the percentage of blacks with a college degree.

More than 1 million blacks are enrolled in four-year colleges

(number of black students enrolled in college, by type of school, 2009)

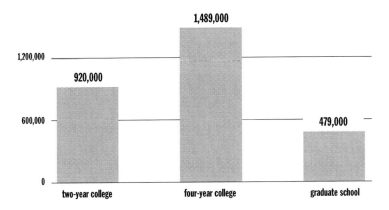

Table 2.9 Total and Black College Enrollment Rate, 1990 to 2009

(percent of total people and blacks aged 16 to 24 having graduated from high school in the previous 12 months who were enrolled in college as of October, and index of black to total, 1990 to 2009; percentage point change in enrollment rate for selected years)

	total people	blacks	index, black to total
2009	70.1%	69.5%	99
2008	68.6	55.7	81
2007	67.2	55.7	83
2006	66.0	55.5	84
2005	68.6	55.7	81
2004	66.7	62.5	94
2003	63.9	57.5	90
2002	65.2	59.4	91
2001	61.8	55.0	89
2000	63.3	54.9	87
1999	62.9	58.9	94
1998	65.6	61.9	94
1997	67.0	58.5	87
1996	65.0	56.0	86
1995	61.9	51.2	83
1994	61.9	50.8	82
1993	62.6	55.6	89
1992	61.9	48.2	78
1991	62.5	46.4	74
1990	60.1	46.8	78
Percentage point change			
2000 to 2009	6.8	14.6	–
1990 to 2009	10.0	22.7	–

Note: The index is calculated by dividing the black enrollment rate by the total enrollment rate and multiplying by 100. "–" means not applicable.
Source: National Center for Education Statistics, Digest of Education Statistics: 2010, Table 209, Internet site http://nces.ed.gov/programs/digest/d10/

Table 2.10 Total and Black College Enrollment, 1976 to 2009

(number of total people and blacks aged 15 or older enrolled in institutions of higher education, and black share of total, selected years 1976 to 2009; numbers in thousands)

	total enrolled	black	
		number	share of total
2009	20,428	2,920	14.3%
2008	19,103	2,584	13.5
2007	18,248	2,383	13.1
2006	17,759	2,280	12.8
2005	17,488	2,215	12.7
2004	17,272	2,165	12.5
2003	16,901	2,069	12.2
2002	16,612	1,979	11.9
2001	15,928	1,850	11.6
2000	15,312	1,730	11.3
1999	14,791	1,641	11.1
1998	14,507	1,583	10.9
1997	14,502	1,551	10.7
1996	14,368	1,506	10.5
1995	14,262	1,474	10.3
1990	13,819	1,247	9.0
1980	12,087	1,107	9.2
1976	10,986	1,033	9.4

Note: Enrollment figures are based on a survey of institutions of higher education. They differ from enrollment figures in other tables, which are based on household surveys.
Source: National Center for Education Statistics, Digest of Education Statistics: 2010, Table 236, Internet site http://nces .ed.gov/programs/digest/d10/

Table 2.11 Total and Black College Enrollment by Age, 2009

(total number of people aged 15 or older enrolled in college, number of blacks enrolled, and black share of total, by age, October 2009; numbers in thousands)

	total	black number	share of total
Total enrolled in college	**19,765**	**2,889**	**14.6%**
Under age 20	4,495	594	13.2
Aged 20 to 21	4,034	495	12.3
Aged 22 to 24	3,749	550	14.7
Aged 25 to 29	2,769	410	14.8
Aged 30 to 34	1,524	253	16.6
Aged 35 to 44	1,848	364	19.7
Aged 45 to 54	998	164	16.4
Aged 55 or older	347	59	17.0

Note: Blacks are those who identify themselves as being of the race alone.
Source: Bureau of the Census, School Enrollment—Social and Economic Characteristics of Students: October 2009, Internet site http://www.census.gov/population/www/socdemo/school/cps2009.html; calculations by New Strategist

Table 2.12 Black Share of College Enrollment by Attendance Status and Type of School, 2009

(total number of people aged 15 or older enrolled in college, number of blacks enrolled, and black share of total, by attendance status and type of school, October 2009; numbers in thousands)

	total	blacks number	blacks share of total
Total enrolled in college	**19,765**	**2,889**	**14.6%**
Two-year college	5,551	920	16.6
Four-year college	10,461	1,489	14.2
Graduate school	3,753	479	12.8
Enrolled full-time	**14,364**	**2,061**	**14.3**
Two-year college	3,633	628	17.3
Four-year college	8,685	1,180	13.6
Graduate school	2,046	252	12.3
Enrolled part-time	**5,401**	**828**	**15.3**
Two-year college	1,918	292	15.2
Four-year college	1,776	309	17.4
Graduate school	1,707	227	13.3

Note: Blacks are those who identify themselves as being of the race alone.
Source: Bureau of the Census, School Enrollment—Social and Economic Characteristics of Students: October 2009, Internet site http://www.census.gov/population/www/socdemo/school/cps2009.html; calculations by New Strategist

Table 2.13 College Enrollment of Blacks by Type of School and Attendance Status, 2009

(number and percent distribution of blacks aged 15 or older enrolled in college by type of school and attendance status, October 2009; numbers in thousands)

	total	full-time	part-time
Total blacks enrolled	**2,889**	**2,061**	**828**
Two-year college	920	628	292
Four-year college	1,489	1,180	309
Graduate school	479	252	227
PERCENT DISTRIBUTION BY ATTENDANCE STATUS			
Total blacks enrolled	**100.0%**	**71.3%**	**28.7%**
Two-year college	100.0	68.3	31.7
Four-year college	100.0	79.2	20.8
Graduate school	100.0	52.6	47.4
PERCENT DISTRIBUTION BY TYPE OF SCHOOL			
Total blacks enrolled	**100.0%**	**100.0%**	**100.0%**
Two-year college	31.8	30.5	35.3
Four-year college	51.5	57.3	37.3
Graduate school	16.6	12.2	27.4

Note: Blacks are those who identify themselves as being of the race alone.
Source: Bureau of the Census, School Enrollment—Social and Economic Characteristics of Students: October 2009, Internet site http://www.census.gov/population/www/socdemo/school/cps2009.html; calculations by New Strategist

Blacks Earn 10 Percent of Bachelor's Degrees

They earn a larger 13 percent of associate's degrees.

Of the 1.6 million bachelor's degrees awarded in 2008–09, blacks earned 10 percent, including 23 percent of degrees in public administration. At the master's level, blacks earned 11 percent of degrees, including 14 percent of degrees in business, 19 percent of degrees in public administration, and 21 percent of degrees in security and protective services.

Blacks earned a relatively small 7 percent of first-professional degrees awarded in 2008–09, but in theology they accounted for a larger 16 percent of degrees. Blacks earned 7 percent of degrees in medicine in 2008–09.

■ Blacks are making inroads on higher education, but the rising cost of college is limiting their gains.

Blacks earn one in eight associate's degrees

(percent of degrees earned by blacks, by level of degree, 2008–09)

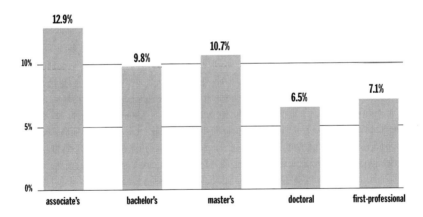

Table 2.14 Associate's Degrees Earned by Total People and Blacks by Field of Study, 2008–09

(total number of associate's degrees conferred and number and percent earned by blacks, by field of study, 2008–09)

		earned by blacks	
	total	number	share of total
Total associate's degrees	**787,325**	**101,487**	**12.9%**
Agriculture and natural resources	5,724	49	0.9
Architecture and related services	596	23	3.9
Area, ethnic, cultural, and gender studies	173	26	15.0
Biological and biomedical sciences	2,364	183	7.7
Business	127,848	20,326	15.9
Communications, journalism, and related programs	2,722	261	9.6
Communications technologies	4,803	542	11.3
Computer and information sciences	30,006	4,705	15.7
Construction trades	4,252	359	8.4
Education	14,123	2,102	14.9
Engineering	2,181	174	8.0
Engineering technologies	30,434	3,423	11.2
English language and literature/letters	1,525	104	6.8
Family and consumer sciences	9,020	1,931	21.4
Foreign languages, literatures, and linguistics	1,627	91	5.6
Health professions and related clinical sciences	165,163	21,824	13.2
Legal professions and studies	9,062	1,606	17.7
Liberal arts and sciences, general studies, and humanities	263,853	30,433	11.5
Library science	116	3	2.6
Mathematics and statistics	930	38	4.1
Mechanics and repair technologies	16,066	1,418	8.8
Military technologies	721	84	11.7
Multi/interdisciplinary studies	15,459	1,214	7.9
Parks, recreation, leisure, and fitness studies	1,587	192	12.1
Philosophy and religious studies	191	25	13.1
Physical sciences and science technologies	3,617	307	8.5
Precision production	2,126	88	4.1
Psychology	3,949	419	10.6
Public administration and social service professions	4,178	1,200	28.7
Security and protective services	33,033	5,363	16.2
Social sciences and history	9,142	1,031	11.3
Theology and religious vocations	675	157	23.3
Transportation and materials moving	1,430	108	7.6
Visual and performing arts	18,629	1,678	9.0

Source: National Center for Education Statistics, Digest of Education Statistics 2010, Table 294, Internet site http://nces.ed.gov/ programs/digest/d10/; calculations by New Strategist

Table 2.15 Bachelor's Degrees Earned by Total People and Blacks by Field of Study, 2008–09

(total number of bachelor's degrees conferred and number and percent earned by blacks, by field of study, 2008–09)

	total	earned by blacks number	earned by blacks share of total
Total bachelor's degrees	**1,601,368**	**156,615**	**9.8%**
Agriculture and natural resources	24,988	742	3.0
Architecture and related services	10,119	486	4.8
Area, ethnic, cultural, and gender studies	8,772	1,192	13.6
Biological and biomedical sciences	80,756	6,379	7.9
Business	347,985	39,532	11.4
Communications, journalism, and related programs	78,009	7,636	9.8
Communications technologies	5,100	462	9.1
Computer and information sciences	37,994	4,322	11.4
Construction trades	168	13	7.7
Education	101,708	6,645	6.5
Engineering	69,133	3,259	4.7
Engineering technologies	15,112	1,373	9.1
English language and literature/letters	55,462	4,225	7.6
Family and consumer sciences	21,905	2,437	11.1
Foreign languages, literatures, and linguistics	21,158	919	4.3
Health professions and related clinical sciences	120,488	13,827	11.5
Legal professions and studies	3,822	656	17.2
Liberal arts and sciences, general studies, and humanities	47,096	6,701	14.2
Library science	78	2	2.6
Mathematics and statistics	15,496	876	5.7
Mechanics and repair technologies	223	20	9.0
Military technologies	55	2	3.6
Multi/interdisciplinary studies	37,444	3,522	9.4
Parks, recreation, leisure, and fitness studies	31,667	3,118	9.8
Philosophy and religious studies	12,444	761	6.1
Physical sciences and science technologies	22,466	1,315	5.9
Precision production	29	1	3.4
Psychology	94,271	11,270	12.0
Public administration and social service professions	23,851	5,498	23.1
Security and protective services	41,800	8,011	19.2
Social sciences and history	168,500	15,183	9.0
Theology and religious vocations	8,940	591	6.6
Transportation and materials moving	5,189	304	5.9
Visual and performing arts	89,140	5,335	6.0

Source: National Center for Education Statistics, Digest of Education Statistics 2010, Table 297, Internet site http://nces.ed.gov/ programs/digest/d10/; calculations by New Strategist

Table 2.16 Master's Degrees Earned by Total People and Blacks by Field of Study, 2008–09

(total number of master's degrees conferred and number and percent earned by blacks, by field of study, 2008–09)

	total	earned by blacks number	earned by blacks share of total
Total master's degrees	**656,784**	**70,010**	**10.7%**
Agriculture and natural resources	4,877	167	3.4
Architecture and related services	6,587	280	4.3
Area, ethnic, cultural, and gender studies	1,779	199	11.2
Biological and biomedical sciences	9,898	560	5.7
Business	168,375	23,220	13.8
Communications, journalism, and related programs	7,092	798	11.3
Communications technologies	475	53	11.2
Computer and information sciences	17,907	1,107	6.2
Education	178,564	18,697	10.5
Engineering	34,750	993	2.9
Engineering technologies	3,455	238	6.9
English language and literature/letters	9,261	460	5.0
Family and consumer sciences	2,453	304	12.4
Foreign languages, literatures, and linguistics	3,592	98	2.7
Health professions and related clinical sciences	62,620	6,716	10.7
Legal professions and studies	5,150	311	6.0
Liberal arts and sciences, general studies, and humanities	3,728	356	9.5
Library science	7,091	350	4.9
Mathematics and statistics	5,211	153	2.9
Military technologies	3	0	0.0
Multi/interdisciplinary studies	5,344	391	7.3
Parks, recreation, leisure, and fitness studies	4,822	443	0.0
Philosophy and religious studies	1,859	99	5.3
Physical sciences and science technologies	5,658	187	3.3
Precision production	10	0	0.0
Psychology	23,415	3,317	14.2
Public administration and social service professions	33,933	6,419	18.9
Security and protective services	6,128	1,263	20.6
Social sciences and history	19,240	1,349	7.0
Theology and religious vocations	7,541	716	9.5
Transportation and materials moving	1,048	59	5.6
Visual and performing arts	14,918	707	4.7

Source: National Center for Education Statistics, Digest of Education Statistics 2010, Table 300, Internet site http://nces.ed.gov/programs/digest/d10/; calculations by New Strategist

Table 2.17 Doctoral Degrees Earned by Total People and Blacks by Field of Study, 2008–09

(total number of doctoral degrees conferred and number and percent earned by blacks, by field of study, 2008–09)

	total	earned by blacks number	share of total
Total doctoral degrees	**67,716**	**4,434**	**6.5%**
Agriculture and natural resources	1,328	31	2.3
Architecture and related services	212	7	3.3
Area, ethnic, cultural, and gender studies	239	41	17.2
Biological and biomedical sciences	6,957	264	3.8
Business	2,123	267	12.6
Communications, journalism, and related programs	533	41	7.7
Communications technologies	2	0	0.0
Computer and information sciences	1,580	34	2.2
Education	9,028	1,585	17.6
Engineering	7,931	156	2.0
Engineering technologies	59	4	6.8
English language and literature/letters	1,271	63	5.0
Family and consumer sciences	333	43	12.9
Foreign languages, literatures, and linguistics	1,111	16	1.4
Health professions and related clinical sciences	12,112	651	5.4
Legal professions and studies	259	14	5.4
Liberal arts and sciences, general studies, and humanities	67	10	14.9
Library science	35	3	8.6
Mathematics and statistics	1,535	30	2.0
Multi/interdisciplinary studies	1,273	98	7.7
Parks, recreation, leisure, and fitness studies	285	15	5.3
Philosophy and religious studies	686	41	6.0
Physical sciences and science technologies	5,048	89	1.8
Psychology	5,477	390	7.1
Public administration and social service professions	812	104	12.8
Security and protective services	97	5	5.2
Social sciences and history	4,234	198	4.7
Theology and religious vocations	1,520	189	12.4
Visual and performing arts	1,569	45	2.9

Source: National Center for Education Statistics, Digest of Education Statistics 2010, Table 303, Internet site http://nces.ed.gov/programs/digest/d10/; calculations by New Strategist

Table 2.18 First-Professional Degrees Earned by Total People and Blacks by Field of Study, 2008–09

(total number of first-professional degrees conferred and number and percent earned by blacks, by field of study, 2008–09)

		earned by blacks	
	total	number	share of total
Total first-professional degrees	**92,004**	**6,571**	**7.1%**
Dentistry (D.D.S. or D.M.D.)	4,918	275	5.6
Medicine (M.D.)	15,987	1,095	6.8
Optometry (O.D.)	1,338	40	3.0
Osteopathic medicine (D.O.)	3,665	150	4.1
Pharmacy (Pharm.D.)	11,291	801	7.1
Podiatry (Pod.D., D.P., or D.P.M.)	431	39	9.0
Veterinary medicine (D.V.M.)	2,377	75	3.2
Chiropractic (D.C. or D.C.M.)	2,512	94	3.7
Naturopathic medicine	78	5	6.4
Law (LL.B. or J.D.)	44,045	3,162	7.2
Theology (M.Div., M.H.L., B.D., or Ord.)	5,362	835	15.6

Source: National Center for Education Statistics, Digest of Education Statistics 2010, Table 306, Internet site http://nces.ed.gov/ programs/digest/d10/; calculations by New Strategist

Health

■ Only 42.5 percent of blacks aged 18 or older say their health is excellent or very good, which is well below the 56 percent of all adults who rate their health highly.

■ Only 40 percent of black adults are current regular drinkers compared with a much larger 51 percent of all adults.

■ Seventy-one percent of black adults are overweight. Thirty-eight percent are obese.

■ Of the 4.1 million births in the United States in 2009, blacks accounted for a substantial 15 percent. Seventy-two percent of black births are to unmarried women.

■ The 79 percent majority of blacks had health insurance coverage in 2009. The percentage of blacks without health insurance reaches a high of 36 percent in the 18-to-24 age group.

■ At birth, blacks can expect to live 74.3 years, well below the 78.2 years of life expectancy at birth for the average American.

Blacks Are Less Likely to Say Their Health Is Excellent or Very Good

The percentage of blacks who rate their health as excellent or very good has declined.

Only 42.5 percent of blacks aged 18 or older say their health is excellent or very good, according to the federal government's Behavioral Risk Factor Surveillance System. This is well below the 56.0 percent of all adults who rate their health highly. Blacks are more likely than the average person to say their health is only fair or poor.

Between 2000 and 2009, the percentage of blacks who rated their health as excellent fell by 2 percentage points. During those same years, the proportion of those who rated their health as only good or fair climbed 1 to 2 percentage points. Five percent of blacks reported poor health in 2009, about the same as in 2000.

■ A lack of health insurance and problems accessing health care services could be affecting the health status of blacks.

Blacks are less likely than the average American to rate their health highly

(percent of total people and blacks aged 18 or older who rate their health as excellent or very good, 2009)

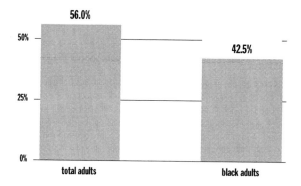

Table 3.1 Health Status of Total and Black Adults, 2009

(percent distribution of total people and blacks aged 18 or older by self-reported health status, and index of black to total, 2009)

	total	black	index black to total
Total people	100.0%	100.0%	–
Excellent	21.0	15.9	76
Very good	35.0	26.6	76
Good	29.9	35.3	118
Fair	10.5	15.2	145
Poor	3.7	5.0	135

Note: Numbers may not add to total because "not stated" is not shown. "–" means not applicable.
Source: Centers for Disease Control and Prevention, Behavioral Risk Factor Surveillance System, Prevalence Data, Internet site http://apps.nccd.cdc.gov/brfss/index.asp; calculations by New Strategist

Table 3.2 Black Health Status, 2000 and 2009

(percent distribution of blacks aged 18 or older by self-reported health status, 2000 and 2009; percentage point change, 2000–09)

	2009	2000	percentage point change
Total blacks	100.0%	100.0%	–
Excellent	15.9	18.3	–2.4
Very good	26.6	28.9	–2.3
Good	35.3	33.3	2.0
Fair	15.2	13.8	1.4
Poor	5.0	5.1	–0.1

Note: Numbers may not add to total because "not stated" is not shown. "–" means not applicable.
Source: Centers for Disease Control and Prevention, Behavioral Risk Factor Surveillance System, Prevalence Data, Internet site http://apps.nccd.cdc.gov/brfss/index.asp; calculations by New Strategist

Among Blacks, One in Five Smokes Cigarettes

Blacks are much less likely than the average American to drink alcohol.

Blacks smoke cigarettes at an average rate. Twenty-one percent of blacks aged 18 or older are current smokers, the same percentage as among all adults in the United States. Sixty-four percent of blacks aged 18 or older have never smoked, a larger share than the 57 percent of all Americans who never started smoking.

Only 40 percent of blacks are current regular drinkers, meaning they have had more than 12 alcoholic drinks in the past year. This compares with a much larger 51 percent of all adults who are current regular drinkers. Twenty-eight percent of blacks are lifetime abstainers versus a smaller 20 percent of all Americans.

■ Only 14 percent of blacks are former smokers compared with 22 percent of all adults.

Blacks are equally likely to smoke, but less likely to drink, than the average American

(percent of total people and blacks aged 18 or older by smoking and drinking status, 2009)

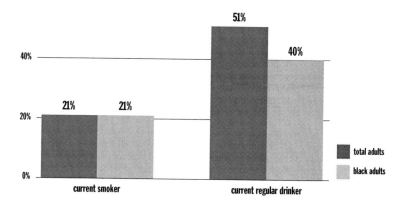

Table 3.3 Smoking Status of Total People and Black Adults, 2009

(number and percent distribution of total people and blacks aged 18 or older, by smoking status, 2009)

	total		blacks	
	number	percent distribution	number	percent distribution
Total people	**227,371**	**100.0%**	**27,374**	**100.0%**
All current smokers	46,641	20.5	5,732	20.9
Every-day smoker	36,434	16.0	4,232	15.5
Some-day smoker	10,206	4.5	1,500	5.5
Former smoker	49,878	21.9	3,962	14.5
Nonsmoker	130,045	57.2	17,595	64.3

Note: Current smokers have smoked at least 100 cigarettes in lifetime and still smoke; every-day smokers are current smokers who smoke every day; some-day smokers are current smokers who smoke on some days; former smokers have smoked at least 100 cigarettes in lifetime but currently do not smoke; nonsmokers have smoked fewer than 100 cigarettes in lifetime. Numbers by smoking status may not add to total because "unknown" is not shown. Blacks are those who identify themselves as being of the race alone.
Source: National Center for Health Statistics, Summary Health Statistics for U.S. Adults: National Health Interview Survey, 2009, Vital and Health Statistics, Series 10, No. 249, 2010, Internet site http://www.cdc.gov/nchs/nhis.htm; calculations by New Strategist

Table 3.4 Drinking Status of Total and Black Adults, 2009

(number and percent distribution of total people and blacks aged 18 or older, by drinking status, 2009)

	total		blacks	
	number	percent distribution	number	percent distribution
Total people	**227,371**	**100.0%**	**27,374**	**100.0%**
Current regular drinker	116,236	51.1	10,951	40.0
Current infrequent drinker	28,945	12.7	3,680	13.4
Former drinker	33,567	13.9	4,529	14.5
Lifetime abstainer	44,661	19.6	7,718	28.2

Note: A lifetime abstainer had fewer than 12 drinks in lifetime; a former drinker had 12 or more drinks in lifetime, but no drinks in past year; a current drinker had 12 or more drinks in lifetime and had a drink in the past year; an infrequent drinker had fewer than 12 drinks in past year; a regular drinker had 12 or more drinks in past year. Numbers by drinking status may not add to total because "unknown" is not shown. Blacks are those who identify themselves as being of the race alone.
Source: National Center for Health Statistics, Summary Health Statistics for U.S. Adults: National Health Interview Survey, 2009, Vital and Health Statistics, Series 10, No. 249, 2010, Internet site http://www.cdc.gov/nchs/nhis.htm; calculations by New Strategist

Most Blacks Are Overweight

More than one in three are obese.

Black men aged 20 or older weigh nearly 200 pounds, on average, according to a government study that put a representative sample of Americans on a scale to measure their weight. Black women aged 20 or older weigh 185 pounds, on average. Among black adults, weight does not vary much by age.

Blacks are significantly more likely to be overweight than is the general population. Seventy-one percent of blacks are overweight, that is, they have a body mass index of 25.0 or more. Among all adults, a smaller 63 percent are overweight. Thirty-eight percent of blacks are obese—they have a body mass index of 30.0 or more. Among all adults, 28 percent are obese.

■ Only 28 percent of blacks aged 18 or older have a healthy weight compared with 35 percent of all adults.

Few blacks have a healthy weight

(percent distribution of blacks aged 18 or older by weight status, 2009)

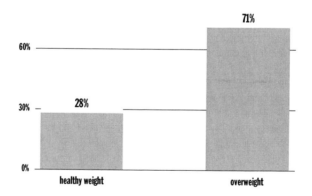

Table 3.5 Average Measured Weight of Blacks by Age and Sex, 2003–06

(average weight in pounds of non-Hispanic blacks aged 20 or older by age and sex, 2003–06)

	men	women
Total blacks	**199.8**	**184.8**
Aged 20 to 39	202.4	181.6
Aged 40 to 59	201.0	190.1
Aged 60 or older	189.0	180.8

Note: Data are based on measured weight of a sample of the civilian noninstitutionalized population.
Source: National Center for Health Statistics, Anthropometric Reference Data for Children and Adults: United States, 2003–2006, National Health Statistics Reports, No. 10, 2008, Internet site http://www.cdc.gov/nchs/products/nhsr.htm

Table 3.6 Weight Status of Total and Black Adults, 2009

(percent distribution of total people and blacks aged 18 or older by body weight status, and index of black to total, 2009)

	total	blacks	index black to total
Total people	**100.0%**	**100.0%**	–
Underweight	1.7	1.3	76
Healthy weight	35.1	27.6	79
Overweight, total	63.2	71.1	113
Obese	27.6	37.6	136

Note: Underweight is a body mass index (BMI) below 18.5; healthy weight is a BMI of 18.5 to 24.9; overweight is a BMI of 25.0 or higher; obese is a BMI of 30.0 or more. BMI is calculated by dividing weight in kilograms by height in meters squared. Data are based on self-reported heights and weights of a representative sample of the civilian noninstitutional population. Numbers may not add to total because "weight unknown" is not shown. Blacks are those who identify themselves as being of the race alone. "–" means not applicable.
Source: National Center for Health Statistics, Summary Health Statistics for U.S. Adults: National Health Interview Survey, 2009, Vital and Health Statistics, Series 10, No. 249, 2010, Internet site http://www.cdc.gov/nchs/nhis.htm; calculations by New Strategist

Most Black Children Are Born to Single Mothers

More than 70 percent of black births are to unmarried women.

Of the 4.1 million births in the United States in 2009, non-Hispanic blacks accounted for a substantial 15 percent. Blacks account for nearly one in four births to women aged 15 to 19.

In 2008, the 72 percent majority of non-Hispanic black births were to unmarried women (the latest data available on non-Hispanic black births to unmarried women by age). The percentage of births to single mothers falls with age, from virtually all births to black women under age 20 to less than half of births to black women aged 30 or older.

Although non-Hispanic blacks account for 15 percent of births nationwide, in some states the black share is much higher. The black share of births is at least 30 percent in Alabama, Georgia, Louisiana, Maryland, Mississippi, and South Carolina.

■ Because single mothers are such a large proportion of black families, the black poverty rate is well above average.

The percentage of babies born to single mothers falls with age

(percent of non-Hispanic black babies born to unmarried mothers, by age of mother, 2008)

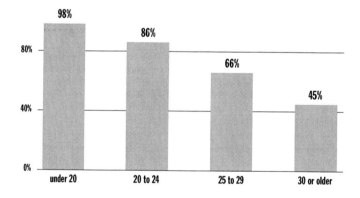

Table 3.7 Births to Total and Non-Hispanic Black Women by Age, 2009

(total number of births, number and percent distribution of births to non-Hispanic blacks, and black share of total, by age, 2009)

| | | non-Hispanic black | | |
	total	number	percent distribution	share of total
Total births	**4,131,019**	**609,552**	**100.0%**	**14.8%**
Under age 15	5,030	1,704	0.3	33.9
Aged 15 to 19	409,840	98,425	16.1	24.0
Aged 20 to 24	1,006,055	194,103	31.8	19.3
Aged 25 to 29	1,166,904	153,217	25.1	13.1
Aged 30 to 34	955,300	98,903	16.2	10.4
Aged 35 to 39	474,143	50,006	8.2	10.5
Aged 40 to 44	105,813	12,319	2.0	11.6
Aged 45 to 54	7,934	875	0.1	11.0

Source: National Center for Health Statistics, Births: Preliminary Data for 2009, National Vital Statistics Reports, Vol. 59, No. 3, 2010, Internet site http://www.cdc.gov/nchs/births.htm; calculations by New Strategist

Table 3.8 Births to Non-Hispanic Black Women by Age and Marital Status, 2008

(total number of births to non-Hispanic blacks, number of births to unmarried non-Hispanic blacks, and unmarried share of total, by age, 2008)

| | | unmarried | |
	total	number	share of total
Births to non-Hispanic blacks	**623,029**	**450,546**	**72.3%**
Under age 15	2,131	2,128	99.9
Aged 15 to 19	104,559	101,926	97.5
Aged 20 to 24	198,116	170,504	86.1
Aged 25 to 29	156,472	102,563	65.5
Aged 30 to 34	98,062	47,704	48.6
Aged 35 to 39	50,506	20,540	40.7
Aged 40 or older	13,183	5,181	39.3

Source: National Center for Health Statistics, Births: Final Data for 2008, National Vital Statistics Reports, Vol. 59, No. 1, 2010, Internet site http://www.cdc.gov/nchs/births.htm; calculations by New Strategist

Table 3.9 Births to Total and Non-Hispanic Black Women by Birth Order, 2009

(total number of births, number and percent distribution of births to non-Hispanic blacks, and black share of total, by birth order, 2009)

	total	non-Hispanic black		
		number	percent distribution	share of total
Total births	**4,131,019**	**609,552**	**100.0%**	**14.8%**
First child	1,660,342	239,262	39.3	14.4
Second child	1,291,155	170,181	27.9	13.2
Third child	679,183	102,078	16.7	15.0
Fourth or later child	473,735	91,425	15.0	19.3

Note: Numbers do not add to total because "not stated" is not shown.
Source: National Center for Health Statistics, Births: Preliminary Data for 2009, National Vital Statistics Reports, Vol. 59, No. 3, 2010, Internet site http://www.cdc.gov/nchs/births.htm; calculations by New Strategist

Table 3.10 Births to Total and Non-Hispanic Black Women by State, 2008

(total number of births, number and percent distribution of births to non-Hispanic blacks, and black share of total, by state, 2008)

| | | non-Hispanic black births | | |
	total	number	percent distribution	share of total
Total births	**4,131,019**	**609,552**	**100.0%**	**14.8%**
Alabama	62,476	19,230	3.2	30.8
Alaska	11,325	409	0.1	3.6
Arizona	92,816	4,136	0.7	4.5
Arkansas	39,853	7,649	1.3	19.2
California	527,011	31,090	5.1	5.9
Colorado	68,627	3,120	0.5	4.5
Connecticut	38,896	4,971	0.8	12.8
Delaware	11,562	3,178	0.5	27.5
District of Columbia	9,044	4,720	0.8	52.2
Florida	221,391	50,723	8.3	22.9
Georgia	141,375	46,242	7.6	32.7
Hawaii	18,888	411	0.1	2.2
Idaho	23,731	136	0.0	0.6
Illinois	171,255	29,947	4.9	17.5
Indiana	86,698	10,076	1.7	11.6
Iowa	39,700	1,907	0.3	4.8
Kansas	41,396	3,063	0.5	7.4
Kentucky	57,558	5,438	0.9	9.4
Louisiana	64,988	25,150	4.1	38.7
Maine	13,470	392	0.1	2.9
Maryland	75,061	24,992	4.1	33.3
Massachusetts	75,104	7,228	1.2	9.6
Michigan	117,293	22,071	3.6	18.8
Minnesota	70,648	6,475	1.1	9.2
Mississippi	42,905	19,043	3.1	44.4
Missouri	78,920	12,026	2.0	15.2
Montana	12,261	65	0.0	0.5
Nebraska	26,937	1,759	0.3	6.5
Nevada	37,627	3,602	0.6	9.6
New Hampshire	13,378	217	0.0	1.6
New Jersey	110,324	17,131	2.8	15.5
New Mexico	29,002	513	0.1	1.8
New York	248,110	40,982	6.7	16.5
North Carolina	126,846	30,317	5.0	23.9
North Dakota	9,001	162	0.0	1.8
Ohio	144,772	23,834	3.9	16.5
Oklahoma	54,574	5,086	0.8	9.3
Oregon	47,199	1,144	0.2	2.4
Pennsylvania	146,432	21,482	3.5	14.7

| | total | non-Hispanic black births | | |
		number	percent distribution	share of total
Rhode Island	11,443	906	0.1%	7.9%
South Carolina	60,632	19,480	3.2	32.1
South Dakota	11,935	247	0.0	2.1
Tennessee	82,213	17,405	2.9	21.2
Texas	402,011	45,493	7.5	11.3
Utah	53,887	548	0.1	1.0
Vermont	6,109	76	0.0	1.2
Virginia	105,056	23,021	3.8	21.9
Washington	89,284	4,083	0.7	4.6
West Virginia	21,270	831	0.1	3.9
Wisconsin	70,840	7,288	1.2	10.3
Wyoming	7,884	56	0.0	0.7

Source: National Center for Health Statistics, Births: Preliminary Data for 2009, National Vital Statistics Reports, Vol. 59, No. 3, 2010, Internet site http://www.cdc.gov/nchs/births.htm; calculations by New Strategist

The Plurality of Blacks Has Private Health Insurance

One in five has no health insurance.

The 79 percent majority of blacks had health insurance coverage in 2009, including 89 percent of black children. Although the 49 percent plurality of blacks has private health insurance, only 25 percent have employment-based coverage through their own employer. An even larger share, 28 percent, is covered by Medicaid (the government's health insurance program for the poor), and 12 percent of blacks are on Medicare (the government's health insurance program for people aged 65 or older). Twenty-one percent of blacks are without health insurance.

The proportion of blacks with employment-based coverage through their own job tops 50 percent among blacks ranging in age from 35 to 64. The percentage of blacks without health insurance reaches a high of 36 percent in the 18-to-24 age group.

■ Many of the nation's uninsured seek care at emergency rooms, driving up health care costs.

Blacks are more likely to be covered by private than government insurance

(percent distribution of blacks by health insurance coverage, 2009)

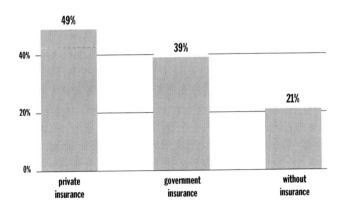

Table 3.11 Health Insurance Coverage of Total People and Blacks by Age, 2009

(number of total people and blacks with and without health insurance coverage and black share of total, 2009; numbers in thousands)

	with health insurance			without health insurance		
	total	black	black share of total	total	black	black share of total
Total people	**253,606**	**32,543**	**12.8%**	**50,674**	**8,414**	**16.6%**
Under age 65	215,669	29,232	13.6	49,998	8,320	16.6
Under age 18	67,527	11,349	16.8	7,513	1,388	18.5
Aged 18 to 24	20,389	2,890	14.2	8,923	1,628	18.2
Aged 25 to 34	29,122	3,796	13.0	11,963	2,004	16.8
Aged 35 to 44	31,689	3,905	12.3	8,759	1,345	15.4
Aged 45 to 54	36,481	4,161	11.4	7,906	1,304	16.5
Aged 55 to 64	30,462	3,131	10.3	4,933	651	13.2
Aged 65 or older	37,937	3,311	8.7	676	94	13.9

Note: Blacks are those who identify themselves as being of the race alone or as being of the race in combination with other races.
Source: Bureau of the Census, Health Insurance, Table HI01, Internet site http://www.census.gov/hhes/www/cpstables/032010/ health/toc.htm; calculations by New Strategist

Table 3.12 Health Insurance Coverage of Blacks by Age, 2009

(number and percent distribution of blacks by age and health insurance coverage status, 2009; numbers in thousands)

	total	with health insurance coverage during year			not covered at any time during the year
		total	private	government	
Total blacks	**40,957**	**32,543**	**19,901**	**16,166**	**8,414**
Under age 65	37,552	29,232	18,535	13,018	8,320
Under age 18	12,737	11,349	5,530	6,931	1,388
Aged 18 to 24	4,518	2,890	1,798	1,325	1,628
Aged 25 to 34	5,800	3,796	2,724	1,274	2,004
Aged 35 to 44	5,250	3,905	3,094	1,037	1,345
Aged 45 to 54	5,464	4,161	3,169	1,218	1,304
Aged 55 to 64	3,782	3,131	2,220	1,233	651
Aged 65 or older	3,405	3,311	1,366	3,148	94
PERCENT DISTRIBUTION BY COVERAGE STATUS					
Total blacks	**100.0%**	**79.5%**	**48.6%**	**39.5%**	**20.5%**
Under age 65	100.0	77.8	49.4	34.7	22.2
Under age 18	100.0	89.1	43.4	54.4	10.9
Aged 18 to 24	100.0	64.0	39.8	29.3	36.0
Aged 25 to 34	100.0	65.4	47.0	22.0	34.6
Aged 35 to 44	100.0	74.4	58.9	19.8	25.6
Aged 45 to 54	100.0	76.2	58.0	22.3	23.9
Aged 55 to 64	100.0	82.8	58.7	32.6	17.2
Aged 65 or older	100.0	97.2	40.1	92.5	2.8

Note: Blacks are those who identify themselves as being of the race alone or as being of the race in combination with other races. Numbers may not add to total because some people have more than one type of health insurance.
Source: Bureau of the Census, Health Insurance, Table HI01, Internet site http://www.census.gov/hhes/www/cpstables/032010/health/toc.htm; calculations by New Strategist

Table 3.13 Blacks with Private Health Insurance Coverage by Age, 2009

(number and percent distribution of blacks by age and private health insurance coverage status, 2009; numbers in thousands)

| | | with private health insurance | | | |
| | | | employment based | | direct |
	total	total	total	own	purchase
Total blacks	**40,957**	**19,901**	**18,259**	**10,080**	**1,825**
Under age 65	37,552	18,535	17,246	9,217	1,390
Under age 18	12,737	5,530	5,193	39	406
Aged 18 to 24	4,518	1,798	1,477	462	158
Aged 25 to 34	5,800	2,724	2,521	2,112	239
Aged 35 to 44	5,250	3,094	2,971	2,408	177
Aged 45 to 54	5,464	3,169	3,011	2,440	234
Aged 55 to 64	3,782	2,220	2,074	1,756	177
Aged 65 or older	3,405	1,366	1,013	863	435
PERCENT DISTRIBUTION BY COVERAGE STATUS					
Total blacks	**100.0%**	**48.6%**	**44.6%**	**24.6%**	**4.5%**
Under age 65	100.0	49.4	45.9	24.5	3.7
Under age 18	100.0	43.4	40.8	0.3	3.2
Aged 18 to 24	100.0	39.8	32.7	10.2	3.5
Aged 25 to 34	100.0	47.0	43.5	36.4	4.1
Aged 35 to 44	100.0	58.9	56.6	45.9	3.4
Aged 45 to 54	100.0	58.0	55.1	44.7	4.3
Aged 55 to 64	100.0	58.7	54.8	46.4	4.7
Aged 65 or older	100.0	40.1	29.8	25.3	12.8

Note: Blacks are those who identify themselves as being of the race alone or as being of the race in combination with other races. Numbers do not add to total because some people have more than one type of health insurance.
Source: Bureau of the Census, Health Insurance, Table HI01, Internet site http://www.census.gov/hhes/www/cpstables/032010/health/toc.htm; calculations by New Strategist

Table 3.14 Blacks with Government Health Insurance Coverage by Age, 2009

(number and percent distribution of blacks by age and government health insurance coverage status, 2009; numbers in thousands)

	total	with government health insurance			
		total	Medicaid	Medicare	military
Total blacks	**40,957**	**16,166**	**11,384**	**4,731**	**1,704**
Under age 65	37,552	13,018	10,787	1,606	1,475
Under age 18	12,737	6,931	6,439	205	466
Aged 18 to 24	4,518	1,325	1,173	68	121
Aged 25 to 34	5,800	1,274	998	150	199
Aged 35 to 44	5,250	1,037	780	192	165
Aged 45 to 54	5,464	1,218	796	370	257
Aged 55 to 64	3,782	1,233	601	620	266
Aged 65 or older	3,405	3,148	596	3,125	229
PERCENT DISTRIBUTION BY COVERAGE STATUS					
Total blacks	**100.0%**	**39.5%**	**27.8%**	**11.6%**	**4.2%**
Under age 65	100.0	34.7	28.7	4.3	3.9
Under age 18	100.0	54.4	50.6	1.6	3.7
Aged 18 to 24	100.0	29.3	26.0	1.5	2.7
Aged 25 to 34	100.0	22.0	17.2	2.6	3.4
Aged 35 to 44	100.0	19.8	14.9	3.7	3.1
Aged 45 to 54	100.0	22.3	14.6	6.8	4.7
Aged 55 to 64	100.0	32.6	15.9	16.4	7.0
Aged 65 or older	100.0	92.5	17.5	91.8	6.7

Note: Blacks are those who identify themselves as being of the race alone or as being of the race in combination with other races. Numbers may not add to total because some people have more than one type of health insurance.
Source: Bureau of the Census, Health Insurance, Table HI01, Internet site http://www.census.gov/hhes/www/cpstables/032010/health/toc.htm; calculations by New Strategist

Thirteen Percent of Blacks Have Diabetes

Blacks account for a disproportionate share of Americans experiencing a number of chronic conditions.

Blacks aged 18 or older suffer from a variety of health conditions at a higher-than-average rate. Thirty-two percent of black adults have high blood pressure, 27 percent have chronic lower back pain, and 23 percent have arthritis. Blacks account for 12 percent of the population, but are an even larger share of those with hypertension, stroke, asthma, diabetes, kidney disease, migraines, vision problems, and the absence of all natural teeth.

Black children are more likely than the average child to experience a variety of health conditions. Twenty-two percent have been diagnosed with asthma, and blacks account for more than one-fourth of all children who currently have asthma. Black children account for 17 percent of all those with a learning disability, and 9 percent of black children have been diagnosed as learning disabled. Fourteen percent have taken prescription medicine regularly for at least three months.

Seventeen percent of blacks aged 18 and older have difficulties in physical functioning. Blacks make up the largest share of cumulative AIDS cases, at 42 percent. Non-Hispanic whites account for a smaller 39 percent of the nation's total AIDS cases.

■ The poorer health of the black population is due in part to their lower socioeconomic status and lesser access to health care services.

Among AIDS cases, blacks outnumber non-Hispanic whites

(percent distribution of cumulative AIDS cases by race and Hispanic origin, through 2008)

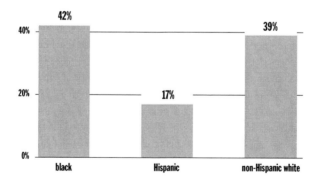

Table 3.15 Health Conditions among Total and Blacks Adults, 2009

(number of total people and blacks aged 18 or older with selected health conditions, percent of blacks with condition, and black share of total with condition, 2009; numbers in thousands)

	total	blacks number	blacks percent with condition	blacks share of total
Total people aged 18 or older	**227,371**	**27,374**	**100.0%**	**12.0%**
Selected circulatory diseases				
Heart disease, all types	26,845	2,825	11.2	10.5
Coronary	14,740	1,637	6.7	11.1
Hypertension	56,582	8,283	32.2	14.6
Stroke	6,011	901	3.8	15.0
Selected respiratory conditions				
Emphysema	4,895	360	1.5	7.4
Asthma, ever	29,734	3,854	13.8	13.0
Asthma, still	17,456	2,380	8.6	13.6
Hay fever	17,738	1,551	5.6	8.7
Sinusitis	29,305	3,513	13.0	12.0
Chronic bronchitis	9,908	1,082	3.9	10.9
Selected types of cancer				
Any cancer	18,648	1,078	4.4	5.8
Breast cancer	3,304	287	1.2	8.7
Cervical cancer	1,289	94	0.6	7.3
Prostate cancer	2,233	200	2.2	9.0
Other selected diseases and conditions				
Diabetes	20,490	3,269	13.1	16.0
Ulcers	17,665	1,746	6.6	9.9
Kidney disease	4,483	617	2.5	13.8
Liver disease	3,287	250	0.9	7.6
Arthritis	52,107	5,938	23.1	11.4
Chronic joint symptoms	64,929	6,871	26.2	10.6
Migraines or severe headaches	35,973	4,811	17.0	13.4
Pain in neck	34,954	3,569	12.9	10.2
Pain in lower back	64,810	7,286	26.7	11.2
Pain in face or jaw	11,501	1,115	4.0	9.7
Selected sensory problems				
Hearing	34,488	2,594	10.3	7.5
Vision	19,441	2,787	10.4	14.3
Absence of all natural teeth	17,271	2,279	9.8	13.2

Note: The conditions shown are those that have ever been diagnosed by a doctor, except as noted. Hay fever, sinusitis, and chronic bronchitis have been diagnosed in the past 12 months. Kidney and liver diseases have been diagnosed in the past 12 months and exclude kidney stones, bladder infections, and incontinence. Chronic joint symptoms are shown if respondent had pain, aching, or stiffness in or around a joint (excluding back and neck) and the condition began more than three months ago. Migraines, and pain in neck, lower back, face, or jaw are shown only if pain lasted a whole day or more.
Source: National Center for Health Statistics, Summary Health Statistics for U.S. Adults: National Health Interview Survey, 2009, Vital and Health Statistics, Series 10, No. 249, 2010, Internet site http://www.cdc.gov/nchs/nhis.htm; calculations by New Strategist

Table 3.16 Health Conditions among Total and Black Children, 2009

(number of total people and blacks under age 18 with selected health conditions, percent of blacks with condition, and black share of total, 2009; numbers in thousands)

| | | blacks | | |
	total	number	percent with condition	share of total
Total children	**73,996**	**11,293**	**100.0%**	**15.3%**
Asthma				
Ever had	10,196	2,441	21.9	23.9
Still have	7,111	1,893	17.0	26.6
Experienced in last 12 months				
Hay fever	7,198	835	7.5	11.6
Respiratory allergies	8,206	1,242	11.2	15.1
Food allergies	3,854	625	5.5	16.2
Skin allergies	8,913	2,005	17.9	22.5
Ever told had*				
Learning disability	5,059	863	9.3	17.1
Attention deficit hyperactivity disorder	5,288	904	9.8	17.1
Prescription medication taken regularly for at least three months	**9,873**	**1,560**	**13.9**	**15.8**

* Ever told by a school representative or health professional. Data exclude children under age 3.
Source: National Center for Health Statistics, Summary Health Statistics for U.S. Children: National Health Interview Survey, 2009, Series 10, No. 247, 2010, Internet site http://www.cdc.gov/nchs/nhis.htm

---

Table 3.17 Health Care Visits by Total People and Blacks, 2009

(total number of people and blacks aged 18 or older and percent distribution by number of visits to a doctor or other health care professional in past 12 months, and index of black to total, 2009; numbers in thousands)

	total	black	index, black to total
Total people aged 18 or older, number	**227,371**	**27,374**	–
Total people aged 18 or older, percent	**100.0%**	**100.0%**	–
No health care visits	**19.0**	**19.7**	**104**
One or more health care visits	**81.1**	**80.3**	**99**
One	16.6	16.2	98
Two to three	26.2	25.9	99
Four to nine	24.2	24.3	100
Ten or more	14.1	13.9	99

Note: The index is calculated by dividing the percentage of blacks with the number of visits by the percentage of total people with the number of visits and multiplying by 100. "–" means not applicable.
Source: National Center for Health Statistics, Summary Health Statistics for U.S. Adults: National Health Interview Survey, 2009, Vital and Health Statistics, Series 10, No. 249, 2010, Internet site http://www.cdc.gov/nchs/nhis.htm; calculations by New Strategist

Table 3.18 Difficulties in Physical Functioning among Total People and Black Adults, 2009

(number of total people and blacks aged 18 or older, number with difficulties in physical functioning, percent of blacks with difficulty, and black share of total, by type of difficulty, 2009; numbers in thousands)

	total	black number	black percent with difficulty	black share of total
Total people	**227,371**	**27,374**	**100.0%**	**12.0%**
Total with any physical difficulty	35,600	4,663	17.0	13.1
Walk quarter of a mile	15,937	2,413	8.8	15.1
Climb up 10 steps without resting	11,455	1,927	7.0	16.8
Stand for two hours	21,228	2,875	10.5	13.5
Sit for two hours	7,898	1,112	4.1	14.1
Stoop, bend, or kneel	20,651	2,659	9.7	12.9
Reach over head	5,415	809	3.0	14.9
Grasp or handle small objects	4,042	527	1.9	13.0
Lift or carry 10 pounds	9,538	1,518	5.5	15.9
Push or pull large objects	14,209	2,228	8.1	15.7

Note: Respondents were classified as having difficulties if they responded "very difficult" or "can't do at all."
Source: National Center for Health Statistics, Summary Health Statistics for U.S. Adults: National Health Interview Survey, 2009, Vital and Health Statistics, Series 10, No. 249, 2010, Internet site http://www.cdc.gov/nchs/nhis.htm; calculations by New Strategist

Table 3.19 Cumulative Number of AIDS Cases by Race and Hispanic Origin, through 2008

(cumulative number and percent distribution of AIDS cases by race and Hispanic origin, through 2008)

	number	percent distribution
Total cases	**1,073,128**	**100.0%**
American Indian	3,741	0.3
	8,253	0.8
Black	452,916	42.2
Hispanic	180,061	16.8
Non-Hispanic white	419,905	39.1

Note: Numbers do not add to total because not all races are shown and Hispanics may be of any race.
Source: Centers for Disease Control and Prevention, HIV/AIDS, Internet site http://www.cdc.gov/hiv/surveillance/resources/reports/2008report/table2a.htm

Heart Disease Is the Leading Cause of Death among Blacks

Cancer ranks second as a cause of death.

Heart disease, the leading cause of death among blacks, accounted for 26 percent of all black deaths in 2007. Cancer is the only other disease that accounted for at least 20 percent of black deaths.

Cerebrovascular disease (stroke) accounts for 6 percent of deaths among blacks and ranks third among causes of death among blacks, while accidents rank fourth and diabetes fifth. Homicide is the sixth leading cause of death among blacks, and HIV infection is ninth.

At birth, blacks can expect to live 74.3 years. This is well below the 78.2 years of life expectancy for the average American. At age 65, blacks can expect to live 17.5 more years, or 1.3 years below average.

■ Although black life expectancy has been rising, it is still below the life expectancy of the average American.

Black life expectancy is nearly five years below average

(average years of life remaining for total people and blacks at birth, 2009)

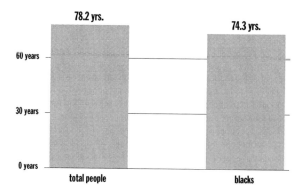

Table 3.20 Leading Causes of Death among Blacks, 2007

(number and percent distribution of deaths to blacks accounted for by the 10 leading causes of death among blacks, 2007)

	number	percent distribution
Total deaths among blacks	**289,585**	**100.0%**
1. Diseases of the heart (1)	71,209	24.6
2. Malignant neoplasms (cancer) (2)	64,049	22.1
3. Cerebrovascular diseases (3)	17,085	5.9
4. Accidents (5)	13,559	4.7
5. Diabetes mellitus (6)	12,459	4.3
6. Homicide (15)	8,870	3.1
7. Nephritis, nephrotic syndrome, nephrosis (9)	8,392	2.9
8. Chronic lower respiratory disease (4)	7,901	2.7
9. Human immunodeficiency virus infection	6,470	2.2
10. Septicemia (10)	6,297	2.2
All other causes	73,294	25.3

Note: Number in parentheses shows rank for all Americans if the cause of death is among top 15.
Source: National Center for Health Statistics, Healthm United States, 2010, Internet site http://www.cdc.gov/nchs/hus.htm; calculations by New Strategist

Table 3.21 Life Expectancy of Total People and Blacks at Birth and Age 65, 2009

(expected number of years of life remaining for total people and blacks at birth and age 65 and difference between total and black, by sex, 2009)

	total	black	difference
Life expectancy at birth			
Total	78.2	74.3	–3.9
Female	80.6	77.4	–3.2
Male	75.7	70.9	–4.8
Life expectancy at age 65			
Total	18.8	17.5	–1.3
Female	20.0	18.9	–1.1
Male	17.3	15.5	–1.8

Source: National Center for Health Statistics, Deaths: Preliminary Deaths for 2009, National Vital Statistics Report, Vol. 59, No. 4, 2011, Internet site http://www.cdc.gov/nchs/deaths.htm; calculations by New Strategist

4

Housing

■ Forty-five percent of the nation's black householders owned their home in 2010, down from a peak of 49 percent in 2004.

■ Black homeownership surpasses 60 percent among householders aged 55 or older.

■ Among black households in the South, the 52 percent majority are homeowners. Sixty-one percent of all black homeowners live in the South.

■ Among household types, black married couples are most likely to own their home. In 2009, black couples had a homeownership rate of 71 percent.

■ More than 84 percent of black homeowners have three or more bedrooms in their home. Fifty-five percent have two or more bathrooms.

■ Twenty-two percent of black homeowners report crime to be a problem in their neighborhood. Eighty-two percent are satisfied with the local public elementary school.

■ The median value of the homes owned by blacks stood at $120,000 in 2009, well below the $170,000 median value of all owned homes.

■ With a mobility rate of 17 percent, blacks are significantly more likely to move in a given year than is the average American.

The Black Homeownership Rate Has Declined

Black homeownership is well below average.

Forty-five percent of the nation's black households owned their home in 2010. This is well below the 67 percent homeownership rate for all households. Homeownership among blacks has fallen by 1.8 percentage points since 2000 and 3.7 percentage points since its peak in 2004.

The black homeownership rate rises with age, surpassing 50 percent in the 45-to-54 age group. It rises as high as 66 percent among black householders aged 75 or older. Blacks account for 9 percent of the nation's homeowners and for a larger 21 percent of the nation's renters.

■ Because so many black households are female-headed families—one of the poorest household types—black homeownership is well below average.

Black homeownership has fallen more than the overall homeownership rate

(percent of total and black households that own their home, 2000 and 2010)

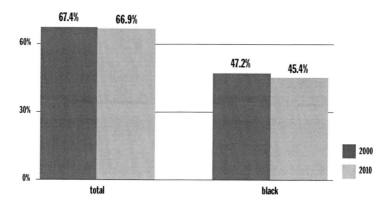

Table 4.1 Total and Black Homeownership Rate, 2000 to 2010

(homeownership rate of total and black households and index of black to total, 2000 to 2010; percentage point change in homeownership rate for selected years)

| | homeownership rate | | index, |
	total	black	black to total
2010	66.9%	45.4%	68
2009	67.4	46.2	69
2008	67.8	47.4	70
2007	68.1	47.2	69
2006	68.8	47.9	70
2005	68.9	48.2	70
2004	69.0	49.1	71
2003	68.3	48.1	70
2002	67.9	47.3	70
2001	67.8	47.7	70
2000	67.4	47.2	70
Percentage point change			
2004 to 2010	−2.1	−3.7	–
2000 to 2010	−0.5	−1.8	–

Note: Blacks include only those who identify themselves as being of the race alone. The index is calculated by dividing the black homeownership rate by the total rate and multiplying by 100. "–" means not applicable.
Source: Bureau of the Census, Housing Vacancy Surveys, Internet site http://www.census.gov/hhes/www/housing/hvs/hvs.html; calculations by New Strategist

Table 4.2 Total and Black Homeownership Rate by Age of Householder, 2009

(percent of total and black households owning a home, by age of householder, 2009)

| | homeownership rate | | index, |
	total	black	black to total
Total households	**68.4%**	**46.8%**	**68**
Under age 25	21.1	7.8	37
Aged 25 to 29	41.1	19.3	47
Aged 30 to 34	54.8	27.4	50
Aged 35 to 44	68.2	46.6	68
Aged 45 to 54	75.5	54.8	73
Aged 55 to 64	80.6	61.1	76
Aged 65 to 74	82.2	64.5	78
Aged 75 or older	77.6	65.8	85

Note: Blacks are those who identify themselves as being of the race alone. The index is calculated by dividing the black homeownership rate by the total rate and multiplying by 100.
Source: Bureau of the Census, American Housing Survey for the United States: 2009, Internet site http://www.census.gov/hhes/www/housing/ahs/ahs09/ahs09.html; calculations by New Strategist

Table 4.3 Total and Black Homeowners by Age of Householder, 2009

(number of total homeowners, number and percent distribution of black homeowners, and black share of total, by age, 2009; numbers in thousands)

| | total | black owners | | |
		number	percent distribution	share of total
Total homeowners	**76,428**	**6,547**	**100.0%**	**8.6%**
Under age 25	1,284	74	1.1	5.8
Aged 25 to 29	3,541	240	3.7	6.8
Aged 30 to 34	5,532	352	5.4	6.4
Aged 35 to 44	14,932	1,399	21.4	9.4
Aged 45 to 54	17,743	1,669	25.5	9.4
Aged 55 to 64	14,924	1,352	20.7	9.1
Aged 65 to 74	9,818	887	13.5	9.0
Aged 75 or older	8,653	573	8.8	6.6

Note: Blacks are those who identify themselves as being of the race alone.
Source: Bureau of the Census, American Housing Survey for the United States: 2009, Internet site http://www.census.gov/hhes/ www/housing/ahs/ahs09/ahs09.html; calculations by New Strategist

Table 4.4 Total Black Renters by Age of Householder, 2009

(number of total renters, number and percent distribution of black renters, and black share of total, by age, 2009; numbers in thousands)

| | total | black renters | | |
		number	percent distribution	share of total
Total renters	**35,378**	**7,446**	**100.0%**	**21.0%**
Under age 25	4,799	874	11.7	18.2
Aged 25 to 29	5,072	1,005	13.5	19.8
Aged 30 to 34	4,561	934	12.5	20.5
Aged 35 to 44	6,976	1,606	21.6	23.0
Aged 45 to 54	5,762	1,379	18.5	23.9
Aged 55 to 64	3,585	861	11.6	24.0
Aged 65 to 74	2,120	487	6.5	23.0
Aged 75 or older	2,503	298	4.0	11.9

Note: Blacks are those who identify themselves as being of the race alone.
Source: Bureau of the Census, American Housing Survey for the United States: 2009, Internet site http://www.census.gov/hhes/ www/housing/ahs/ahs09/ahs09.html; calculations by New Strategist

Table 4.5 Black Homeownership Status by Age of Householder, 2009

(number and percent distribution of black households by age of householder and homeownership status, 2009; numbers in thousands)

	total	owner	renter
Total black households	**13,993**	**6,547**	**7,446**
Under age 25	949	74	874
Aged 25 to 29	1,245	240	1,005
Aged 30 to 34	1,287	352	934
Aged 35 to 44	3,005	1,399	1,606
Aged 45 to 54	3,049	1,669	1,379
Aged 55 to 64	2,214	1,352	861
Aged 65 to 74	1,374	887	487
Aged 75 or older	872	573	298
PERCENT DISTRIBUTION BY HOMEOWNERSHIP STATUS			
Total black households	**100.0%**	**46.8%**	**53.2%**
Under age 25	100.0	7.8	92.2
Aged 25 to 29	100.0	19.3	80.7
Aged 30 to 34	100.0	27.4	72.6
Aged 35 to 44	100.0	46.6	53.4
Aged 45 to 54	100.0	54.8	45.2
Aged 55 to 64	100.0	61.1	38.9
Aged 65 to 74	100.0	64.5	35.5
Aged 75 or older	100.0	65.8	34.2

Note: Blacks are those who identify themselves as being of the race alone.
Source: Bureau of the Census, American Housing Survey for the United States: 2009, Internet site http://www.census.gov/hhes/ www/housing/ahs/ahs09/ahs09.html; calculations by New Strategist

Most Black Homeowners Live in the South

The black homeownership rate is also highest in the South.

Among the 8 million black households in the South, the 52 percent majority owns their home. The South is the only region in which the majority of black households are homeowners. Sixty-one percent of all black homeowners live in the region. The black homeownership rate is lowest in the Northeast, at just 37 percent.

Blacks account for only 9 percent of the nation's homeowners, but in the South the proportion is a larger 14 percent. Blacks account for nearly 30 percent of renters in the South. The black share of renters is also substantial in the Northeast (22 percent) and Midwest (20 percent). Because few blacks live in the West, they account for a small share of homeowners or renters in the region.

■ Blacks account for only 3 percent of homeowners in the West.

Black homeownership is lowest in the Northeast

(percent of black households that own their home, by region, 2009)

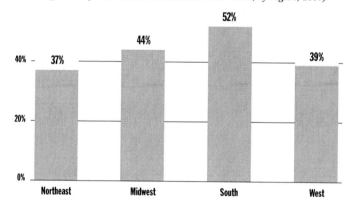

Table 4.6 Total and Black Homeownership Rate by Region, 2009

(percent of total and black households owning a home by region, and index of black to total, 2009)

| | homeownership rate | | index, |
	total	black	black to total
Total households	**68.4%**	**46.8%**	**68**
Northeast	65.4	37.2	57
Midwest	71.9	44.2	61
South	70.2	52.0	74
West	64.0	38.9	61

Note: Blacks are those who identify themselves as being of the race alone. The index is calculated by dividing the black homeownership rate by the total rate and multiplying by 100.
Source: Bureau of the Census, American Housing Survey for the United States: 2009, Internet site http://www.census.gov/hhes/ www/housing/ahs/ahs09/ahs09.html; calculations by New Strategist

Table 4.7 Total and Black Homeowners by Region, 2009

(number of total homeowners, number and percent distribution of black homeowners, and black share of total, by region, 2009; numbers in thousands)

| | | black owners | | share |
	total	number	percent distribution	of total
Total homeowners	**76,428**	**6,547**	**100.0%**	**8.6%**
Northeast	13,378	903	13.8	6.7
Midwest	18,249	1,120	17.1	6.1
South	29,193	4,014	61.3	13.7
West	15,607	510	7.8	3.3

Note: Blacks are those who identify themselves as being of the race alone.
Source: Bureau of the Census, American Housing Survey for the United States: 2009, Internet site http://www.census.gov/hhes/ www/housing/ahs/ahs09/ahs09.html; calculations by New Strategist

Table 4.8 Total and Black Renters by Region, 2009

(number of total renters, number and percent distribution of black renters, and black share of total, by region, 2009; numbers in thousands)

		black renters		
	total	number	percent distribution	share of total
Total renters	**35,378**	**7,446**	**100.0%**	**21.0%**
Northeast	7,073	1,525	20.5	21.6
Midwest	7,119	1,413	19.0	19.8
South	12,392	3,706	49.8	29.9
West	8,794	802	10.8	9.1

Note: Blacks are those who identify themselves as being of the race alone.
Source: Bureau of the Census, American Housing Survey for the United States: 2009, Internet site http://www.census.gov/hhes/www/housing/ahs/ahs09/ahs09.html; calculations by New Strategist

Table 4.9 Black Homeownership Status by Region, 2009

(number and percent distribution of black households by homeownership status and region, 2009; numbers in thousands)

	total	owners	renters
Total black households	**13,993**	**6,547**	**7,446**
Northeast	2,428	903	1,525
Midwest	2,533	1,120	1,413
South	7,720	4,014	3,706
West	1,312	510	802
PERCENT DISTRIBUTION BY HOMEOWNERSHIP STATUS			
Total black households	**100.0%**	**46.8%**	**53.2%**
Northeast	100.0	37.2	62.8
Midwest	100.0	44.2	55.8
South	100.0	52.0	48.0
West	100.0	38.9	61.1

Note: Blacks are those who identify themselves as being of the race alone.
Source: Bureau of the Census, American Housing Survey for the United States: 2009, Internet site http://www.census.gov/hhes/www/housing/ahs/ahs09/ahs09.html; calculations by New Strategist

Most Black Married Couples Are Homeowners

Among blacks, no other household type is likely to own their home.

Among the 14.6 million black households in the United States in 2009, just under half (46 percent) owned their home according to estimates from the Census Bureau's Current Population Survey. Fully 71 percent of black married couples own their home.

Among all married couples who own their home, blacks account for only 6 percent of the total. Among all female-headed families who own their home, blacks account for a much higher 21 percent.

■ The 71 percent homeownership rate of black married couples is well below the 82 percent rate of all married couples.

Black homeownership is above 50 percent only among married couples

(percent of black households that own their home, by household type, 2009)

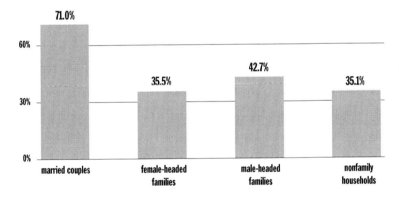

Table 4.10 Total and Black Homeownership Rate by Household Type, 2009

(percent of total and black households owning a home by household type, and index of black to total, 2009)

	homeownership rate		index,
	total	black	black to total
Total households	**67.3%**	**46.4%**	**69**
Married couples	82.5	71.0	86
Female-headed families	47.8	35.5	74
Male-headed families	57.8	42.7	74
Nonfamily households	52.3	35.1	67

Note: Blacks are those who identify themselves as being of the race alone. The index is calculated by dividing the black homeownership rate by the total rate and multiplying by 100.
Source: Bureau of the Census, Current Population Survey, Internet site http://www.census.gov/population/www/socdemo/race/black.html; calculations by New Strategist

Table 4.11 Total and Black Homeowners by Household Type, 2009

(number of total homeowners, number and percent distribution of black homeowners and black share of total, by household type, 2009; numbers in thousands)

		black owners		
	total	number	percent distribution	share of total
Total homeowners	**78,825**	**6,774**	**100.0%**	**8.6%**
Married couples	48,799	3,113	46.0	6.4
Female-headed families	6,929	1,476	21.8	21.3
Male-headed families	3,038	347	5.1	11.4
Nonfamily households	20,059	1,838	27.1	9.2

Note: Blacks are those who identify themselves as being of the race alone.
Source: Bureau of the Census, Current Population Survey, Internet site http://www.census.gov/population/www/socdemo/race/black.html; calculations by New Strategist

Table 4.12 Total and Black Renters by Household Type, 2009

(number of total renters, number and percent distribution of black renters and black share of total, by household type, 2009; numbers in thousands)

	total	black renters		
		number	percent distribution	share of total
Total renters	**38,356**	**7,820**	**100.0%**	**20.4%**
Married couples	10,318	1,274	16.3	12.3
Female-headed families	7,551	2,683	34.3	35.5
Male-headed families	2,214	465	5.9	21.0
Nonfamily households	18,272	3,399	43.5	18.6

Note: Blacks are those who identify themselves as being of the race alone.
Source: Bureau of the Census, Current Population Survey, Internet site http://www.census.gov/population/www/socdemo/race/black.html; calculations by New Strategist

Table 4.13 Black Homeownership Status by Household Type, 2009

(number and percent distribution of black households by homeownership status and household type, 2009; numbers in thousands)

	total	owners	renters
Total black households	**14,595**	**6,774**	**7,820**
Married couples	4,386	3,113	1,274
Female-headed families	4,159	1,476	2,683
Male-headed families	812	347	465
Nonfamily households	5,238	1,838	3,399
PERCENT DISTRIBUTION BY HOMEOWNERSHIP STATUS			
Total black households	**100.0%**	**46.4%**	**53.6%**
Married couples	100.0	71.0	29.0
Female-headed families	100.0	35.5	64.5
Male-headed families	100.0	42.7	57.3
Nonfamily households	100.0	35.1	64.9

Note: Blacks are those who identify themselves as being of the race alone.
Source: Bureau of the Census, Current Population Survey, Internet site http://www.census.gov/population/www/socdemo/race/black.html; calculations by New Strategist

Black Homeowners Are Achieving the American Dream

Most black homeowners have three or more bedrooms in their home.

Black homeowners are much better off than black renters, and the differences can be seen in the housing statistics. More than three out of four black homeowners live in a single-family, detached unit. Among renters, only 23 percent live in a single-family home, while 68 percent live in an apartment.

More than 84 percent of black homeowners have three or more bedrooms in their home. Among black renters, a smaller 33 percent have that many bedrooms. Fifty-five percent of black homeowners have two or more bathrooms compared with only 21 percent of renters. Not surprisingly, black home-owners are more likely than renters to have porches, garages, and fireplaces. Twenty-nine percent of black renters do not have a vehicle available for their use.

■ Nearly one in three black homeowners has a room in their home used for business.

Most black homeowners live in a single-family detached house

(percent of black households living in a single-family detached house, by homeownership status, 2009)

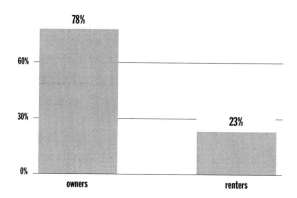

Table 4.14 Structure of Housing Units Occupied by Blacks, 2009

(number and percent distribution of housing units occupied by blacks by type of structure and homeownership status, 2009; numbers in thousands)

	total black households	owners number	owners percent distribution	renters number	renters percent distribution
Total black households	**13,993**	**6,547**	**100.0%**	**7,446**	**100.0%**
One, detached	6,850	5,100	77.9	1,750	23.5
One, attached	1,095	594	9.1	501	6.7
Multi-unit structure	5,407	351	5.4	5,056	67.9
Two to four	1,699	165	2.5	1,533	20.6
Five to nine	1,184	43	0.7	1,141	15.3
10 to 19	1,004	42	0.6	962	12.9
20 to 49	719	44	0.7	674	9.1
50 or more	801	57	0.9	745	10.0
Mobile home or trailer	643	503	7.7	140	1.9
Median square footage of unit*	1,500	1,656	–	1,280	–

* Single-family detached and mobile/manufactured homes only.
Note: Blacks are those who identify themselves as being of the race alone. "–" means not applicable.
Source: Bureau of the Census, American Housing Survey for the United States: 2009, Internet site http://www.census.gov/hhes/ www/housing/ahs/ahs09/ahs09.html; calculations by New Strategist

Table 4.15 Rooms in Housing Units Occupied by Blacks, 2009

(number and percent distribution of housing units occupied by blacks by number of rooms and homeownership status, 2009; numbers in thousands)

	total black households	owners number	owners percent distribution	renters number	renters percent distribution
NUMBER OF BEDROOMS					
Total black households	**13,993**	**6,547**	**100.0%**	**7,446**	**100.0%**
None	100	0	0.0	100	1.3
One	2,067	140	2.1	1,927	25.9
Two	3,891	902	13.8	2,989	40.1
Three	5,715	3,752	57.3	1,963	26.4
Four or more	2,220	1,753	26.8	467	6.3
NUMBER OF BATHROOMS					
Total black households	**13,993**	**6,547**	**100.0**	**7,446**	**100.0**
None	58	17	0.3	42	0.6
One	6,665	1,681	25.7	4,984	66.9
One-and-one-half	2,130	1,277	19.5	853	11.5
Two or more	5,140	3,573	54.6	1,567	21.0
ROOM USED FOR BUSINESS					
Total black households	**13,993**	**6,547**	**100.0**	**7,446**	**100.0**
With room(s) used for business	3,632	2,036	31.1	1,596	21.4

Note: Blacks are those who identify themselves as being of the race alone.
Source: Bureau of the Census, American Housing Survey for the United States: 2009, Internet site http://www.census.gov/hhes/ www/housing/ahs/ahs09/ahs09.html; calculations by New Strategist

Table 4.16 Amenities in Housing Units Occupied by Blacks, 2009

(number and percent of housing units occupied by blacks by selected amenities and homeownership status, 2009; numbers in thousands)

	total black households	owners number	owners percent	renters number	renters percent
Total black households	**13,993**	**6,547**	**100.0%**	**7,446**	**100.0%**
Porch, deck, balcony, or patio	10,717	5,668	86.6	5,049	67.8
Usable fireplace	2,866	2,207	33.7	659	8.9
Separate dining room	6,273	3,975	60.7	2,298	30.9
Two or more living or recreation rooms	2,578	2,156	32.9	421	5.7
Garage or carport					
Yes	6,194	4,257	65.0	1,937	26.0
No, but off-street parking is included	6,150	1,824	27.9	4,326	58.1
No cars, trucks, or vans	2,541	400	6.1	2,141	28.8

Note: Blacks are those who identify themselves as being of the race alone.
Source: Bureau of the Census, American Housing Survey for the United States: 2009, Internet site http://www.census.gov/hhes/ www/housing/ahs/ahs09/ahs09.html; calculations by New Strategist

Many Black Renters Live in Gated Communities

Thirty-five percent of black homeowners live near open space, parks, or woods.

Eighteen percent of black renters live in communities in which access is secured with walls or fences. Among homeowners, only 6 percent live in a gated community. Thirty-five percent of black homeowners say they live within 300 feet of open space, park, woods, farm, or ranch land. Among black renters, the proportion is 32 percent. Thirty percent of black renters report four-lane highways, railroads, or airports within 300 feet of their home compared with a smaller 19 percent of black homeowners.

Street noise and crime are the two most common neighborhood problems reported by black householders. One-third of black renters and one-fourth of black homeowners say street noise is a problem. Twenty-seven percent of black renters and 22 percent of black homeowners say crime has been a problem in their neighborhood in the past 12 months. Eighty-two percent of black homeowners are satisfied with the local public elementary school, as are 79 percent of renters. Most black householders are also satisfied with neighborhood shopping and police protection.

■ Fifty-seven percent of black homeowners and 79 percent of black renters have access to public transportation in their neighborhood.

Most black households are satisfied with the local public elementary school

(percent of black households with children under age 14 who are satisfied with the local public elementary school, by homeownership status, 2009)

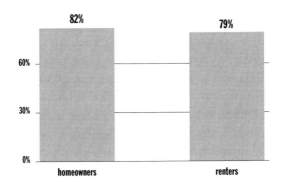

Table 4.17 Neighborhood Characteristics of Black Households, 2009

(number and percent distribution of black households by selected neighborhood characteristics and homeownership status, 2009; numbers in thousands)

	total black households	owners		renters	
		number	percent distribution	number	percent distribution
Total black households	**13,993**	**6,547**	**100.0%**	**7,446**	**100.0%**
SECURED COMMUNITIES					
Total households	**13,993**	**6,547**	**100.0**	**7,446**	**100.0**
Community access secured with walls or fences	1,738	367	5.6	1,371	18.4
Special entry system present	940	150	2.3	790	10.6
Special entry system not present	791	213	3.3	577	7.8
Community access not secured	12,152	6,124	93.5	6,028	81.0
SENIOR CITIZEN COMMUNITIES					
Households with persons aged 55 or older	**4,975**	**3,132**	**100.0**	**1,842**	**100.0**
Community age restricted	389	89	2.9	300	16.3
No age restriction	4,585	3,043	97.1	1,542	83.7
Community age specific	1,058	793	25.3	265	14.4
Community not age specific	3,174	2,006	64.1	1,168	63.4
COMMUNITY AMENITIES					
Total households	**13,993**	**6,547**	**100.0**	**7,446**	**100.0**
Community center or clubhouse	3,260	1,181	18.0	2,078	27.9
Golf in community	1,082	611	9.3	471	6.3
Trails in community	2,000	983	15.0	1,017	13.7
Shuttle bus available	1,124	422	6.4	702	9.4
Daycare center	2,454	1,157	17.7	1,297	17.4
Private or restricted beach, park, or shoreline	1,979	925	14.1	1,053	14.1
DESCRIPTION OF AREA WITHIN 300 FEET OF HOME					
Total households	**13,993**	**6,547**	**100.0**	**7,446**	**100.0**
Single-family detached homes	11,377	5,906	90.2	5,471	73.5
Single-family attached homes	3,870	1,330	20.3	2,541	34.1
Multiunit residential buildings	6,524	1,457	22.3	5,067	68.0
One-to-three-story multiunit is tallest	4,638	1,046	16.0	3,592	48.2
Four-to-six-story multiunit is tallest	1,056	263	4.0	793	10.6
Seven-or-more-story multiunit is tallest	746	130	2.0	615	8.3
Manufactured/mobile homes	1,272	824	12.6	448	6.0
Commercial or institutional establishments	6,563	2,240	34.2	4,324	58.1
Industrial or factories	1,147	401	6.1	746	10.0
Open space, park, woods, farm, or ranch	4,658	2,289	35.0	2,369	31.8
Four-or-more-lane highway, railroad, or airport	3,450	1,215	18.6	2,236	30.0

	total black households	owners		renters	
		number	percent distribution	number	percent distribution
BODIES OF WATER WITHIN 300 FEET OF HOME					
Total households	**13,993**	**6,547**	**100.0%**	**7,446**	**100.0%**
Water in area	1,548	714	10.9	834	11.2
With waterfront property	152	59	0.9	93	1.3
With flood plain	232	115	1.8	117	1.6
No water in area	12,339	5,769	88.1	6,570	88.2

Note: Blacks are those who identify themselves as being of the race alone. Numbers may not add to total because "not re-ported" is not shown.
Source: Bureau of the Census, American Housing Survey for the United States: 2009, Internet site http://www.census.gov/hhes/www/housing/ahs/ahs09/ahs09.html; calculations by New Strategist

Table 4.18 Neighborhood Problems of Black Households, 2009

(number and percent of black households by neighborhood problems and homeownership status, 2009; numbers in thousands)

	total black households	owners		renters	
		number	percent	number	percent
Total black households	**13,993**	**6,547**	**100.0%**	**7,446**	**100.0%**
Bothersome street noise or heavy traffic	4,099	1,639	25.0	2,460	33.0
Serious crime in neighborhood in past 12 months	3,473	1,428	21.8	2,045	27.5
Bothersome odor problem	944	330	5.0	614	8.2
Noise problem	473	176	2.7	296	4.0
Litter or housing deterioration	399	196	3.0	203	2.7
Poor city or county services	181	80	1.2	101	1.4
Undesirable commercial, institutional, industrial establishments	62	25	0.4	37	0.5
People problem	758	298	4.6	460	6.2
Other problems	1,415	705	10.8	710	9.5

Note: Blacks are those who identify themselves as being of the race alone.
Source: Bureau of the Census, American Housing Survey for the United States: 2009, Internet site http://www.census.gov/hhes/www/housing/ahs/ahs09/ahs09.html; calculations by New Strategist

Table 4.19 Public Services Available to Black Households, 2009

(number and percent distribution of black households by public services available in neighborhood and homeownership status, 2009; numbers in thousands)

	total black households	owners		renters	
		number	percent distribution	number	percent distribution
Total black households	13,993	6,547	100.0%	7,446	100.0%
LOCAL ELEMENTARY SCHOOL					
Households with children under age 14	4,467	1,786	100.0	2,681	100.0
Satisfactory public elementary school	3,583	1,462	81.8	2,121	79.1
Unsatisfactory public elementary school	431	172	9.6	259	9.7
Unsatisfactory public elementary school	431	172	100.0	259	100.0
Better than other area elementary schools	53	15	8.8	38	14.6
Same as other area elementary schools	115	53	30.8	62	24.0
Worse than other area elementary schools	237	91	52.8	146	56.4
Households with children under age 14	4,467	1,786	100.0	2,681	100.0
Public elementary school less than one mile	3,068	1,110	62.2	1,957	73.0
Public elementary school more than one mile	1,179	589	33.0	590	22.0
PUBLIC TRANSPORTATION IN AREA					
Total black households	13,993	6,547	100.0	7,446	100.0
With public transportation	9,575	3,719	56.8	5,856	78.6
No public transportation	4,128	2,689	41.1	1,438	19.3
With public transportation, travel time to nearest stop	9,575	3,719	100.0	5,856	100.0
Less than 5 minutes	3,688	1,221	32.8	2,468	42.1
5 to 9 minutes	3,554	1,438	38.7	2,116	36.1
10 to 14 minutes	1,308	570	15.3	738	12.6
15 to 29 minutes	542	305	8.2	237	4.0
30 minutes or longer	88	42	1.1	46	0.8
With public transportation	9,575	3,719	100.0	5,856	100.0
Household uses it regularly for commute to school or work	2,679	720	19.4	1,959	33.5
Household does not use it regularly for commute to school or work	6,801	2,963	79.7	3,838	65.5
SHOPPING IN AREA					
Total black households	13,993	6,547	100.0	7,446	100.0
Grocery stores or drugstores within 15 minutes of home	13,275	6,155	94.0	7,120	95.6
Satisfactory	12,658	5,922	90.5	6,736	90.5
Not satisfactory	535	202	3.1	334	4.5
No grocery stores or drugstores within 15 minutes of home	519	293	4.5	226	3.0

	total black households	owners		renters	
		number	percent distribution	number	percent distribution
POLICE PROTECTION					
Total black households	**13,993**	**6,547**	**100.0%**	**7,446**	**100.0%**
Satisfactory police protection	12,163	5,837	89.2	6,325	85.0
Unsatisfactory police protection	1,351	516	7.9	835	11.2

Note: Blacks are those who identify themselves as being of the race alone. Numbers may not add to total because "not reported" is not shown.
Source: Bureau of the Census, American Housing Survey for the United States: 2009, Internet site http://www.census.gov/hhes/ www/housing/ahs/ahs09/ahs09.html; calculations by New Strategist

Most Black Homeowners Rate Their House Highly

The homes owned by blacks are below average in value, however.

The median value of the homes owned by blacks stood at $120,000 in 2009, well below the $170,000 median value of all owned homes. Only 15 percent of black homeowners valued their home at $300,000 or more compared with a larger 26 percent of all homeowners.

Despite the lower value of the homes owned by blacks, most black homeowners rate their house and neighborhood highly. On a scale of 1 (worst) to 10 (best), 73 percent of black homeowners give their house an 8 or higher. Sixty-five percent give their neighborhood a rating of 8 or higher. Black renters are not as enthusiastic, with only 54 percent rating their dwelling an 8 or higher and 52 percent giving their neighborhood a high rating.

■ The lower value of the homes owned by blacks reduces the net worth of black households.

The median value of black homes is below average

(median value for all homeowners and black homeowners, 2009)

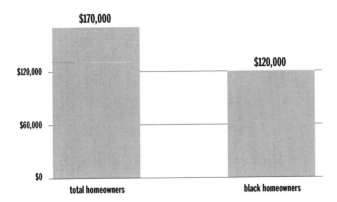

Table 4.20 Housing Value for Total and Black Homeowners, 2009

(number and percent distribution of total and black homeowners by value of home, black share of total, and median value of home, 2009; number of homeowners in thousands)

| | total | | black | | |
	number	percent distribution	number	percent distribution	share of total
Total homeowners	**76,428**	**100.0%**	**6,547**	**100.0%**	**8.6%**
Under $100,000	19,685	25.8	2,551	39.0	13.0
$100,000 to $119,999	4,980	6.5	551	8.4	11.1
$120,000 to $149,999	7,629	10.0	693	10.6	9.1
$150,000 to $199,999	11,141	14.6	882	13.5	7.9
$200,000 to $299,999	13,494	17.7	893	13.6	6.6
$300,000 to $399,999	7,924	10.4	463	7.1	5.8
$400,000 to $499,999	4,200	5.5	236	3.6	5.6
$500,000 to $749,999	4,577	6.0	211	3.2	4.6
$750,000 or more	2,798	3.7	67	1.0	2.4
Median home value	$170,000	–	$120,000	–	–

Note: Blacks are those who identify themselves as being of the race alone. "–" means not applicable.
Source: Bureau of the Census, American Housing Survey for the United States: 2009, Internet site http://www.census.gov/hhes/www/housing/ahs/ahs09/ahs09.html; calculations by New Strategist

Table 4.21 Opinion of Housing Unit and Neighborhood among Blacks, 2009

(number and percent distribution of black households by opinion of housing unit and neighborhood, by homeownership status, 2009; numbers in thousands)

	total black households	owners		renters	
		number	percent distribution	number	percent distribution
OPINION OF HOUSING UNIT					
Total black households	**13,993**	**6,547**	**100.0%**	**7,446**	**100.0%**
1 (worst)	154	38	0.6	117	1.6
2	93	20	0.3	73	1.0
3	151	21	0.3	129	1.7
4	229	48	0.7	181	2.4
5	969	271	4.1	698	9.4
6	889	290	4.4	598	8.0
7	2,037	791	12.1	1,246	16.7
8	3,582	1,660	25.3	1,922	25.8
9	1,568	923	14.1	645	8.7
10 (best)	3,660	2,206	33.7	1,454	19.5
Not reported	662	279	4.3	383	5.1
OPINION OF NEIGHBORHOOD					
Total black households	**13,993**	**6,547**	**100.0**	**7,446**	**100.0**
1 (worst)	291	51	0.8	240	3.2
2	170	34	0.5	136	1.8
3	195	71	1.1	124	1.7
4	291	77	1.2	214	2.9
5	1,250	438	6.7	812	10.9
6	959	388	5.9	571	7.7
7	2,028	931	14.2	1,097	14.7
8	3,379	1,709	26.1	1,670	22.4
9	1,725	953	14.6	772	10.4
10 (best)	3,019	1,605	24.5	1,414	19.0
Not reported	677	284	4.3	393	5.3

Note: Blacks are those who identify themselves as being of the race alone.
Source: Bureau of the Census, American Housing Survey for the United States: 2009, Internet site http://www.census.gov/hhes/www/housing/ahs/ahs09/ahs09.html; calculations by New Strategist

Black Mobility Is above Average

Most black movers stay within the same county.

Nearly 7 million blacks moved between March 2009 and March 2010, according to the Census Bureau. With a mobility rate of 17 percent, blacks are significantly more likely to move in a given year than the average American. Among black movers, 74 percent moved within the same county, and only 9 percent moved to a different state.

As is true for all movers in the United States, most moves by blacks are spurred by housing-related needs. Among black movers, the need to establish an independent household and the need for a larger house or apartment were the two top reasons for moving. When choosing their new home, the largest share of black movers said financial reasons were behind their choice, followed by room layout, and the size of the home.

■ Black mobility is above average because most blacks are renters, and renters are more likely to move than homeowners.

Seventeen percent of blacks moved between 2009 and 2010

(percent of total people and blacks aged 1 or older who moved between March 2009 and March 2010)

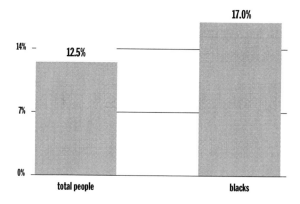

Table 4.22 Total and Black Movers by Age, 2009–10

(number of total people and blacks aged 1 or older who moved and black share of total, percent of total people and blacks aged 1 or older moving, and index of black mobility rate to total, by age, March 20089 to March 2010; numbers in thousands)

	total	black	black share of total
NUMBER MOVING			
Total movers	**37,540**	**6,829**	**18.2%**
Aged 1 to 4	3,384	842	24.9
Aged 5 to 9	2,985	710	23.8
Aged 10 to 14	2,243	548	24.4
Aged 15 to 17	1,311	344	26.2
Aged 18 to 19	1,172	210	17.9
Aged 20 to 24	5,655	879	15.5
Aged 25 to 29	5,563	864	15.5
Aged 30 to 34	3,681	559	15.2
Aged 35 to 39	2,653	401	15.1
Aged 40 to 44	2,093	418	20.0
Aged 45 to 49	1,851	295	15.9
Aged 50 to 54	1,642	311	18.9
Aged 55 to 59	1,066	147	13.8
Aged 60 to 61	366	74	20.2
Aged 62 to 64	452	66	14.6
Aged 65 or older	1,422	162	11.4

	total	black	index, black to total
PERCENT MOVING			
Total movers	**12.5%**	**17.0%**	**136**
Aged 1 to 4	19.6	27.3	139
Aged 5 to 9	14.4	20.8	145
Aged 10 to 14	11.3	16.6	148
Aged 15 to 17	10.1	15.3	151
Aged 18 to 19	14.4	16.2	113
Aged 20 to 24	26.7	27.3	102
Aged 25 to 29	25.9	28.0	108
Aged 30 to 34	18.8	20.6	110
Aged 35 to 39	13.3	15.3	115
Aged 40 to 44	10.2	15.8	156
Aged 45 to 49	8.2	10.5	128
Aged 50 to 54	7.5	11.7	156
Aged 55 to 59	5.6	7.1	128
Aged 60 to 61	5.2	9.5	183
Aged 62 to 64	4.9	7.0	142
Aged 65 or older	3.7	4.8	130

Note: Blacks are those who identify themselves as being of the race alone and those who identify themselves as being of the race in combination with other races. The index is calculated by dividing the black mobility rate by the total rate and multiplying by 100.
Source: Bureau of the Census, Geographic Mobility: 2009 to 2010, Detailed Tables, Internet site http://www.census.gov/hhes/ migration/data/cps/cps2010.html; calculations by New Strategist

Table 4.23 Geographical Mobility of Blacks by Age, 2009–10

(total number of blacks aged 1 or older, number who moved between March 2009 and March 2010, and percent distribution of movers, by age and type of move; numbers in thousands)

	total	total movers	same county	different county, same state	different state	from abroad
				movers		
Total blacks	**40,261**	**6,829**	**5,061**	**1,059**	**609**	**101**
Aged 1 to 4	3,084	842	674	88	70	11
Aged 5 to 9	3,415	710	522	111	69	8
Aged 10 to 14	3,294	548	397	93	56	2
Aged 15 to 17	2,248	344	251	70	22	1
Aged 18 to 19	1,296	210	166	36	9	0
Aged 20 to 24	3,222	879	642	147	72	18
Aged 25 to 29	3,084	864	625	128	94	18
Aged 30 to 34	2,716	559	402	87	62	8
Aged 35 to 39	2,613	401	306	57	30	9
Aged 40 to 44	2,638	418	303	69	36	10
Aged 45 to 49	2,814	295	221	40	30	4
Aged 50 to 54	2,651	311	240	47	17	7
Aged 55 to 59	2,061	147	100	29	18	0
Aged 60 to 61	776	74	54	13	5	2
Aged 62 to 64	946	66	42	19	2	3
Aged 65 or older	3,405	162	116	26	18	2

PERCENT DISTRIBUTION BY MOBILITY STATUS

		total movers	same county	different county, same state	different state	from abroad
Total blacks	–	**100.0%**	**74.1%**	**15.5%**	**8.9%**	**1.5%**
Aged 1 to 4	–	100.0	80.0	10.5	8.3	1.3
Aged 5 to 9	–	100.0	73.5	15.6	9.7	1.1
Aged 10 to 14	–	100.0	72.4	17.0	10.2	0.4
Aged 15 to 17	–	100.0	73.0	20.3	6.4	0.3
Aged 18 to 19	–	100.0	79.0	17.1	4.3	0.0
Aged 20 to 24	–	100.0	73.0	16.7	8.2	2.0
Aged 25 to 29	–	100.0	72.3	14.8	10.9	2.1
Aged 30 to 34	–	100.0	71.9	15.6	11.1	1.4
Aged 35 to 39	–	100.0	76.3	14.2	7.5	2.2
Aged 40 to 44	–	100.0	72.5	16.5	8.6	2.4
Aged 45 to 49	–	100.0	74.9	13.6	10.2	1.4
Aged 50 to 54	–	100.0	77.2	15.1	5.5	2.3
Aged 55 to 59	–	100.0	68.0	19.7	12.2	0.0
Aged 60 to 61	–	100.0	73.0	17.6	6.8	2.7
Aged 62 to 64	–	100.0	63.6	28.8	3.0	4.5
Aged 65 or older	–	100.0	71.6	16.0	11.1	1.2

Note: Blacks are those who identify themselves as being of the race alone and those who identify themselves as being of the race in combination with other races. "–" means not applicable.
Source: Bureau of the Census, Geographic Mobility: 2009 to 2010, Detailed Tables, Internet site http://www.census.gov/hhes/ migration/data/cps/cps2010.html; calculations by New Strategist

Table 4.24 Reasons for Moving among Black Movers, 2009

(number and percent distribution of black households with respondents who moved in the past 12 months by main reason for move and for choosing new neighborhood and house, 2009; numbers in thousands)

	total black movers	
	number	percent distribution
MAIN REASON FOR LEAVING PREVIOUS HOUSING UNIT		
Total black respondents who moved	**2,965**	**100.0%**
All reported reasons equal	89	3.0
Private displacement	18	0.6
Government displacement	8	0.3
Disaster loss (fire, flood, etc.)	37	1.3
New job or job transfer	191	6.4
To be closer to work/school/other	237	8.0
Other financial, employment related	125	4.2
To establish own household	353	11.9
Needed larger house or apartment	328	11.1
Married, widowed, divorced, or separated	113	3.8
Other family, personal reasons	183	6.2
Wanted better home	257	8.7
Change from owner to renter or renter to owner	86	2.9
Wanted lower rent or maintenance	190	6.4
Other housing related reasons	155	5.2
Evicted from residence	18	0.6
Other	362	12.2
Not reported	215	7.2
MAIN REASON FOR CHOOSING PRESENT NEIGHBORHOOD		
Total black respondents who moved	**2,965**	**100.0**
All reported reasons equal	284	9.6
Convenient to job	521	17.6
Convenient to friends or relatives	432	14.6
Convenient to leisure activities	18	0.6
Convenient to public transportation	73	2.5
Good schools	190	6.4
Other public services	66	2.2
Looks/design of neighborhood	316	10.6
House was most important consideration	285	9.6
Other	620	20.9
Not reported	161	5.4

| | total black movers | |
	number	percent distribution
MAIN REASON FOR CHOOSING PRESENT HOME		
Total black respondents who moved	**2,965**	**100.0%**
All reported reasons equal	304	10.2
Financial reasons	852	28.7
Room layout/design	467	15.8
Kitchen	22	0.7
Size	378	12.7
Exterior appearance	87	2.9
Yard/trees/view	60	2.0
Quality of construction	53	1.8
Only one available	135	4.5
Other	423	14.3
Not reported	185	6.2

Note: Blacks are those who identify themselves as being of the race alone.
Source: Bureau of the Census, American Housing Survey for the United States: 2009, Internet site http://www.census.gov/hhes/
www/housing/ahs/ahs09/ahs09.html; calculations by New Strategist

5

Income

■ The median income of black households stood at $32,750 in 2009, well below the all-household median of $49,777. Since 2000, the median income of black households has fallen 11 percent, after adjusting for inflation.

■ Black households have a relatively low median income because so many are headed by female-headed families, the poorest household type. Black married couples have above-average incomes, a median of $61,553 in 2009.

■ Until the Great Recession, the median income of black men and women had been growing much faster than the median income of all men and women. Between 2000 and 2009, the median income of black men fell 11 percent. The median income of black women fell 2 percent during those years.

■ Earnings rise with educational attainment. Black men with no more than a high school diploma who work full-time earned a median of $32,339 in 2009. Those with at least a bachelor's degree earned a much larger $57,806.

■ The black share of the nation's poor fell from 29 to 24 percent between 1990 and 2009. Today, Hispanics are a larger share of the poverty population than blacks.

The Great Recession Is Hurting Black Households

Since 2000, black household income has fallen sharply.

Black households had a median income of $32,750 in 2009, well below the all-household median of $49,777. The median household income of blacks is lower than the median household income of Asians, Hispanics, or non-Hispanic whites.

Until recently, black households had been making gains. Between 1990 and 2009, the median income of black households grew 10 percent, after adjusting for inflation—more than the 4 percent gain for all households during those years. Since 2000, however, black households have lost ground. The median income of black households fell 11 percent between 2000 and 2009, after adjusting for inflation. This loss was greater than the 5 percent decline in the median income of all households during those years.

Despite recent income losses, black households are still better off than they were in 1990. The median household income of blacks was 66 percent as high as the all-household median in 2009, up from 62 percent in 1990.

■ Black households have lower incomes than Asian, Hispanic, or non-Hispanic white households because they are less likely to be headed by married couples—the most affluent household type.

The median income of black households is below average

(median income of total and black households, 2009)

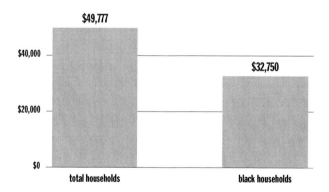

Table 5.1 Median Income of Total and Black Households, 1990 to 2009

(median income of total and black households, and index of black to total, 1990 to 2009; percent change in income, 2000–09 and 1990–2009; in 2009 dollars)

| | median income | | |
	total households	black households	index, black to total
2009	$49,777	$32,750	66
2008	50,112	34,215	68
2007	51,965	35,267	68
2006	51,278	34,183	67
2005	50,899	34,009	67
2004	50,343	34,333	68
2003	50,519	34,624	69
2002	50,563	34,787	69
2001	51,161	35,704	70
2000	52,301	36,952	71
1999	52,388	35,928	69
1998	51,100	33,315	65
1997	49,309	33,379	68
1996	48,315	31,966	66
1995	47,622	31,295	66
1994	46,175	30,093	65
1993	45,665	28,552	63
1992	45,888	28,092	61
1991	46,269	28,884	62
1990	47,637	29,712	62
Percent change			
2000 to 2009	–4.8%	–11.4%	–
1990 to 2009	4.5	10.2	–

Note: Beginning in 2002, data for blacks are for those who identify themselves as being of the race alone or being of the race in combination with other races. "–" means not applicable.
Source: Bureau of the Census, Historical Income Tables—Households, Internet site http://www.census.gov/hhes/www/income/histinc/h05.html; calculations by New Strategist

Most Black Couples Have Incomes above $60,000

The median income of black female-headed families was less than half the income of black married couples.

Among black households, married couples have the highest median income, at $61,553 in 2009. In contrast, black female-headed families had a median income of just $26,479. Because female-headed families are almost as numerous as married couples among black households, the median income of all black households is relatively modest, at $32,750 in 2009—lower than the median household income of any other racial or ethnic group.

Black household incomes rise with age to a peak of $72,835 among black couples aged 45 to 54. Black women aged 65 or older who live alone had a median income of just $13,543.

Education greatly increases household income. Black householders with a college degree had a median income of $63,798. Those with no more than a high school diploma had a median income of just $28,192.

■ Nearly 1 million black married couples had an income of $100,000 or more in 2009—22 percent of all black couples.

Black married couples have incomes far above average

(median income of black households, by type of household, 2009)

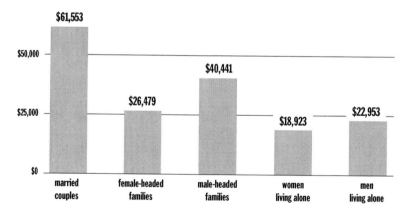

Table 5.2 Household Income by Household Type, 2009: Black Households

(number and percent distribution of black households by household income and type of householder, 2009; households in thousands as of 2010)

		family households				nonfamily households				
							female householders		male householders	
	total	total	married couples	female hh, no spouse present	male hh, no spouse present	total	total	living alone	total	living alone
Black households	**15,212**	**9,652**	**4,427**	**4,257**	**968**	**5,560**	**3,103**	**2,779**	**2,457**	**2,060**
Under $25,000	5,900	2,930	636	2,011	284	2,971	1,769	1,671	1,201	1,094
$25,000 to $49,999	4,253	2,745	1,117	1,310	318	1,510	796	703	715	583
$50,000 to $74,999	2,308	1,691	930	542	221	617	325	266	292	235
$75,000 to $99,999	1,322	1,068	768	227	73	254	124	77	131	80
$100,000 to $124,999	641	535	411	89	36	105	46	32	58	36
$125,000 to $149,999	316	264	212	32	18	53	29	25	23	15
$150,000 to $174,999	203	179	141	32	6	24	9	3	16	5
$175,000 to $199,999	76	73	63	7	4	3	1	0	2	2
$200,000 or more	189	167	148	10	9	22	3	2	19	9
Median income	$32,750	$40,695	$61,553	$26,479	$40,441	$22,726	$20,693	$18,923	$25,692	$22,953
Black households	**100.0%**	**100.0%**	**100.0%**	**100.0%**	**100.0%**	**100.0%**	**100.0%**	**100.0%**	**100.0%**	**100.0%**
Under $25,000	38.8	30.4	14.4	47.2	29.3	53.4	57.0	60.1	48.9	53.1
$25,000 to $49,999	28.0	28.4	25.2	30.8	32.9	27.2	25.7	25.3	29.1	28.3
$50,000 to $74,999	15.2	17.5	21.0	12.7	22.8	11.1	10.5	9.6	11.9	11.4
$75,000 to $99,999	8.7	11.1	17.3	5.3	7.5	4.6	4.0	2.8	5.3	3.9
$100,000 to $124,999	4.2	5.5	9.3	2.1	3.7	1.9	1.5	1.2	2.4	1.7
$125,000 to $149,999	2.1	2.7	4.8	0.8	1.9	1.0	0.9	0.9	0.9	0.7
$150,000 to $174,999	1.3	1.9	3.2	0.8	0.6	0.4	0.3	0.1	0.7	0.2
$175,000 to $199,999	0.5	0.8	1.4	0.2	0.4	0.1	0.0	0.0	0.1	0.1
$200,000 or more	1.2	1.7	3.3	0.2	0.9	0.4	0.1	0.1	0.8	0.4

Note: Blacks are those who identify themselves as being of the race alone and those who identify themselves as being of the race in combination with other races.
Source: Bureau of the Census, 2010 Current Population Survey, Internet site http://www.census.gov/hhes/www/cpstables/032010/hhinc/toc.htm; calculations by New Strategist

Table 5.3 Household Income by Age of Householder, 2009: Black Households

(number and percent distribution of black households by household income and age of householder, 2009; households in thousands as of 2010)

	total	under 25	25 to 34	35 to 44	45 to 54	55 to 64	65 or older
Total black households	**15,212**	**1,074**	**2,937**	**3,134**	**3,284**	**2,413**	**2,370**
Under $25,000	5,900	630	1,155	929	1,048	900	1,241
$25,000 to $49,999	4,253	302	920	963	815	638	615
$50,000 to $74,999	2,308	87	396	576	630	362	259
$75,000 to $99,999	1,322	25	256	309	353	243	137
$100,000 to $124,999	641	15	101	166	201	109	50
$125,000 to $149,999	316	5	59	76	88	66	23
$150,000 to $174,999	203	2	26	59	65	33	19
$175,000 to $199,999	76	2	1	27	24	16	7
$200,000 or more	189	5	22	30	61	50	21
Median income	$32,750	$20,708	$31,181	$40,291	$41,727	$34,978	$23,549
Total black households	**100.0%**	**100.0%**	**100.0%**	**100.0%**	**100.0%**	**100.0%**	**100.0%**
Under $25,000	38.8	58.7	39.3	29.6	31.9	37.3	52.4
$25,000 to $49,999	28.0	28.1	31.3	30.7	24.8	26.4	25.9
$50,000 to $74,999	15.2	8.1	13.5	18.4	19.2	15.0	10.9
$75,000 to $99,999	8.7	2.3	8.7	9.9	10.7	10.1	5.8
$100,000 to $124,999	4.2	1.4	3.4	5.3	6.1	4.5	2.1
$125,000 to $149,999	2.1	0.5	2.0	2.4	2.7	2.7	1.0
$150,000 to $174,999	1.3	0.2	0.9	1.9	2.0	1.4	0.8
$175,000 to $199,999	0.5	0.2	0.0	0.9	0.7	0.7	0.3
$200,000 or more	1.2	0.5	0.7	1.0	1.9	2.1	0.9

Note: Blacks are those who identify themselves as being of the race alone and those who identify themselves as being of the race in combination with other races.
Source: Bureau of the Census, 2010 Current Population Survey, Internet site http://www.census.gov/hhes/www/cpstables/032010/hhinc/toc.htm; calculations by New Strategist

Table 5.4 Median Household Income by Type of Household and Age of Householder, 2009: Black Households

(median income of black households by household type and age of householder, and index of black median by type/age to $49,777 national median, 2009)

	total	under 25	25 to 34	35 to 44	45 to 54	55 to 64	65 or older
Total black households	**$32,750**	**$20,708**	**$31,181**	**$40,291**	**$41,727**	**$34,978**	**$23,549**
Married couples	61,553	–	54,709	66,178	72,835	62,220	39,713
Female householder, no spouse present	26,479	15,643	21,427	28,144	34,300	35,104	29,453
Male householder, no spouse present	40,441	32,958	40,504	42,411	41,890	43,876	39,194
Women living alone	18,923	17,515	26,805	28,858	23,716	18,650	13,543
Men living alone	22,953	13,457	27,438	32,508	22,940	20,398	16,069
INDEX							
Total black households	**66**	**42**	**63**	**81**	**84**	**70**	**47**
Married couples	124	–	110	133	146	125	80
Female householder, no spouse present	53	31	43	57	69	71	59
Male householder, no spouse present	81	66	81	85	84	88	79
Women living alone	38	35	54	58	48	37	27
Men living alone	46	27	55	65	46	41	32

Note: Blacks are those who identify themselves as being of the race alone and those who identify themselves as being of the race in combination with other races. "–" means sample is too small to make a reliable estimate.
Source: Bureau of the Census, 2010 Current Population Survey, Internet site http://www.census.gov/hhes/www/cpstables/032010/hhinc/toc.htm; calculations by New Strategist

Table 5.5 Income of Black Households by Educational Attainment of Householder, 2009

(number and percent distribution of black households headed by people aged 25 or older by household income and educational attainment of householder, 2009; households in thousands as of 2010)

	total	less than 9th grade	9th–12th grade, no diploma	high school graduate	some college, no degree	associate's degree	bachelor's degree or more total	bachelor's degree	master's degree	professional degree	doctoral degree
Total black households	**14,138**	**607**	**1,624**	**4,589**	**2,912**	**1,443**	**2,964**	**1,964**	**801**	**110**	**89**
Under $25,000	5,271	450	986	2,047	964	431	393	282	86	18	8
$25,000 to $49,999	3,953	105	410	1,326	898	480	733	556	153	13	10
$50,000 to $74,999	2,220	34	148	652	540	238	607	390	196	15	5
$75,000 to $99,999	1,296	11	60	307	281	168	471	300	134	10	27
$100,000 to $124,999	626	4	11	149	115	65	283	167	84	18	13
$125,000 to $149,999	311	2	4	53	51	30	173	99	58	6	9
$150,000 to $174,999	201	2	1	25	29	12	134	86	33	3	11
$175,000 to $199,999	74	0	0	8	9	9	46	22	24	0	0
$200,000 or more	184	2	3	18	27	11	123	59	33	25	6
Median income	$34,384	$14,031	$18,585	$28,192	$36,459	$37,417	$63,798	$59,175	$70,081	$97,434	$86,662
Total black households	**100.0%**	**100.0%**	**100.0%**	**100.0%**	**100.0%**	**100.0%**	**100.0%**	**100.0%**	**100.0%**	**100.0%**	**100.0%**
Under $25,000	37.3	74.1	60.7	44.6	33.1	29.9	13.3	14.4	10.7	16.4	9.0
$25,000 to $49,999	28.0	17.3	25.2	28.9	30.8	33.3	24.7	28.3	19.1	11.8	11.2
$50,000 to $74,999	15.7	5.6	9.1	14.2	18.5	16.5	20.5	19.9	24.5	13.6	5.6
$75,000 to $99,999	9.2	1.8	3.7	6.7	9.6	11.6	15.9	15.3	16.7	9.1	30.3
$100,000 to $124,999	4.4	0.7	0.7	3.2	3.9	4.5	9.5	8.5	10.5	16.4	14.6
$125,000 to $149,999	2.2	0.3	0.2	1.2	1.8	2.1	5.8	5.0	7.2	5.5	10.1
$150,000 to $174,999	1.4	0.3	0.1	0.5	1.0	0.8	4.5	4.4	4.1	2.7	12.4
$175,000 to $199,999	0.5	0.0	0.0	0.2	0.3	0.6	1.6	1.1	3.0	0.0	0.0
$200,000 or more	1.3	0.3	0.2	0.4	0.9	0.8	4.1	3.0	4.1	22.7	6.7

Note: Blacks are those who identify themselves as being of the race alone or the race in combination with other races.
Source: Bureau of the Census, 2010 Current Population Survey, Internet site http://www.census.gov/hhes/www/cpstables/032010/hhinc/toc.htm; calculations by New Strategist

Table 5.6 Income of Black Households by Region, 2009

(number and percent distribution of black households by household income and region, 2009; households in thousands as of 2010)

	total	Northeast	Midwest	South	West
Total black households	**15,212**	**2,602**	**2,761**	**8,419**	**1,430**
Under $25,000	5,900	952	1,188	3,249	512
$25,000 to $49,999	4,253	762	745	2,375	372
$50,000 to $74,999	2,308	371	413	1,292	232
$75,000 to $99,999	1,322	256	202	723	142
$100,000 to $124,999	641	116	99	363	64
$125,000 to $149,999	316	45	43	181	46
$150,000 to $174,999	203	43	20	109	32
$175,000 to $199,999	76	17	16	36	9
$200,000 or more	189	43	35	90	21
Median income	$32,750	$33,987	$29,698	$33,231	$37,253
Total black households	**100.0%**	**100.0%**	**100.0%**	**100.0%**	**100.0%**
Under $25,000	38.8	36.6	43.0	38.6	35.8
$25,000 to $49,999	28.0	29.3	27.0	28.2	26.0
$50,000 to $74,999	15.2	14.3	15.0	15.3	16.2
$75,000 to $99,999	8.7	9.8	7.3	8.6	9.9
$100,000 to $124,999	4.2	4.5	3.6	4.3	4.5
$125,000 to $149,999	2.1	1.7	1.6	2.1	3.2
$150,000 to $174,999	1.3	1.7	0.7	1.3	2.2
$175,000 to $199,999	0.5	0.7	0.6	0.4	0.6
$200,000 or more	1.2	1.7	1.3	1.1	1.5

Note: Blacks are those who identify themselves as being of the race alone or the race in combination with other races.
Source: Bureau of the Census, 2010 Current Population Survey, Internet site http://www.census.gov/hhes/www/cpstables/032010/hhinc/toc.htm; calculations by New Strategist

Black Men and Women Were Making Gains

The median income of black men and women was growing rapidly until the Great Recession.

The median income of black men stood at $23,674 in 2009, up 16 percent since 1990, after adjusting for inflation. The median income of black women grew even faster during those years, up 47 percent.

Between 2000 and 2009, the median income of black men and women fell 2 percent for women and 11 percent for men. Despite these declines, blacks are still ahead of where they were in 1990. In 2009, the median income of black men was 74 percent as high as the median income of all men, up from 63 percent in 1990. Black women saw their median income rise relative to the median for all women from 83 to 93 percent during those years.

■ The Great Recession has hurt blacks more than Asians, Hispanics, or non-Hispanic whites.

Black men have lost ground since 2000

(median income of black men for selected years 1990 to 2009; in 2009 dollars)

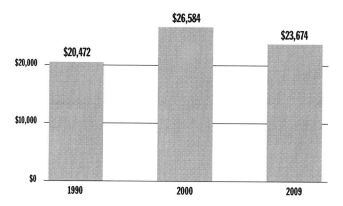

Table 5.7 Median Income of Total and Black Men, 1990 to 2009

(median income of total and black men aged 15 or older with income, and index of black to total, 1990 to 2009; percent change in income for selected years; in 2009 dollars)

	median income		
	total men	black men	index, black to total
2009	$32,184	$23,674	74
2008	33,035	25,023	76
2007	34,341	26,681	78
2006	34,324	26,676	78
2005	34,362	24,841	72
2004	34,652	25,792	74
2003	34,907	25,581	73
2002	34,860	25,645	74
2001	35,257	26,007	74
2000	35,303	26,584	75
1999	35,134	26,314	75
1998	34,814	25,391	73
1997	33,595	24,113	72
1996	32,445	22,449	69
1995	31,531	22,369	71
1994	31,085	21,442	69
1993	30,845	21,348	69
1992	30,639	19,568	64
1991	31,437	19,908	63
1990	32,284	20,472	63
Percent change			
2000 to 2009	−8.8%	−10.9%	–
1990 to 2009	−0.3	15.6	–

Note: Beginning in 2002, data for blacks are for those who identify themselves as being of the race alone or being of the race in combination with other races. The black/total indexes are calculated by dividing the median income of black men by the median income of total men and multiplying by 100. "–" means not applicable.
Source: Bureau of the Census, Current Population Surveys, Internet site http://www.census.gov/hhes/www/income/data/historical/people/index.html; calculations by New Strategist

Table 5.8 Median Income of Total and Black Women, 1990 to 2009

(median income of total and black women aged 15 or older with income, and index of black to total, 1990 to 2009; percent change in income for selected years; in 2009 dollars)

	median income		
	total women	black women	index, black to total
2009	$20,957	$19,413	93
2008	20,788	20,126	97
2007	21,643	20,392	94
2006	21,291	20,282	95
2005	20,410	19,332	95
2004	20,062	19,698	98
2003	20,128	19,290	96
2002	20,045	19,876	99
2001	20,129	19,726	98
2000	20,007	19,781	99
1999	19,701	19,021	97
1998	18,963	17,264	91
1997	18,259	17,386	95
1996	17,445	16,025	92
1995	16,952	15,318	90
1994	16,410	15,090	92
1993	16,146	13,898	86
1992	16,048	13,311	83
1991	16,089	13,540	84
1990	16,020	13,249	83
Percent change			
2000 to 2009	4.7%	−1.9%	–
1990 to 2009	30.8	46.5	–

Note: Beginning in 2002, data for blacks are for those who identify themselves as being of the race alone or being of the race in combination with other races. The black/total indexes are calculated by dividing the median income of black women by the median income of total women and multiplying by 100. "–" means not applicable.
Source: Bureau of the Census, Current Population Surveys, Internet site http://www.census.gov/hhes/www/income/data/ historical/people/index.html; calculations by New Strategist

Income of Black Men Peaks in 35-to-44 Age Group

The percentage of men who work full-time also peaks in the 35-to-44 age group.

The median income of black men peaks at $34,165 in the 35-to-44 age group. Behind the income peak is labor force participation. Sixty-one percent of black men aged 35 to 44 work full-time, more than in any other age group. Among those working full-time, median income is $41,545. Median income peaks at $46,124 among black men aged 55 to 64 who work full-time.

The median income of black women also peaks in the 35-to-44 age group, at $27,122, well below the median of black men. The labor force participation of black women is highest among those aged 35-to-44 as well, with 56 percent working full-time. Among full-time workers, women's median income peaks at $36,989 in the 45-to-54 age group.

Black men who work full-time have a median income 80 percent as high as the average man with a full-time job, up from 74 percent in 1990. Black women who work full-time have a median income 88 percent as high as the average woman who works full-time—slightly lower than in 1990. Among blacks working full-time, women earn 83 percent as much as men.

■ Black incomes are below average in part because their educational attainment is less than that of non-Hispanic whites or Asians.

Black men are catching up to the average

(index of the median income of black men working full-time to the median income of all men with full-time jobs, for selected years, 1990 to 2009)

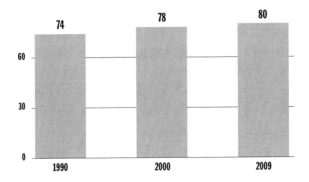

Table 5.9 Income of Black Men by Age, 2009

(number and percent distribution of black men aged 15 or older by income and age, 2009; median income of men with income and of men working full-time, year-round; percent working full-time, year-round; men in thousands as of 2010)

	total	15 to 24	25 to 34	35 to 44	45 to 54	55 to 64	65 or older
Total black men	**13,830**	**3,288**	**2,705**	**2,349**	**2,475**	**1,673**	**1,339**
Without income	2,766	1,680	382	256	243	139	65
With income	11,064	1,608	2,323	2,093	2,232	1,534	1,274
Under $10,000	2,458	921	468	255	346	222	247
$10,000 to $19,999	2,335	336	484	317	400	341	456
$20,000 to $29,999	1,754	204	488	327	338	211	186
$30,000 to $39,999	1,338	85	339	328	281	194	110
$40,000 to $49,999	975	33	191	280	233	148	87
$50,000 to $59,999	721	18	125	198	197	120	62
$60,000 to $69,999	471	0	76	105	141	94	54
$70,000 to $79,999	306	3	61	88	77	57	22
$80,000 to $89,999	186	4	31	53	55	28	15
$90,000 to $99,999	122	0	7	40	42	26	9
$100,000 or more	399	3	52	100	125	92	27
Median income of men with income	$23,674	$8,602	$24,449	$34,165	$30,740	$29,473	$18,084
Median income of full-time workers	39,280	23,752	31,819	41,545	42,358	46,124	44,425
Percent working full-time	38.8%	10.9%	48.8%	60.7%	56.0%	44.4%	9.6%
PERCENT DISTRIBUTION							
Total black men	**100.0%**	**100.0%**	**100.0%**	**100.0%**	**100.0%**	**100.0%**	**100.0%**
Without income	20.0	51.1	14.1	10.9	9.8	8.3	4.9
With income	80.0	48.9	85.9	89.1	90.2	91.7	95.1
Under $10,000	17.8	28.0	17.3	10.9	14.0	13.3	18.4
$10,000 to $19,999	16.9	10.2	17.9	13.5	16.2	20.4	34.1
$20,000 to $29,999	12.7	6.2	18.0	13.9	13.7	12.6	13.9
$30,000 to $39,999	9.7	2.6	12.5	14.0	11.4	11.6	8.2
$40,000 to $49,999	7.0	1.0	7.1	11.9	9.4	8.8	6.5
$50,000 to $59,999	5.2	0.5	4.6	8.4	8.0	7.2	4.6
$60,000 to $69,999	3.4	0.0	2.8	4.5	5.7	5.6	4.0
$70,000 to $79,999	2.2	0.1	2.3	3.7	3.1	3.4	1.6
$80,000 to $89,999	1.3	0.1	1.1	2.3	2.2	1.7	1.1
$90,000 to $99,999	0.9	0.0	0.3	1.7	1.7	1.6	0.7
$100,000 or more	2.9	0.1	1.9	4.3	5.1	5.5	2.0

Note: Blacks are those who identify themselves as being of the race alone and those who identify themselves as being of the race in combination with other races.
Source: Bureau of the Census, 2010 Current Population Survey, Internet site http://www.census.gov/hhes/www/cpstables/ 032010/perinc/toc.htm; calculations by New Strategist

Table 5.10 Income of Black Women by Age, 2009

(number and percent distribution of black women aged 15 or older by income and age, 2009; median income of women with income and of women working full-time, year-round; percent working full-time, year-round; women in thousands as of 2010)

	total	15 to 24	25 to 34	35 to 44	45 to 54	55 to 64	65 or older
Total black women	16,638	3,478	3,095	2,902	2,989	2,109	2,066
Without income	2,845	1,565	386	285	300	183	127
With income	13,793	1,913	2,709	2,617	2,689	1,926	1,939
Under $10,000	3,581	1,036	551	434	504	413	641
$10,000 to $19,999	3,460	515	662	504	508	540	730
$20,000 to $29,999	2,315	218	559	510	482	325	223
$30,000 to $39,999	1,674	107	395	397	374	259	140
$40,000 to $49,999	989	7	216	309	258	132	64
$50,000 to $59,999	635	13	133	149	196	91	51
$60,000 to $69,999	389	8	69	108	123	44	35
$70,000 to $79,999	252	1	48	66	79	39	21
$80,000 to $89,999	150	0	27	47	49	22	6
$90,000 to $99,999	90	1	7	30	29	19	5
$100,000 or more	257	5	40	58	90	41	23
Median income of women with income	$19,413	$8,914	$22,175	$27,122	$26,604	$20,199	$12,873
Median income of full-time workers	32,723	22,573	31,354	35,921	36,989	33,901	36,752
Percent working full-time	36.4%	13.4%	47.3%	55.7%	53.2%	37.4%	6.6%
PERCENT DISTRIBUTION							
Total black women	100.0%	100.0%	100.0%	100.0%	100.0%	100.0%	100.0%
Without income	17.1	45.0	12.5	9.8	10.0	8.7	6.1
With income	82.9	55.0	87.5	90.2	90.0	91.3	93.9
Under $10,000	21.5	29.8	17.8	15.0	16.9	19.6	31.0
$10,000 to $19,999	20.8	14.8	21.4	17.4	17.0	25.6	35.3
$20,000 to $29,999	13.9	6.3	18.1	17.6	16.1	15.4	10.8
$30,000 to $39,999	10.1	3.1	12.8	13.7	12.5	12.3	6.8
$40,000 to $49,999	5.9	0.2	7.0	10.6	8.6	6.3	3.1
$50,000 to $59,999	3.8	0.4	4.3	5.1	6.6	4.3	2.5
$60,000 to $69,999	2.3	0.2	2.2	3.7	4.1	2.1	1.7
$70,000 to $79,999	1.5	0.0	1.6	2.3	2.6	1.8	1.0
$80,000 to $89,999	0.9	0.0	0.9	1.6	1.6	1.0	0.3
$90,000 to $99,999	0.5	0.0	0.2	1.0	1.0	0.9	0.2
$100,000 or more	1.5	0.1	1.3	2.0	3.0	1.9	1.1

Note: Blacks are those who identify themselves as being of the race alone and those who identify themselves as being of the race in combination with other races.
Source: Bureau of the Census, 2010 Current Population Survey, Internet site http://www.census.gov/hhes/www/cpstables/032010/perinc/toc.htm; calculations by New Strategist

Table 5.11 Median Income of Total and Black Men Who Work Full-Time, 1990 to 2009

(median income of total and black men who work full-time, year-round, and index of black to total, 1990 to 2009;
percent change in income for selected years; in 2009 dollars)

	median income of full-time workers		
	total men	black men	index, black to total
2009	$49,164	$39,280	80
2008	47,598	38,219	80
2007	47,818	38,048	80
2006	47,828	37,777	79
2005	46,352	37,514	81
2004	47,315	36,009	76
2003	48,402	39,027	81
2002	48,296	38,112	79
2001	48,626	38,674	80
2000	48,441	37,976	78
1999	48,209	38,817	81
1998	47,640	36,102	76
1997	46,968	35,840	76
1996	45,655	36,940	81
1995	44,999	34,656	77
1994	45,242	34,928	77
1993	45,426	34,447	76
1992	46,182	34,437	75
1991	46,583	34,753	75
1990	46,103	34,174	74
Percent change			
2000 to 2009	1.5%	3.4%	–
1990 to 2009	6.6	14.9	–

Note: Beginning in 2002, data for blacks are for those who identify themselves as being of the race alone or the race in combination with other races. The black/total indexes are calculated by dividing the median income of black men by the median income of total men and multiplying by 100. "–" means not applicable.
Source: Bureau of the Census, Current Population Surveys, Internet site http://www.census.gov/hhes/www/income/data/historical/people/index.html; calculations by New Strategist

Table 5.12 Median Income of Total and Black Women Who Work Full-Time, 1990 to 2009

(median income of total and black women who work full-time, year-round, and index of black to total, 1990 to 2009; percent change in income for selected years; in 2009 dollars)

	median income of full-time workers		
	total women	black women	index, black to total
2009	$37,234	$32,723	88
2008	36,549	32,082	88
2007	37,414	32,764	88
2006	37,222	32,962	89
2005	36,539	33,363	91
2004	36,469	33,150	91
2003	36,915	32,276	87
2002	36,925	33,030	89
2001	36,855	33,071	90
2000	36,274	32,073	88
1999	35,228	32,364	92
1998	35,291	31,361	89
1997	34,683	30,333	87
1996	33,943	29,935	88
1995	33,229	29,458	89
1994	33,296	29,522	89
1993	32,843	29,695	90
1992	33,092	30,344	92
1991	32,629	29,387	90
1990	32,758	29,502	90
Percent change			
2000 to 2009	2.6%	2.0%	–
1990 to 2009	13.7	10.9	–

Note: Beginning in 2002, data for blacks are for those who identify themselves as being of the race alone or the race in combination with other races. The black/total indexes are calculated by dividing the median income of black women by the median income of total women and multiplying by 100. "–" means not applicable.
Source: Bureau of the Census, Current Population Surveys, Internet site http://www.census.gov/hhes/www/income/data/historical/people/index.html; calculations by New Strategist

Table 5.13 Median Income of Blacks Working Full-Time by Sex, 1990 to 2009

(median income of blacks working full-time, year-round, by sex, and black women's income as a percent of black men's income, 1990 to 2009; percent change in income for selected years; in 2009 dollars)

	median income of full-time workers		women's income as a percent of men's income
	black men	black women	
2009	$39,280	$32,723	83.3%
2008	38,219	32,082	83.9
2007	38,048	32,764	86.1
2006	37,777	32,962	87.3
2005	37,514	33,363	88.9
2004	36,009	33,150	92.1
2003	39,027	32,276	82.7
2002	38,112	33,030	86.7
2001	38,674	33,071	85.5
2000	37,976	32,073	84.5
1999	38,817	32,364	83.4
1998	36,102	31,361	86.9
1997	35,840	30,333	84.6
1996	36,940	29,935	81.0
1995	34,656	29,458	85.0
1994	34,928	29,522	84.5
1993	34,447	29,695	86.2
1992	34,437	30,344	88.1
1991	34,753	29,387	84.6
1990	34,174	29,502	86.3
Percent change			
2000 to 2009	3.4%	2.0%	–
1990 to 2009	14.9	10.9	–

Note: Beginning in 2002, data for blacks are for those who identify themselves as being of the race alone or the race in combination with other races. "–" means not applicable.
Source: Bureau of the Census, Current Population Surveys, Internet site http://www.census.gov/hhes/www/income/data/historical/people/index.html; calculations by New Strategist

Black Earnings Rise with Education

Eighteen percent of black men with at least a bachelor's degree earn more than $100,000.

The earnings of black men and women who work full-time rise with educational attainment. Among black men with no more than a high school diploma who work full-time, median earnings were just $32,339 in 2009. Those with at least a bachelor's degree earned a much larger $57,806.

The pattern is the same for black women, although their earnings are less than those of black men. Black women who graduated from high school and work full-time earned a median of $26,907 in 2009. Those with at least a bachelor's degree earned a much larger $49,371. Thirty-two percent of black women with a professional degree who work full-time earned $100,000 or more.

■ As black educational attainment increases, so do black earnings.

Many educated black men earn $100,000 or more

(percent of black men aged 25 or older working full-time, year-round, who earn $100,000 or more, by educational attainment, 2009)

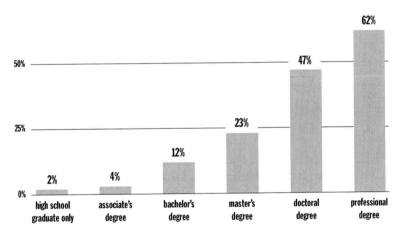

Table 5.14 Earnings of Black Men Who Work Full-Time by Education, 2009

(number and percent distribution of black men aged 25 or older working full-time, year-round by earnings and educational attainment, and median earnings of those with earnings, 2009; men in thousands as of 2010)

	total	less than 9th grade	9th–12th grade, no diploma	high school graduate	some college, no degree	associate's degree	bachelor's degree or more				
							total	bachelor's degree	master's degree	professional degree	doctoral degree
Black men working full-time	**5,004**	**87**	**342**	**1,835**	**1,028**	**492**	**1,219**	**829**	**292**	**52**	**45**
Under $10,000	90	12	8	46	14	1	11	6	5	0	0
$10,000 to $19,999	536	24	88	267	81	34	42	30	7	3	1
$20,000 to $29,999	950	20	110	451	194	84	91	83	8	1	0
$30,000 to $39,999	920	12	74	366	215	100	152	112	37	2	1
$40,000 to $49,999	764	12	22	286	163	86	193	157	31	3	2
$50,000 to $59,999	568	4	17	206	125	83	134	81	49	3	0
$60,000 to $69,999	380	4	6	85	103	37	146	92	43	4	7
$70,000 to $79,999	248	0	14	56	55	23	103	78	19	0	5
$80,000 to $89,999	148	0	2	29	25	14	79	48	21	3	7
$90,000 to $99,999	92	0	0	10	20	10	50	40	9	1	0
$100,000 or more	306	0	2	33	32	19	220	101	66	32	21
Median earnings	$40,026	$23,786	$26,362	$32,339	$40,241	$41,583	$57,806	$51,643	$61,037	–	–
Black men working full-time	**100.0%**	**100.0%**	**100.0%**	**100.0%**	**100.0%**	**100.0%**	**100.0%**	**100.0%**	**100.0%**	**100.0%**	**100.0%**
Under $10,000	1.8	13.8	2.3	2.5	1.4	0.2	0.9	0.7	1.7	0.0	0.0
$10,000 to $19,999	10.7	27.6	25.7	14.6	7.9	6.9	3.4	3.6	2.4	5.8	2.2
$20,000 to $29,999	19.0	23.0	32.2	24.6	18.9	17.1	7.5	10.0	2.7	1.9	0.0
$30,000 to $39,999	18.4	13.8	21.6	19.9	20.9	20.3	12.5	13.5	12.7	3.8	2.2
$40,000 to $49,999	15.3	13.8	6.4	15.6	15.9	17.5	15.8	18.9	10.6	5.8	4.4
$50,000 to $59,999	11.4	4.6	5.0	11.2	12.2	16.9	11.0	9.8	16.8	5.8	0.0
$60,000 to $69,999	7.6	4.6	1.8	4.6	10.0	7.5	12.0	11.1	14.7	7.7	15.6
$70,000 to $79,999	5.0	0.0	4.1	3.1	5.4	4.7	8.4	9.4	6.5	0.0	11.1
$80,000 to $89,999	3.0	0.0	0.6	1.6	2.4	2.8	6.5	5.8	7.2	5.8	15.6
$90,000 to $99,999	1.8	0.0	0.0	0.5	1.9	2.0	4.1	4.8	3.1	1.9	0.0
$100,000 or more	6.1	0.0	0.6	1.8	3.1	3.9	18.0	12.2	22.6	61.5	46.7

Note: Blacks are those who identify themselves as being of the race alone and those who identify themselves as being of the race in combination with other races. "–" means sample is too small to make a reliable estimate.
Source: Bureau of the Census, 2010 Current Population Survey, Internet site http://www.census.gov/hhes/www/cpstables/032010/perinc/toc.htm; calculations by New Strategist

Table 5.15 Earnings of Black Women Who Work Full-Time by Education, 2009

(number and percent distribution of black women aged 25 or older working full-time, year-round by earnings and educational attainment, and median earnings of those with earnings, 2009; women in thousands as of 2010)

	total	less than 9th grade	9th–12th grade, no diploma	high school graduate	some college, no degree	associate's degree	bachelor's degree or more				
							total	bachelor's degree	master's degree	professional degree	doctoral degree
Black women working full-time	**5,592**	**60**	**287**	**1,563**	**1,273**	**694**	**1,716**	**1,180**	**427**	**66**	**42**
Under $10,000	121	5	17	44	25	11	22	14	4	2	2
$10,000 to $19,999	766	26	100	365	137	88	49	38	8	2	2
$20,000 to $29,999	1,342	21	95	507	368	187	165	149	11	2	2
$30,000 to $39,999	1,206	7	36	370	323	163	307	237	64	2	4
$40,000 to $49,999	818	1	25	158	200	100	334	232	84	17	0
$50,000 to $59,999	483	0	4	52	121	75	229	152	66	4	7
$60,000 to $69,999	312	0	11	31	43	34	194	130	58	7	0
$70,000 to $79,999	196	0	0	20	21	12	144	90	45	4	5
$80,000 to $89,999	132	0	0	2	13	15	101	52	44	0	5
$90,000 to $99,999	52	0	0	2	6	2	43	28	8	6	2
$100,000 or more	163	0	0	12	15	7	128	59	36	21	13
Median earnings	$33,134	–	$22,429	$26,907	$31,760	$32,117	$49,371	$46,297	$55,824	–	–
Black women working full-time	**100.0%**	**100.0%**	**100.0%**	**100.0%**	**100.0%**	**100.0%**	**100.0%**	**100.0%**	**100.0%**	**100.0%**	**100.0%**
Under $10,000	2.2	8.3	5.9	2.8	2.0	1.6	1.3	1.2	0.9	3.0	4.8
$10,000 to $19,999	13.7	43.3	34.8	23.4	10.8	12.7	2.9	3.2	1.9	3.0	4.8
$20,000 to $29,999	24.0	35.0	33.1	32.4	28.9	26.9	9.6	12.6	2.6	3.0	4.8
$30,000 to $39,999	21.6	11.7	12.5	23.7	25.4	23.5	17.9	20.1	15.0	3.0	9.5
$40,000 to $49,999	14.6	1.7	8.7	10.1	15.7	14.4	19.5	19.7	19.7	25.8	0.0
$50,000 to $59,999	8.6	0.0	1.4	3.3	9.5	10.8	13.3	12.9	15.5	6.1	16.7
$60,000 to $69,999	5.6	0.0	3.8	2.0	3.4	4.9	11.3	11.0	13.6	10.6	0.0
$70,000 to $79,999	3.5	0.0	0.0	1.3	1.6	1.7	8.4	7.6	10.5	6.1	11.9
$80,000 to $89,999	2.4	0.0	0.0	0.1	1.0	2.2	5.9	4.4	10.3	0.0	11.9
$90,000 to $99,999	0.9	0.0	0.0	0.1	0.5	0.3	2.5	2.4	1.9	9.1	4.8
$100,000 or more	2.9	0.0	0.0	0.8	1.2	1.0	7.5	5.0	8.4	31.8	31.0

Note: Blacks are those who identify themselves as being of the race alone and those who identify themselves as being of the race in combination with other races. "–" means sample is too small to make a reliable estimate.
Source: Bureau of the Census, 2010 Current Population Survey, Internet site http://www.census.gov/hhes/www/cpstables/032010/perinc/toc.htm; calculations by New Strategist

More than One in Four Blacks Are Poor

The black poverty rate has fallen since 1990.

In 2009, 25.9 percent of blacks were poor, down from 31.9 percent in 1990. The black share of the poverty population fell from 29 to 24 percent during those years. Since the Great Recession began in 2007, the black poverty rate has grown, but the black share of the poor has continued to decline.

More than one in three black children are poor. The black poverty rate is lowest (15.3 percent) among 65-to-74-year-olds. Black women are more likely than black men to be poor.

Family type has a strong effect on black poverty. Only 8.6 percent of black married couples were poor in 2009. This compares with a poverty rate of 36.8 percent among black female-headed families. Fully 44.3 percent of black female-headed families with children are poor. This is a lower poverty rate than in 1990, however, when the 56.1 percent majority of black female-headed families with children were poor.

■ Once the economy gets back on track, the black poverty rate should continue to decline as black educational attainment grows.

The black poverty rate bottomed out in 2000

(percent of blacks below poverty level for selected years, 1990 to 2009)

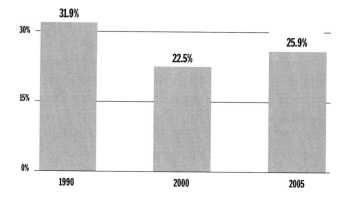

Table 5.16 Total People and Blacks below Poverty Level, 1990 to 2009

(number and percent of total people and blacks below poverty level, and black share of poor, 1990 to 2009; people in thousands as of the following year)

	total people in poverty		blacks in poverty		black share
	number	percent	number	percent	of total
2009	43,569	14.3%	10,575	25.9%	24.3%
2008	39,829	13.2	9,882	24.6	24.8
2007	37,276	12.5	9,668	24.4	25.9
2006	36,460	12.3	9,447	24.2	25.9
2005	36,950	12.6	9,517	24.7	25.8
2004	37,040	12.7	9,411	24.7	25.4
2003	35,861	12.5	9,108	24.3	25.4
2002	34,570	12.1	8,884	23.9	25.7
2001	32,907	11.7	8,136	22.7	24.7
2000	31,581	11.3	7,982	22.5	25.3
1999	32,791	11.9	8,441	23.6	25.7
1998	34,476	12.7	9,091	26.1	26.4
1997	35,574	13.3	9,116	26.5	25.6
1996	36,529	13.7	9,694	28.4	26.5
1995	36,425	13.8	9,872	29.3	27.1
1994	38,059	14.5	10,196	30.6	26.8
1993	39,265	15.1	10,877	33.1	27.7
1992	38,014	14.8	10,827	33.4	28.5
1991	35,708	14.2	10,242	32.7	28.7
1990	33,585	13.5	9,837	31.9	29.3

Note: Beginning in 2002, data for blacks are for those who identify themselves as being of the race alone or as being of the race in combination with other races.
Source: Bureau of the Census, Current Population Surveys, Internet site http://www.census.gov/hhes/www/poverty/data/ historical/index.html; calculations by New Strategist

Table 5.17 Total People and Blacks below Poverty Level by Age, 2009

(number and percent of total people and blacks below poverty level by age, and black share of total, 2009; numbers in thousands)

	total		black		
	number	percent	number	percent	share of total
Total people in poverty	**43,569**	**14.3%**	**10,575**	**25.9%**	**24.3%**
Under age 18	15,451	20.7	4,480	35.4	29.0
Under age 5	5,211	24.5	1,552	41.4	29.8
Aged 5 to 17	10,241	19.2	2,927	32.9	28.6
Aged 18 to 64	24,684	12.9	5,441	21.9	22.0
Aged 18 to 24	6,071	20.7	1,392	30.8	22.9
Aged 25 to 34	6,123	14.9	1,382	23.8	22.6
Aged 35 to 44	4,756	11.8	994	18.9	20.9
Aged 45 to 54	4,421	10.0	984	18.0	22.3
Aged 55 to 59	1,792	9.3	385	18.7	21.5
Aged 60 to 64	1,520	9.4	304	17.6	20.0
Aged 65 or older	3,433	8.9	655	19.2	19.1
Aged 65 to 74	1,675	8.0	300	15.3	17.9
Aged 75 or older	1,758	10.0	355	24.5	20.2

Note: Blacks are those who identify themselves as being of the race alone or in combination with other races.
Source: Bureau of the Census, 2010 Current Population Survey, Internet site http://www.census.gov/hhes/www/cpstables/032010/pov/toc.htm; calculations by New Strategist

Table 5.18 Blacks below Poverty Level by Age and Sex, 2009

(number and percent of blacks below poverty level by age and sex, and female share of poor, 2009; numbers in thousands)

	total	males		females		
		number	percent	number	percent	share of poor
Total blacks in poverty	**10,575**	**4,571**	**24.0%**	**6,004**	**27.5%**	**56.8%**
Under age 18	4,480	2,278	35.7	2,202	35.1	49.2
Under age 5	1,552	805	42.5	747	40.3	48.1
Aged 5 to 17	2,927	1,473	32.8	1,455	32.9	49.7
Aged 18 to 64	5,441	2,083	18.3	3,357	25.0	61.7
Aged 18 to 24	1,392	567	26.2	825	35.0	59.3
Aged 25 to 34	1,382	495	18.3	887	28.7	64.2
Aged 35 to 44	994	348	14.8	646	22.3	65.0
Aged 45 to 54	984	403	16.3	580	19.4	58.9
Aged 55 to 59	385	143	15.1	241	21.7	62.6
Aged 60 to 64	304	126	17.4	177	17.8	58.2
Aged 65 or older	655	210	15.7	445	21.5	67.9
Aged 65 to 74	300	103	12.3	197	17.5	65.7
Aged 75 or older	355	108	21.2	248	26.3	69.9

Note: Blacks are those who identify themselves as being of the race alone or in combination with other races.
Source: Bureau of the Census, 2010 Current Population Survey, Internet site http://www.census.gov/hhes/www/cpstables/032010/pov/toc.htm; calculations by New Strategist

Table 5.19 Number and Percent of Black Families below Poverty Level by Family Type, 1990 to 2009

(number and percent of black families below poverty level by family type, 1990 to 2009; families in thousands as of the following year)

	total black families in poverty		married couples		female householder, no spouse present		male householder, no spouse present	
	number	percent	number	percent	number	percent	number	percent
2009	2,193	22.7%	383	8.6%	1,569	36.8%	241	24.9%
2008	2,112	21.9	365	8.0	1,580	37.1	167	19.8
2007	2,091	22.0	313	7.0	1,570	37.2	208	25.1
2006	2,041	21.5	356	7.9	1,506	36.4	180	20.4
2005	2,050	22.0	348	8.2	1,524	36.2	178	21.3
2004	2,082	22.8	386	9.1	1,538	37.6	158	20.7
2003	2,021	22.1	331	7.8	1,496	36.8	194	24.1
2002	1,958	21.4	340	8.0	1,454	35.7	165	20.8
2001	1,829	20.7	328	7.8	1,351	35.2	150	19.4
2000	1,686	19.3	266	6.3	1,300	34.3	120	16.3
1999	1,887	21.8	295	7.1	1,487	39.2	105	14.8
1998	1,981	23.4	290	7.3	1,557	40.8	134	20.3
1997	1,985	23.6	312	8.0	1,563	39.8	111	19.7
1996	2,206	26.1	352	9.1	1,724	43.7	130	19.8
1995	2,127	26.4	314	8.5	1,701	45.1	112	19.5
1994	2,212	27.3	336	8.7	1,715	46.2	161	30.1
1993	2,499	31.3	458	12.3	1,908	49.9	133	29.6
1992	2,484	31.1	490	13.0	1,878	50.2	116	24.8
1991	2,343	30.4	399	11.0	1,834	51.2	110	21.9
1990	2,193	29.3	448	12.6	1,648	48.1	97	20.6

Note: Beginning in 2002, data for blacks are for those who identify themselves as being of the race alone or of the race in combination with other races.
Source: Bureau of the Census, Current Population Surveys, Internet site http://www.census.gov/hhes/www/poverty/data/historical/index.html; calculations by New Strategist

Table 5.20 **Number and Percent of Black Families with Children below Poverty Level by Family Type, 1990 to 2009**

(number and percent of black families with related children under age 18 below poverty level by family type, 1990 to 2009; families in thousands as of the following year)

	total black families with children in poverty		married couples		female householder, no spouse present		male householder, no spouse present	
	number	percent	number	percent	number	percent	number	percent
2009	1,787	30.4%	259	11.4%	1,365	44.3%	163	30.5%
2008	1,756	29.6	225	9.8	1,416	44.4	115	25.5
2007	1,706	29.0	194	8.5	1,385	43.7	128	29.5
2006	1,686	28.1	221	9.1	1,347	43.3	117	25.8
2005	1,679	28.3	213	9.2	1,335	42.0	131	29.6
2004	1,655	28.6	213	9.3	1,339	43.3	102	25.3
2003	1,698	28.6	210	9.1	1,341	42.7	146	30.7
2002	1,597	27.2	199	8.5	1,288	41.3	110	26.3
2001	1,524	26.6	205	8.7	1,220	40.8	99	24.6
2000	1,411	25.3	157	6.7	1,177	41.0	76	21.7
1999	1,603	28.9	199	8.7	1,320	46.0	84	21.7
1998	1,673	30.5	189	8.6	1,397	47.5	88	24.8
1997	1,721	30.5	205	9.0	1,436	46.9	81	25.8
1996	1,941	34.1	239	11.0	1,593	51.0	109	27.2
1995	1,821	34.1	209	9.9	1,533	53.2	79	23.4
1994	1,954	35.9	245	11.4	1,591	53.9	118	34.6
1993	2,171	39.3	298	13.9	1,780	57.7	93	31.6
1992	2,132	39.1	343	15.4	1,706	57.4	83	33.5
1991	2,016	39.2	263	12.4	1,676	60.5	77	31.7
1990	1,887	37.2	301	14.3	1,513	56.1	73	27.3

Note: Beginning in 2002, data for blacks are for those who identify themselves as being of the race alone or of the race in combination with other races.
Source: Bureau of the Census, Current Population Surveys, Internet site http://www.census.gov/hhes/www/poverty/data/historical/index.html; calculations by New Strategist

6

Labor Force

■ In 2010, blacks accounted for 12 percent of the labor force. Sixty-five percent of black men and 60 percent of black women are in the labor force.

■ Blacks are more likely to be unemployed than the average worker. In 2010, the black unemployment rate was 16.0 percent, substantially above the 9.6 percent rate among all workers.

■ Blacks are more likely to be managers and professionals (29 percent) than service workers (25 percent). They are 12 percent of registered nurses and 15 percent of dietitians.

■ Most black workers have at least some college experience. Twenty-four percent have a bachelor's degree.

■ Black households have fewer workers than average. There are 1.15 workers in black households compared with 1.32 workers in the average household.

■ The black labor force is projected to grow 14 percent between 2008 and 2018, faster than the 8 percent growth projected for the overall labor force.

Two-Thirds of Black Men Are in the Labor Force

Eighteen percent of black men in the labor force are unemployed.

In 2010, the labor force participation rate of black men stood at 65 percent, below the 71 percent rate for all men. At every age, black men are less likely than the average man to be in the labor force, but the gap is most pronounced among the young and the old.

Black women are slightly more likely than the average woman to be in the labor force. In 2010, nearly 60 percent of black women were in the labor force.

Black unemployment is above average. In 2010, 18 percent of black men and 14 percent of black women were unemployed. Among black men aged 16 to 19, the unemployment rate is an astonishing 45.4 percent.

■ The high unemployment rate of black men—particularly teenagers—discourages many from even looking for a job.

Black women are almost as likely as black men to work

(percent of blacks aged 16 or older in the labor force, by sex, 2010)

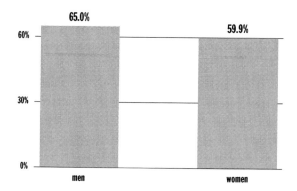

Table 6.1 Total and Black Labor Force by Sex and Age, 2010

(number of total people and blacks aged 16 or older in the civilian labor force, and black share of total, by sex and age; numbers in thousands 2010)

	total	black	black share of total
Total in labor force	**153,889**	**17,862**	**11.6%**
Aged 16 to 19	5,905	676	11.4
Aged 20 to 24	15,028	2,072	13.8
Aged 25 to 34	33,615	4,417	13.1
Aged 35 to 44	33,366	4,095	12.3
Aged 45 to 54	35,960	3,991	11.1
Aged 55 to 64	23,297	2,103	9.0
Aged 65 or older	6,718	506	7.5
Men in labor force	**81,985**	**8,415**	**10.3**
Aged 16 to 19	2,991	339	11.3
Aged 20 to 24	7,864	986	12.5
Aged 25 to 34	18,352	2,118	11.5
Aged 35 to 44	18,119	1,924	10.6
Aged 45 to 54	18,856	1,862	9.9
Aged 55 to 64	12,103	950	7.8
Aged 65 or older	3,701	236	6.4
Women in labor force	**71,904**	**9,447**	**13.1**
Aged 16 to 19	2,914	337	11.6
Aged 20 to 24	7,164	1,086	15.2
Aged 25 to 34	15,263	2,299	15.1
Aged 35 to 44	15,247	2,171	14.2
Aged 45 to 54	17,104	2,129	12.4
Aged 55 to 64	11,194	1,153	10.3
Aged 65 or older	3,017	270	8.9

Note: The civilian labor force equals the number of employed plus the number of unemployed.
Source: Bureau of Labor Statistics, Current Population Survey, Internet site http://www.bls.gov/cps/tables.htm#empstat

Table 6.2 Labor Force Participation Rate of Total People and Blacks by Sex and Age, 2010

(percent of total people and blacks aged 16 or older in the civilian labor force, and index of black to total, by sex and age, 2010)

	total	black	index, black to total
Total people	**64.7%**	**62.2%**	**96**
Aged 16 to 19	34.9	25.5	73
Aged 20 to 24	71.4	66.9	94
Aged 25 to 34	82.2	80.5	98
Aged 35 to 44	83.2	81.4	98
Aged 45 to 54	81.2	75.0	92
Aged 55 to 64	64.9	55.7	86
Aged 65 or older	17.4	15.2	87
Men	**71.2**	**65.0**	**91**
Aged 16 to 19	34.9	25.8	74
Aged 20 to 24	74.5	66.9	90
Aged 25 to 34	89.7	83.4	93
Aged 35 to 44	91.5	86.1	94
Aged 45 to 54	86.8	77.4	89
Aged 55 to 64	70.0	56.8	81
Aged 65 or older	22.1	18.1	82
Women	**58.6**	**59.9**	**102**
Aged 16 to 19	35.0	25.1	72
Aged 20 to 24	68.3	66.9	98
Aged 25 to 34	74.7	77.9	104
Aged 35 to 44	75.2	77.7	103
Aged 45 to 54	75.7	73.0	96
Aged 55 to 64	60.2	54.9	91
Aged 65 or older	13.8	13.3	96

Note: The civilian labor force equals the number of employed plus the number of unemployed. The index is calculated by dividing the black rate by the total rate and multiplying by 100.
Source: Bureau of Labor Statistics, Current Population Survey, Internet site http://www.bls.gov/cps/tables.htm#empstat

Table 6.3 Labor Force Participation Rate of Blacks by Detailed Age and Sex, 2010

(percent of blacks aged 16 or older in the civilian labor force, by age and sex, 2010)

	total	men	women
Total blacks	**62.2%**	**65.0%**	**59.9%**
Aged 16 to 19	25.5	25.8	25.1
Aged 16 to 17	14.1	13.4	14.9
Aged 18 to 19	38.8	40.7	37.0
Aged 20 to 24	66.9	66.9	66.9
Aged 25 to 34	80.5	83.4	77.9
Aged 25 to 29	79.3	82.3	76.7
Aged 30 to 34	81.7	84.7	79.3
Aged 35 to 44	81.4	86.1	77.7
Aged 35 to 39	82.0	86.8	78.2
Aged 40 to 44	80.9	85.5	77.1
Aged 45 to 54	75.0	77.4	73.0
Aged 45 to 49	77.2	79.6	75.3
Aged 50 to 54	72.6	75.1	70.6
Aged 55 to 64	55.7	56.8	54.9
Aged 55 to 59	64.3	65.2	63.6
Aged 60 to 64	45.3	46.7	44.2
Aged 65 or older	15.2	18.1	13.3
Aged 65 to 69	25.9	27.9	24.2
Aged 70 to 74	14.2	16.3	13.0
Aged 75 or older	6.9	9.3	5.6

Note: The civilian labor force equals the number of employed plus the number of unemployed.
Source: Bureau of Labor Statistics, 2010 Current Population Survey, Internet site http://www.bls.gov/cps/tables.htm#empstat

Table 6.4 Employment Status of Blacks by Sex and Age, 2010

(number and percent of blacks aged 16 or older in the civilian labor force by sex, age, and employment status, 2010; numbers in thousands)

	civilian noninstitutional population	civilian labor force			unemployed	
		total	percent of population	employed	number	percent of labor force
Total blacks	**28,708**	**17,862**	**62.2%**	**15,010**	**2,852**	**16.0%**
Aged 16 to 19	2,657	677	25.5	386	291	43.0
Aged 20 to 24	3,097	2,072	66.9	1,532	539	26.0
Aged 25 to 34	5,491	4,418	80.5	3,641	776	17.6
Aged 35 to 44	5,031	4,095	81.4	3,561	534	13.0
Aged 45 to 54	5,322	3,991	75.0	3,531	461	11.5
Aged 55 to 64	3,773	2,104	55.7	1,899	204	9.7
Aged 65 or older	3,337	506	15.2	460	47	9.2
Total black men	**12,939**	**8,415**	**65.0**	**6,865**	**1,550**	**18.4**
Aged 16 to 19	1,313	339	25.8	185	154	45.4
Aged 20 to 24	1,474	986	66.9	692	294	29.8
Aged 25 to 34	2,540	2,118	83.4	1,710	408	19.3
Aged 35 to 44	2,234	1,924	86.1	1,638	286	14.9
Aged 45 to 54	2,406	1,862	77.4	1,594	268	14.4
Aged 55 to 64	1,673	950	56.8	834	116	12.2
Aged 65 or older	1,299	236	18.1	211	24	10.4
Total black women	**15,769**	**9,447**	**59.9**	**8,145**	**1,302**	**13.8**
Aged 16 to 19	1,344	337	25.1	201	137	40.5
Aged 20 to 24	1,623	1,086	66.9	841	245	22.6
Aged 25 to 34	2,951	2,299	77.9	1,931	369	16.0
Aged 35 to 44	2,796	2,171	77.7	1,923	248	11.4
Aged 45 to 54	2,916	2,129	73.0	1,936	193	9.1
Aged 55 to 64	2,101	1,153	54.9	1,065	88	7.6
Aged 65 or older	2,038	270	13.3	248	22	8.2

Note: The civilian labor force equals the number of the employed plus the number of the unemployed. The civilian population equals the number in the labor force plus the number not in the labor force.
Source: Bureau of Labor Statistics, Current Population Survey, Internet site http://www.bls.gov/cps/tables.htm#empstat

Table 6.5 Unemployment Rate of Total People and Blacks by Sex and Age, 2010

(unemployment rate of the total and black civilian labor force and index of black to total, by sex and age, 2010)

	total	black	index, black to total
Total unemployment rate	**9.6%**	**16.0%**	**166**
Aged 16 to 19	25.9	43.0	166
Aged 20 to 24	15.5	26.0	168
Aged 25 to 34	10.1	17.6	174
Aged 35 to 44	8.1	13.0	161
Aged 45 to 54	7.7	11.5	149
Aged 55 to 64	7.1	9.7	136
Aged 65 or older	6.7	9.2	138
Men's unemployment rate	**10.5**	**18.4**	**175**
Aged 16 to 19	28.8	45.4	158
Aged 20 to 24	17.8	29.8	168
Aged 25 to 34	10.9	19.3	177
Aged 35 to 44	8.5	14.9	176
Aged 45 to 54	8.6	14.4	168
Aged 55 to 64	8.0	12.2	153
Aged 65 or older	7.1	10.4	147
Women's unemployment rate	**8.6**	**13.8**	**160**
Aged 16 to 19	22.8	40.5	177
Aged 20 to 24	13.0	22.6	174
Aged 25 to 34	9.1	16.0	175
Aged 35 to 44	7.7	11.4	149
Aged 45 to 54	6.8	9.1	134
Aged 55 to 64	6.2	7.6	122
Aged 65 or older	6.2	8.2	132

Note: The civilian labor force equals the number of employed plus the number of unemployed. The unemployment rate is calculated by dividing the number of unemployed by the civilian labor force. The index is calculated by dividing the black rate by the total rate and multiplying by 100.
Source: Bureau of Labor Statistics, Current Population Survey, Internet site http://www.bls.gov/cps/tables.htm#empstat

Many Blacks Are in Managerial and Professional Occupations

Thirty percent of blacks work in the education and health services industries

Blacks are more likely to be managers and professionals than service workers. In 2010, a substantial 29 percent of employed blacks were in managerial or professional specialty occupations, while a smaller 25 percent were service workers.

Blacks accounted for 11 percent of the overall workforce in 2010, but the black share of workers by occupation varies widely. Only 3 percent of chief executives are black, but blacks are a larger 12 percent of registered nurses and 24 percent of licensed practical nurses. Fifteen percent of dietitians are black.

By industry, blacks are most likely to work in education and health services. Thirty percent of blacks are employed in those types of organizations, where they account for 14 percent of workers.

■ Blacks account for 37 percent of the nation's barbers.

Black managers and professionals outnumber black service workers

(percent distribution of employed black workers aged 16 or older by occupation, 2010)

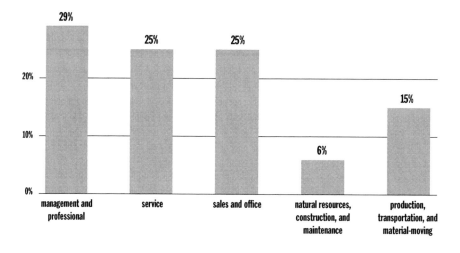

Table 6.6 Total and Black Workers by Occupation, 2010

(total number of employed persons aged 16 or older in the civilian labor force, number and percent distribution of employed blacks, and black share of total, by occupation, 2010; numbers in thousands)

	total	black number	black percent distribution	black share of total
TOTAL EMPLOYED	139,064	15,010	100.0%	10.8%
Management, professional and related occupations	51,743	4,363	29.1	8.4
Management, business and financial operations	20,938	1,537	10.2	7.3
Management	15,001	954	6.4	6.4
Business and financial operations	5,937	583	3.9	9.8
Professional and related occupations	30,805	2,826	18.8	9.2
Computer and mathematical	3,531	237	1.6	6.7
Architecture and engineering	2,619	135	0.9	5.2
Life, physical, and social science	1,409	88	0.6	6.2
Community and social services	2,337	451	3.0	19.3
Legal	1,716	111	0.7	6.5
Education, training, and library	8,628	810	5.4	9.4
Art, design, entertainment, sports, and media	2,759	152	1.0	5.5
Health care practitioner and technical occupations	7,805	842	5.6	10.8
Service occupations	24,634	3,763	25.1	15.3
Health care support	3,332	849	5.7	25.5
Protective service	3,289	585	3.9	17.8
Food preparation and serving related	7,660	866	5.8	11.3
Building and grounds cleaning and maintenance	5,328	722	4.8	13.6
Personal care and service	5,024	741	4.9	14.7
Sales and office occupations	33,433	3,762	25.1	11.3
Sales and related	15,386	1,503	10.0	9.8
Office and administrative support	18,047	2,259	15.0	12.5
Natural resources, construction, maintenance occupations	13,073	876	5.8	6.7
Farming, fishing, and forestry	987	51	0.3	5.2
Construction and extraction	7,175	441	2.9	6.1
Installation, maintenance, and repair	4,911	384	2.6	7.8
Production, transportation, material-moving occupations	16,180	2,247	15.0	13.9
Production	7,998	908	6.0	11.4
Transportation and material moving	8,182	1,339	8.9	16.4

Source: Bureau of Labor Statistics, Current Population Survey, Internet site http://www.bls.gov/cps/tables.htm#empstat; calculations by New Strategist

Table 6.7 Black Workers by Detailed Occupation, 2010

(total number of employed workers agd 16 or older and percent black, by detailed occupation, 2010; numbers in thousands)

	total	percent black
TOTAL EMPLOYED	**139,064**	**10.8%**
Management, professional and related occupations	**51,743**	**8.4**
Management, business and financial operations occupations	20,938	7.3
Management occupations	15,001	6.4
Chief executives	1,505	2.8
General and operations managers	1,007	5.8
Advertising and promotions managers	78	0.8
Marketing and sales managers	959	5.9
Public relations managers	85	4.4
Administrative services managers	104	9.0
Computer and information systems managers	537	6.8
Financial managers	1,141	6.7
Human resources managers	268	9.1
Industrial production managers	254	3.0
Purchasing managers	203	7.6
Transportation, storage, and distribution managers	278	9.5
Farm, ranch, and other agricultural managers	237	0.6
Farmers and ranchers	713	0.6
Construction managers	1,083	3.5
Education administrators	830	11.1
Engineering managers	113	5.4
Food service managers	960	8.5
Lodging managers	143	5.1
Medical and health services managers	549	12.4
Property, real estate, and community association managers	604	7.7
Social and community service managers	326	13.1
Managers, all other	2,898	6.8
Business and financial operations occupations	5,937	9.8
Wholesale and retail buyers, except farm products	180	4.4
Purchasing agents, except wholesale, retail, and farm products	235	8.0
Claims adjusters, appraisers, examiners, and investigators	282	13.8
Compliance officers, except agriculture, construction, health and safety, and transportation	188	11.5
Cost estimators	115	1.5
Human resources, training, and labor relations specialists	824	14.0
Logisticians	68	10.6
Management analysts	658	7.2
Meeting and convention planners	63	9.4
Other business operations specialists	243	10.3
Accountants and auditors	1,646	8.6
Appraisers and assessors of real estate	79	3.0
Financial analysts	97	11.6
Personal financial advisors	369	5.2
Insurance underwriters	125	13.2
Loan counselors and officers	363	9.9
Tax examiners, collectors, and revenue agents	71	25.6
Tax preparers	106	13.0
Financial specialists, all other	84	13.7

	total	percent black
Professional and related occupations	30,805	9.2%
Computer and mathematical occupations	3,531	6.7
Computer scientists and systems analysts	784	7.3
Computer programmers	470	5.1
Computer software engineers	1,026	5.1
Computer support specialists	388	11.3
Database administrators	101	9.0
Network and computer systems administrators	229	5.6
Network systems and data communications analysts	366	6.6
Operations research analysts	107	10.7
Architecture and engineering occupations	2,619	5.2
Architects, except naval	184	2.1
Aerospace engineers	126	6.7
Chemical engineers	63	3.1
Civil engineers	318	4.9
Computer hardware engineers	70	3.1
Electrical and electronics engineers	307	5.3
Industrial engineers, including health and safety	159	5.0
Mechanical engineers	293	3.2
Engineers, all other	334	7.1
Drafters	143	3.6
Engineering technicians, except drafters	374	8.2
Surveying and mapping technicians	61	1.6
Life, physical, and social science occupations	1,409	6.3
Biological scientists	113	8.0
Medical scientists	143	7.0
Chemists and materials scientists	103	9.9
Environmental scientists and geoscientists	108	5.4
Physical scientists, all other	144	4.0
Market and survey researchers	150	5.1
Psychologists	179	3.9
Chemical technicians	62	12.8
Other life, physical, and social science technicians	162	7.4
Community and social services occupations	2,337	19.3
Counselors	702	21.4
Social workers	771	22.8
Miscellaneous community and social service specialists	297	21.6
Clergy	429	12.6
Directors, religious activities and education	53	2.0
Religious workers, all other	84	6.0
Legal occupations	1,716	6.5
Lawyers	1,040	4.3
Judges, magistrates, and other judicial workers	71	12.5
Paralegals and legal assistants	345	8.8
Miscellaneous legal support workers	259	10.4
Education, training, and library occupations	8,628	9.4
Postsecondary teachers	1,300	6.3
Preschool and kindergarten teachers	712	13.4
Elementary and middle school teachers	2,813	9.3
Secondary school teachers	1,221	8.0
Special education teachers	387	6.8
Other teachers and instructors	806	9.6
Archivists, curators, and museum technicians	50	3.3
Librarians	216	9.2

	total	percent black
Teacher assistants	966	12.7%
Other education, training, and library workers	114	16.1
Arts, design, entertainment, sports, and media occupations	2,759	5.5
Artists and related workers	195	2.7
Designers	793	3.3
Producers and directors	152	9.1
Athletes, coaches, umpires, and related workers	260	7.3
Musicians, singers, and related workers	182	13.9
Announcers	52	12.9
News analysts, reporters, and correspondents	81	3.0
Public relations specialists	148	2.8
Editors	162	4.9
Technical writers	56	5.4
Writers and authors	199	3.8
Miscellaneous media and communication workers	83	6.6
Broadcast and sound engineering technicians and radio operators	102	5.7
Photographers	161	6.5
Television, video, and motion picture camera operators and editors	54	5.5
Health care practitioner and technical occupations	7,805	10.8
Chiropractors	57	–
Dentists	175	0.3
Dietitians and nutritionists	105	14.9
Pharmacists	255	5.2
Physicians and surgeons	872	5.8
Physician assistants	99	5.0
Registered nurses	2,843	12.0
Occupational therapists	109	2.5
Physical therapists	187	5.8
Respiratory therapists	131	11.9
Speech-language pathologists	132	2.9
Therapists, all other	138	6.6
Veterinarians	73	2.6
Clinical laboratory technologists and technicians	342	15.1
Dental hygienists	141	4.3
Diagnostic related technologists and technicians	349	7.2
Emergency medical technicians and paramedics	179	4.4
Health diagnosing and treating practitioner support technicians	505	13.6
Licensed practical and licensed vocational nurses	573	24.4
Medical records and health information technicians	118	19.9
Opticians, dispensing	55	15.3
Miscellaneous health technologists and technicians	167	17.6
Other health care practitioners and technical occupations	70	8.7
Service occupations	**24,634**	**15.3**
Health care support occupations	3,332	25.5
Nursing, psychiatric, and home health aides	1,928	34.6
Physical therapist assistants and aides	86	6.2
Massage therapists	162	5.3
Dental assistants	296	5.7
Medical assistants and other health care support occupations	850	17.8
Protective service occupations	3,289	17.8
First-line supervisors/managers of police and detectives	103	8.7
Supervisors, protective service workers, all other	105	19.9
Fire fighters	301	6.4
Bailiffs, correctional officers, and jailers	465	22.0

	total	percent black
Detectives and criminal investigators	159	10.6%
Police and sheriff's patrol officers	714	12.1
Private detectives and investigators	89	5.7
Security guards and gaming surveillance officers	993	28.8
Crossing guards	59	26.4
Lifeguards and other protective service workers	166	4.2
Food preparation and serving related occupations	7,660	11.3
Chefs and head cooks	337	12.0
First-line supervisors/managers of food preparation and serving workers	551	15.4
Cooks	1,951	15.0
Food preparation workers	717	13.4
Bartenders	393	3.8
Combined food preparation and serving workers, including fast food	294	12.8
Counter attendants, cafeteria, food concession, and coffee shop	269	11.3
Waiters and waitresses	2,067	7.1
Food servers, nonrestaurant	174	18.6
Dining room and cafeteria attendants and bartender helpers	371	10.7
Dishwashers	246	10.5
Hosts and hostesses, restaurant, lounge, and coffee shop	284	8.1
Building and grounds cleaning and maintenance occupations	5,328	13.6
First-line supervisors/managers of housekeeping and janitorial workers	234	13.3
First-line supervisors/managers of landscaping, lawn service, and grounds keeping workers	229	3.8
Janitors and building cleaners	2,186	17.1
Maids and housekeeping cleaners	1,407	16.3
Pest control workers	76	5.3
Grounds maintenance workers	1,195	6.3
Personal care and service occupations	5,024	14.8
First-line supervisors/managers of gaming workers	136	5.4
First-line supervisors/managers of personal service workers	185	7.7
Nonfarm animal caretakers	169	2.7
Gaming services workers	121	5.0
Ushers, lobby attendants, and ticket takers	51	24.0
Miscellaneous entertainment attendants and related workers	173	12.8
Barbers	96	37.2
Hairdressers, hairstylists, and cosmetologists	770	10.6
Miscellaneous personal appearance workers	273	7.5
Baggage porters, bellhops, and concierges	77	29.8
Transportation attendants	110	12.2
Child care workers	1,247	16.0
Personal and home care aides	973	23.8
Recreation and fitness workers	379	11.3
Residential advisors	60	25.4
Personal care and service workers, all other	91	5.9
Sales and office occupations	**33,433**	**11.3**
Sales and related occupations	15,386	9.8
First-line supervisors/managers of retail sales workers	3,132	7.9
First-line supervisors/managers of nonretail sales workers	1,131	5.9
Cashiers	3,109	16.1
Counter and rental clerks	150	7.9
Parts salespersons	129	3.7
Retail salespersons	3,286	11.3
Advertising sales agents	214	6.3
Insurance sales agents	513	6.6

	total	percent black
Securities, commodities, and financial services sales agents	308	6.4%
Travel agents	76	9.9
Sales representatives, services, all other	524	9.6
Sales representatives, wholesale and manufacturing	1,284	4.0
Models, demonstrators, and product promoters	61	8.0
Real estate brokers and sales agents	854	5.3
Telemarketers	118	25.0
Door-to-door sales workers, news and street vendors, and related workers	203	12.9
Sales and related workers, all other	268	7.0
Office and administrative support occupations	18,047	12.5
First-line supervisors/managers of office and administrative support workers	1,507	9.7
Bill and account collectors	216	17.5
Billing and posting clerks and machine operators	472	13.7
Bookkeeping, accounting, and auditing clerks	1,297	6.5
Payroll and timekeeping clerks	167	10.4
Tellers	453	11.3
Court, municipal, and license clerks	95	17.9
Customer service representatives	1,896	17.5
Eligibility interviewers, government programs	89	20.2
File clerks	334	16.0
Hotel, motel, and resort desk clerks	129	15.3
Interviewers, except eligibility and loan	210	17.3
Library assistants, clerical	115	5.9
Loan interviewers and clerks	127	11.5
Order clerks	117	8.0
Receptionists and information clerks	1,281	9.8
Reservation and transportation ticket agents and travel clerks	100	24.0
Information and record clerks, all other	116	16.7
Couriers and messengers	270	16.4
Dispatchers	293	13.5
Postal service clerks	124	29.5
Postal service mail carriers	321	11.7
Postal service mail sorters, processors, processing machine operators	76	30.5
Production, planning, and expediting clerks	259	9.5
Shipping, receiving, and traffic clerks	558	12.5
Stock clerks and order fillers	1,456	16.7
Weighers, measurers, checkers, and samplers, recordkeeping	70	10.8
Secretaries and administrative assistants	3,082	8.6
Computer operators	122	10.8
Data entry keyers	338	13.2
Word processors and typists	144	12.3
Insurance claims and policy processing clerks	231	16.5
Mail clerks and mail machine operators, except postal service	94	21.4
Office clerks, general	994	13.0
Office and administrative support workers, all other	501	12.7
Natural resources, construction, and maintenance occupations	**13,073**	**6.7**
Farming, fishing, and forestry occupations	987	5.2
Graders and sorters, agricultural products	103	9.2
Miscellaneous agricultural workers	691	3.9
Logging workers	63	13.6
Construction and extraction occupations	7,175	6.1
First-line supervisors/managers of construction trades, extraction workers	659	4.9
Brickmasons, blockmasons, and stonemasons	162	6.7

	total	percent black
Carpenters	1,242	4.0%
Carpet, floor, and tile installers and finishers	209	3.8
Cement masons, concrete finishers, and terrazzo workers	88	12.0
Construction laborers	1,267	9.0
Operating engineers and other construction equipment operators	363	4.7
Drywall installers, ceiling tile installers, and tapers	171	2.5
Electricians	691	7.0
Painters, construction and maintenance	578	4.8
Pipelayers, plumbers, pipefitters, and steamfitters	526	7.2
Roofers	214	4.0
Sheet metal workers	108	5.8
Structural iron and steel workers	59	0.6
Helpers, construction trades	60	4.5
Construction and building inspectors	104	8.3
Highway maintenance workers	110	14.2
Mining machine operators	60	2.4
Other extraction workers	55	10.0
Installation, maintenance, and repair occupations	4,911	7.8
First-line supervisors/managers of mechanics, installers, repairers	381	7.5
Computer, automated teller, and office machine repairers	305	10.0
Radio and telecommunications equipment installers and repairers	166	9.3
Electronic home entertainment equipment installers and repairers	52	12.1
Security and fire alarm systems installers	60	6.0
Aircraft mechanics and service technicians	136	7.1
Automotive body and related repairers	168	6.3
Automotive service technicians and mechanics	802	6.8
Bus and truck mechanics and diesel engine specialists	339	7.6
Heavy vehicle and mobile equipment service technicians and mechanics	235	4.6
Small-engine mechanics	57	6.4
Misc. vehicle and mobile equipment mechanics, installers, and repairers	99	7.3
Heating, air conditioning, and refrigeration mechanics and installers	392	8.0
Home appliance repairers	53	7.7
Industrial and refractory machinery mechanics	447	8.1
Maintenance and repair workers, general	347	11.1
Electrical power-line installers and repairers	124	8.2
Telecommunications line installers and repairers	163	9.4
Precision instrument and equipment repairers	73	10.8
Other installation, maintenance, and repair workers	197	5.4
Production, transportation, and material-moving occupations	**16,180**	**13.9**
Production occupations	7,998	11.4
First-line supervisors/managers of production and operating workers	702	7.3
Electrical, electronics, and electromechanical assemblers	151	15.1
Miscellaneous assemblers and fabricators	805	15.3
Bakers	206	9.8
Butchers and other meat, poultry, and fish processing workers	331	14.0
Food batchmakers	107	9.7
Computer control programmers and operators	56	6.9
Cutting, punching, press machine setters, operators, tenders, metal, plastic	78	11.1
Grinding, lapping, polishing, and buffing machine tool setters, operators, and tenders, metal and plastic	54	11.3
Machinists	408	4.3
Molders, molding machine setters, operators, tenders, metal and plastic	55	10.7
Tool and die makers	68	1.8

	total	percent black
Welding, soldering, and brazing workers	479	7.0%
Metalworkers and plastic workers, all other	337	11.2
Job printers	50	13.5
Printing machine operators	162	13.7
Laundry and dry-cleaning workers	195	15.9
Pressers, textile, garment, and related materials	59	19.3
Sewing machine operators	170	13.3
Tailors, dressmakers, and sewers	76	4.9
Cabinetmakers and bench carpenters	62	4.0
Stationary engineers and boiler operators	91	9.8
Water and liquid waste treatment plant and system operators	77	6.8
Chemical processing machine setters, operators, and tenders	58	17.6
Crushing, grinding, polishing, mixing, and blending workers	90	16.0
Cutting workers	67	10.1
Inspectors, testers, sorters, samplers, and weighers	669	11.1
Medical, dental, and ophthalmic laboratory technicians	92	5.5
Packaging and filling machine operators and tenders	255	16.4
Painting workers	139	9.3
Production workers, all other	921	14.9
Transportation and material-moving occupations	8,182	16.4
Supervisors, transportation and material-moving workers	263	18.3
Aircraft pilots and flight engineers	110	1.0
Bus drivers	600	25.1
Driver/sales workers and truck drivers	3,028	13.6
Taxi drivers and chauffeurs	390	26.6
Motor vehicle operators, all other	54	7.8
Locomotive engineers and operators	57	5.7
Railroad conductors and yardmasters	58	19.9
Parking lot attendants	75	25.7
Service station attendants	77	8.6
Crane and tower operators	50	6.9
Dredge, excavating, and loading machine operators	51	3.3
Industrial truck and tractor operators	499	22.0
Cleaners of vehicles and equipment	333	14.8
Laborers and freight, stock, and material movers, hand	1,700	16.9
Packers and packagers, hand	403	17.3
Refuse and recyclable material collectors	88	23.9
Material-moving workers, all other	59	13.2

Note: "–" means sample is too small to make a reliable estimate.
Source: Bureau of Labor Statistics, 2010 Current Population Survey, Internet site http://www.bls.gov/cps/tables.htm#empstat

Table 6.8 Black Workers by Industry, 2010

(total number of employed people aged 16 or older in the civilian labor force; number and percent distribution of employed blacks, and black share of total, by industry, 2010; numbers in thousands)

		black		
	total	number	percent distribution	share of total
Total employed	**139,064**	**15,010**	**100.0%**	**10.8%**
Agriculture, forestry, fishing, hunting	2,206	59	0.4	2.7
Mining	731	37	0.2	5.1
Construction	9,077	491	3.3	5.4
Manufacturing	14,081	1,268	8.4	9.0
Wholesale/retail trade	19,739	1,970	13.1	10.0
Transportation and utilities	7,134	1,136	7.6	15.9
Information	3,149	345	2.3	11.0
Financial activities	9,350	841	5.6	9.0
Professional and business services	15,253	1,321	8.8	8.7
Educational and health services	32,062	4,509	30.0	14.1
Leisure and hospitality	12,530	1,335	8.9	10.7
Other services	6,769	624	4.2	9.2
Public administration	6,983	1,075	7.2	15.4

Source: Bureau of Labor Statistics, 2010 Current Population Survey, Internet site http://www.bls.gov/cps/tables.htm#empstat; calculations by New Strategist

Most Black Workers Have College Experience

Twenty-four percent have a bachelor's degree.

Among the 15 million blacks in the labor force in 2010, only 9 percent were not high school gradu-ates. The 57 percent majority of black workers has at least some college experience, and nearly one in four has a bachelor's degree. Black labor force participation increases sharply with education, from a low of 38.8 percent among blacks aged 25 or older without a high school diploma to 79.5 percent among those with a bachelor's degree.

Black job tenure is about average, with 21 percent of blacks having worked for their current employer for 12 months or less. Among all workers, a slightly smaller 19 percent had a year or less job tenure. Blacks are slightly less likely than the average worker to have held their current job for 10 or more years—26 percent of blacks versus 29 percent of all workers.

Most black workers have full-time jobs. Among black men, 78 percent work full-time. Among women, the 72 percent majority has a full-time job.

■ Many blacks who work part-time would prefer a full-time job. Among men aged 25 to 54 who work part-time, 33 percent would prefer a full-time job.

Few black workers are high school dropouts

(percent distribution of black workers aged 25 or older by educational attainment, 2010)

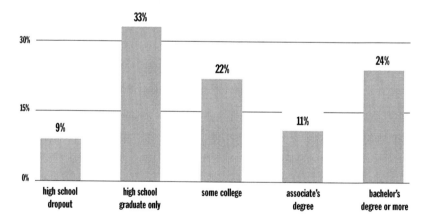

Table 6.9 Black Workers by Educational Attainment, 2010

(number of total people and blacks aged 25 or older in the civilian labor force, black labor force participation rate, distribution of blacks in labor force, and black share of total labor force, by educational attainment, 2010; numbers in thousands)

	total labor force	black labor force number	black labor force participation rate	black labor force percent distribution	black labor force share of total
Total aged 25 or older	**132,954**	**15,113**	**65.8%**	**100.0%**	**11.4%**
Not a high school graduate	11,880	1,423	38.8	9.4	12.0
High school graduate only	38,236	5,029	63.8	33.3	13.2
Some college	22,958	3,299	72.4	21.8	14.4
Associate's degree	13,882	1,661	75.9	11.0	12.0
Bachelor's degree or more	45,998	3,701	79.5	24.5	8.0

Source: Bureau of Labor Statistics, 2010 Current Population Survey, Internet site http://www.bls.gov/cps/tables.htm#empstat; calculations by New Strategist

Table 6.10 Total and Black Workers by Job Tenure, 2010

(number of total and black employed wage and salary workers aged 16 or older, percent distribution by tenure with current employer, and index of black to total, 2010; numbers in thousands)

	total	black	index black to total
Total workers, number	**121,931**	**13,508**	–
Total workers, percent	**100.0%**	**100.0%**	**100**
12 months or less	19.0	20.7	109
13 to 23 months	7.0	6.1	87
Two years	5.8	6.1	105
Three to four years	18.9	20.9	111
Five to nine years	20.5	20.4	100
10 to 14 years	12.2	11.6	95
15 to 19 years	6.1	4.9	80
20 or more years	10.5	9.3	89

Note: The index is calculated by dividing the black figure by the total figure and multiplying by 100. "–" means not applicable.
Source: Bureau of Labor Statistics, Employee Tenure, Internet site http://www.bls.gov/news.release/tenure.toc.htm; calculations by New Strategist

Table 6.11 Black Workers by Full-Time and Part-Time Status, Age, and Sex, 2010

(number and percent distribution of employed blacks aged 16 or older by age, sex, and full- and part-time employment status, 2010; numbers in thousands)

	men			women		
	total	full-time	part-time	total	full-time	part-time
Total employed blacks	**6,734**	**5,279**	**1,455**	**7,930**	**5,727**	**2,203**
Aged 16 to 19	183	44	139	200	46	154
Aged 20 to 24	685	398	287	826	433	393
Aged 25 to 54	4,846	4,061	785	5,629	4,344	1,285
Aged 55 or older	1,020	776	244	1,273	904	369
PERCENT DISTRIBUTION BY EMPLOYMENT STATUS						
Total employed blacks	**100.0%**	**78.4%**	**21.6%**	**100.0%**	**72.2%**	**27.8%**
Aged 16 to 19	100.0	24.0	76.0	100.0	23.0	77.0
Aged 20 to 24	100.0	58.1	41.9	100.0	52.4	47.6
Aged 25 to 54	100.0	83.8	16.2	100.0	77.2	22.8
Aged 55 or older	100.0	76.1	23.9	100.0	71.0	29.0
PERCENT DISTRIBUTION BY AGE						
Total employed blacks	**100.0%**	**100.0%**	**100.0%**	**100.0%**	**100.0%**	**100.0%**
Aged 16 to 19	2.7	0.8	9.6	2.5	0.8	7.0
Aged 20 to 24	10.2	7.5	19.7	10.4	7.6	17.8
Aged 25 to 54	72.0	76.9	54.0	71.0	75.9	58.3
Aged 55 or older	15.1	14.7	16.8	16.1	15.8	16.7

Source: Bureau of Labor Statistics, 2010 Current Population Survey, Internet site http://www.bls.gov/cps/tables.htm#empstat; calculations by New Strategist

Table 6.12 Black Part-Time Workers by Age, Sex, and Reason, 2010

(total number of blacks aged 16 or older who work part-time, and number and percent working part-time for economic reasons, by sex and age, 2010; numbers in thousands)

	total	working part-time for economic reasons	
		number	share of total
Black men working part-time	**1,455**	**419**	**28.8%**
Aged 16 to 19	139	26	18.7
Aged 20 to 24	287	95	33.1
Aged 25 to 54	785	258	32.9
Aged 55 or older	244	40	16.4
Black women working part-time	**2,203**	**528**	**24.0**
Aged 16 to 19	154	24	15.6
Aged 20 to 24	393	112	28.5
Aged 25 to 54	1,285	336	26.1
Aged 55 or older	369	57	15.4

Note: Part-time work is less than 35 hours per week. Part-time workers exclude those who worked less than 35 hours in the previous week because of vacation, holidays, child care problems, weather issues, and other temporary, noneconomic reasons. "Economic reasons" means a worker's hours have been reduced or workers cannot find full-time employment.
Source: Bureau of Labor Statistics, 2010 Current Population Survey, Internet site http://www.bls.gov/cps/tables.htm#empstat; calculations by New Strategist

Blacks Households Have Fewer Earners

Among black couples, most are dual earners.

The average black household has only 1.15 earners, less than the 1.32 earners in the typical American household. Behind the lower figure for blacks is the fact that female-headed families constitute a large share of black households, and many female-headed families have only one earner. Consequently, blacks account for a disproportionately large share of the nation's one-earner households and for a much smaller share of households with two or more earners.

Although black households have fewer earners than average, black couples are more likely than the average married couple to be dual earners. Fifty-seven percent of black couples are dual earners. Among all married couples, the figure is a smaller 54 percent. Only 17 percent of black husbands are the family's sole provider compared with 22 percent of husbands nationally.

■ Among black couples aged 55 to 64, husbands and wives are almost equally likely to be the sole provider.

Among black households, single earners are more common than dual earners

(percent distribution of black households by number of earners, 2010)

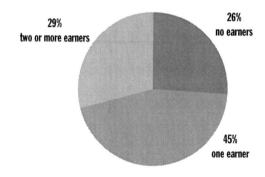

29%
two or more earners

26%
no earners

45%
one earner

Table 6.13 Black Households by Number of Earners, 2010

(number of total households, number and percent distribution of black households and black share of total, by number of earners per household, 2010; numbers in thousands)

	total	black number	black percent distribution	black share of total
Total households	**117,538**	**15,212**	**100.0%**	**12.9%**
No earners	26,172	3,913	25.7	15.0
One earner	43,712	6,829	44.9	15.6
Two or more earners	47,654	4,469	29.4	9.4
Two earners	38,302	3,662	24.1	9.6
Three earners	7,023	648	4.3	9.2
Four or more earners	2,330	159	1.0	6.8
Average number of earners per household	1.32	1.15	–	–

Note: Blacks are those who identify themselves as being of the race alone or as being of the race in combination with other races. "–" means not applicable.
Source: Bureau of the Census, 2010 Current Population Survey, Internet site http://www.census.gov/hhes/www/cpstables/032010/hhinc/toc.htm; calculations by New Strategist

Table 6.14 Labor Force Status of Black Married Couples, 2010

(number and percent distribution of black married-couple family groups aged 20 or older by age of householder and labor force status of husband and wife, 2010; numbers in thousands)

| | total | husband and/or wife in labor force | | | neither husband nor wife in labor force |
		husband and wife	husband only	wife only	
Total black couples	**4,571**	**2,604**	**788**	**457**	**721**
Under age 25	78	48	22	1	8
Aged 25 to 29	299	202	72	15	9
Aged 30 to 34	463	299	126	20	17
Aged 35 to 39	562	437	93	28	3
Aged 40 to 44	527	396	79	38	14
Aged 45 to 54	1,143	767	187	130	59
Aged 55 to 64	865	396	156	144	169
Aged 65 or older	634	59	53	80	441
Total black couples	**100.0%**	**57.0%**	**17.2%**	**10.0%**	**15.8%**
Under age 25	100.0	61.5	28.2	1.3	10.3
Aged 25 to 29	100.0	67.6	24.1	5.0	3.0
Aged 30 to 34	100.0	64.6	27.2	4.3	3.7
Aged 35 to 39	100.0	77.8	16.5	5.0	0.5
Aged 40 to 44	100.0	75.1	15.0	7.2	2.7
Aged 45 to 54	100.0	67.1	16.4	11.4	5.2
Aged 55 to 64	100.0	45.8	18.0	16.6	19.5
Aged 65 or older	100.0	9.3	8.4	12.6	69.6

Note: Blacks are those who identify themselves as being of the race alone or as being of the race in combination with other races.
Source: Bureau of the Census, America's Families and Living Arrangements: 2010, Internet site http://www.census.gov/ population/www/socdemo/hh-fam/cps2010.html; calculations by New Strategist

Few Blacks Earn Minimum Wage or Less

Union representation is higher than average among blacks.

Fifteen percent of blacks are represented by unions, more than the 13 percent share among all workers. Among blacks represented by unions, median weekly earnings ($766) are 30 percent higher than the earnings of those not represented by a union ($589).

Although blacks have lower earnings than the average American worker, few earn the minimum wage or less. In 2010, just 7 percent of black wage and salary workers earned at or below the minimum wage. Blacks account for 15 percent of the nation's minimum wage workers.

Seventy-one percent of black workers drive themselves to work alone, while 10 percent carpool. Eleven percent of blacks use public transportation to get to work. Blacks account for 25 percent of mass transit commuters.

■ Black women are more likely than black men to earn minimum wage or less.

Eleven percent of blacks use mass transportation to get to work

(percent distribution of black workers aged 16 or older by selected principal means of transportation to work, 2009)

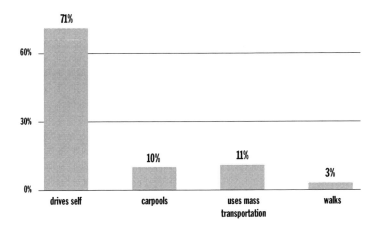

Table 6.15 Black Minimum Wage Workers, 2010

(number and percent distribution of total and black wage and salary workers aged 16 or older paid hourly rates and those paid at or below minimum wage, by sex, 2010; numbers in thousands)

	total paid hourly rates	paid at or below minimum wage
Total workers aged 16 or older	**72,902**	**4,360**
Black workers aged 16 or older	9,436	650
Black men	4,137	244
Black women	5,299	406
PERCENT DISTRIBUTION BY RACE/SEX		
Total workers aged 16 or older	**100.0%**	**100.0%**
Black workers aged 16 or older	12.9	14.9
Black men	5.7	5.6
Black women	7.3	9.3
PERCENT DISTRIBUTION BY WAGE STATUS		
Total workers aged 16 or older	**100.0%**	**6.0%**
Black workers aged 16 or older	100.0	6.9
Black men	100.0	5.9
Black women	100.0	7.7

Source: Bureau of Labor Statistics, 2010 Current Population Survey, Internet site http://www.bls.gov/cps/tables.htm#empstat; calculations by New Strategist

Table 6.16 Union Representation of Total and Black Workers, 2010

(number of total and black employed wage and salary workers aged 16 or older, number and percent represented by unions, and median weekly earnings of those working full-time by union representation status, 2010; number in thousands)

	total	blacks
Total employed	**124,073**	**14,195**
Number represented by unions	16,290	2,115
Percent represented by unions	13.1%	14.9%
Median weekly earnings of full-time workers	**$747**	**$611**
Workers represented by unions	911	766
Workers not represented by unions	717	589

Note: Workers represented by unions are either members of a labor union or similar employee association or workers who report no union affiliation but whose jobs are covered by a union or an employee association contract.
Source: Bureau of Labor Statistics, 2010 Current Population Survey, Internet site http://www.bls.gov/cps/tables.htm#empstat; calculations by New Strategist

Table 6.17 Journey to Work by Blacks, 2009

(number and percent distribution of total and black workers aged 16 or older by principal means of transportation to work, 2009; numbers in thousands)

	total	blacks		
		number	percent distribution	share of total
Total workers	**138,592**	**14,863**	**100.0%**	**10.7%**
Drove car, truck, or van alone	105,476	10,622	71.5	10.1
Carpooled in car, truck, or van	13,917	1,513	10.2	10.9
Used public transportation (incl. taxis)	6,922	1,705	11.5	24.6
Walked	3,966	418	2.8	10.5
Traveled by other means	2,393	243	1.6	10.2
Worked at home	5,918	362	2.4	6.1

Source: Bureau of the Census, 2009 American Community Survey, Internet site http://factfinder.census.gov/servlet/ DatasetMainPageServlet?_program=ACS&_submenuId=&_lang=en&_ts=; calculations by New Strategist

The Black Labor Force Will Grow by More than 2 Million

The black share of the labor force will not change much between now and 2018.

The black labor force will grow by 2.5 million workers between 2008 and 2018, a 14 percent increase. Overall labor force participation rates are projected to decline during the next decade, but black rates are projected to decline more slowly than average.

Blacks will account for a larger share of workers entering than exiting the labor force. Between 2008 and 2018, blacks will account for 14 percent of labor force entrants and for a smaller 11 percent of those exiting the labor force.

■ Black women outnumber black men in the labor force by about 1 million, a number that will not change much during the next decade.

The black labor force is growing somewhat faster than average

(percent change in total and black workers aged 16 or older, 2008–18)

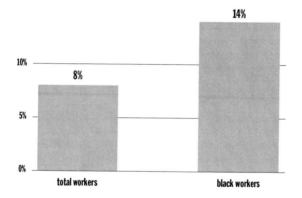

Table 6.18 Black Labor Force Projections, 2008 and 2018

(projected number and percent of total people and blacks aged 16 or older in the civilian labor force by sex, 2008 and 2018; percent change in number and percentage point change in rate, 2008–18; numbers in thousands)

	2008	2018	percent change
NUMBER			
Total labor force	**154,287**	**166,911**	**8.2%**
Black labor force	17,740	20,244	14.1
Total men in labor force	**82,520**	**88,682**	**7.5**
Black men in labor force	8,347	9,579	14.8
Total women in labor force	**71,767**	**78,229**	**9.0**
Black women in labor force	9,393	10,665	13.5

	2008	2018	percentage point change
PARTICIPATION RATE			
Total people	**66.0%**	**64.5%**	**−1.5**
Total blacks	63.7	63.3	−0.4
Total men	**73.0**	**70.6**	**−2.4**
Black men	66.7	65.7	−1.0
Total women	**59.5**	**58.7**	**−0.8**
Black women	61.3	61.2	−0.1

Note: Blacks are those who identified their race as black alone.
Source: Bureau of Labor Statistics, Labor Force Projections to 2018: Older Workers Staying More Active, Monthly Labor Review, November 2009, Internet site http://www.bls.gov/opub/mlr/2009/11/home.htm; calculations by New Strategist

Table 6.19 Black Labor Force Entrants and Leavers, 2008 to 2018

(projected number and percent distribution of total people and blacks aged 16 or older in the civilian labor force in 2008 and 2018, and number and percent distribution of entrants, leavers, and stayers, 2008–18; numbers in thousands)

	2008 labor force	2008–18 entrants	2008–18 leavers	2008–18 stayers	2018 labor force
NUMBER					
Total labor force	**154,287**	**37,632**	**25,008**	**129,279**	**166,911**
Black labor force	17,740	5,403	2,899	14,841	20,244
PERCENT DISTRIBUTION					
Total labor force	**100.0%**	**100.0%**	**100.0%**	**100.0%**	**100.0%**
Black labor force	11.5	14.4	11.6	11.5	12.1

Note: Blacks are those who identified their race as black alone.
Source: Bureau of Labor Statistics, Labor Force Projections to 2018: Older Workers Staying More Active, Monthly Labor Review, November 2009, Internet site http://www.bls.gov/opub/mlr/2009/11/home.htm; calculations by New Strategist

7

Living Arrangements

■ Married couples head only 29 percent of black households—well below their 50 percent share of all households. Female-headed families are almost as numerous, accounting for 28 percent of total black households.

■ Black households are only slightly larger than the average household, with 2.62 people on average in black households versus 2.59 people in households nationally.

■ Forty-five percent of black households include children of any age, a greater proportion than the 40 percent of all U.S. households that include children.

■ Black children are much less likely than the average American child to live with both parents. Among black children under age 18, only 36 percent live with married parents.

■ Fewer than half of blacks are married. Among black men, only 37 percent are currently married. The figure is a smaller 28 percent among black women.

Few Black Households Are Headed by Married Couples

Female-headed families are almost as numerous.

In 2010, there were more than 15 million households headed by blacks in the United States, accounting for 13 percent of the total. Black householders have an average age of 47, three years younger than the average householder.

Married couples head only 29 percent of black households—well below their 50 percent share of all households. Female-headed families are almost as numerous and account for 28 percent of the total, a much higher proportion than their 13 percent share of households nationally.

Female-headed families outnumber married couples among black householders under age 35. Among householders aged 35 or older, married couples outnumber female-headed families.

■ Black household incomes will remain well below average as long as female-headed families account for such a large share of black households.

Black households are diverse

(percent distribution of black households by household type, 2010)

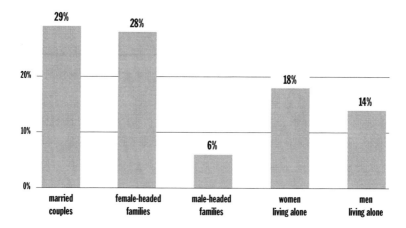

Table 7.1 Total and Black Households by Age of Householder, 2010

(number and percent distribution of total and black households, and black share of total, by age of householder, 2010; numbers in thousands)

| | total | | black | | |
	number	percent distribution	number	percent distribution	share of total
Total households	**117,538**	**100.0%**	**15,212**	**100.0%**	**12.9%**
Under age 25	6,233	5.3	1,074	7.1	17.2
Aged 25 to 29	9,446	8.0	1,430	9.4	15.1
Aged 30 to 34	9,811	8.3	1,508	9.9	15.4
Aged 35 to 39	10,551	9.0	1,610	10.6	15.3
Aged 40 to 44	10,968	9.3	1,523	10.0	13.9
Aged 45 to 49	12,449	10.6	1,695	11.1	13.6
Aged 50 to 54	12,423	10.6	1,589	10.4	12.8
Aged 55 to 64	20,387	17.3	2,413	15.9	11.8
Aged 65 to 74	13,164	11.2	1,359	8.9	10.3
Aged 75 or older	12,106	10.3	1,011	6.6	8.4
Avg. age of householder	50.2	–	47.0	–	–

Note: Blacks are those who identify themselves as being of the race alone or as being of the race in combination with other races. "–" means not applicable.
Source: Bureau of the Census, Current Population Survey Annual Social and Economic Supplement, Internet site http://www .census.gov/hhes/www/income/dinctabs.html; calculations by New Strategist

Table 7.2 Total and Black Households by Household Type, 2010

(number and percent distribution of total and black households, and black share of total, by household type, 2010; numbers in thousands)

	total		black		
	number	percent distribution	number	percent distribution	share of total
TOTAL HOUSEHOLDS	**117,538**	**100.0%**	**15,212**	**100.0%**	**12.9%**
Family households	**78,833**	**67.1**	**9,652**	**63.4**	**12.2**
Married couples	58,410	49.7	4,427	29.1	7.6
With own children under age 18	24,575	20.9	2,013	13.2	8.2
Female householders, no spouse present	14,843	12.6	4,257	28.0	28.7
With own children under age 18	8,419	7.2	2,617	17.2	31.1
Male householders, no spouse present	5,580	4.7	968	6.4	17.3
With own children under age 18	2,224	1.9	416	2.7	18.7
Nonfamily households	**38,705**	**32.9**	**5,560**	**36.6**	**14.4**
Female householders	20,442	17.4	3,103	20.4	15.2
Living alone	17,428	14.8	2,779	18.3	15.9
Male householders	18,263	15.5	2,457	16.2	13.5
Living alone	13,971	11.9	2,060	13.5	14.7

Note: Blacks are those who identify themselves as being of the race alone or as being of the race in combination with other races.
Source: Bureau of the Census, Current Population Survey Annual Social and Economic Supplement, Internet site http://www .census.gov/hhes/www/income/dinctabs.html; calculations by New Strategist

Table 7.3 Black Households by Age of Householder and Household Type, 2010

(number and percent distribution of black households by age of householder and household type, 2010; numbers in thousands)

| | | family households | | | nonfamily households | | | |
| | | | | | female-headed | | male-headed | |
	total	married couples	female hh, no spouse present	male hh, no spouse present	total	living alone	total	living alone
Total black households	**15,212**	**4,427**	**4,257**	**968**	**3,103**	**2,779**	**2,457**	**2,060**
Under age 25	1,074	68	481	145	195	136	184	125
Aged 25 to 29	1,430	279	521	98	283	209	249	190
Aged 30 to 34	1,508	450	566	98	180	157	212	162
Aged 35 to 39	1,610	555	525	127	175	144	229	187
Aged 40 to 44	1,523	507	499	102	198	177	217	183
Aged 45 to 49	1,695	565	457	115	290	266	269	245
Aged 50 to 54	1,589	538	364	89	320	292	278	238
Aged 55 to 64	2,413	850	414	112	630	586	407	354
Aged 65 to 74	1,359	414	241	39	405	387	260	233
Aged 75 or older	1,011	201	190	41	427	425	152	142
PERCENT DISTRIBUTION BY AGE								
Total black households	**100.0%**	**100.0%**	**100.0%**	**100.0%**	**100.0%**	**100.0%**	**100.0%**	**100.0%**
Under age 25	7.1	1.5	11.3	15.0	6.3	4.9	7.5	6.1
Aged 25 to 29	9.4	6.3	12.2	10.1	9.1	7.5	10.1	9.2
Aged 30 to 34	9.9	10.2	13.3	10.1	5.8	5.6	8.6	7.9
Aged 35 to 39	10.6	12.5	12.3	13.1	5.6	5.2	9.3	9.1
Aged 40 to 44	10.0	11.5	11.7	10.5	6.4	6.4	8.8	8.9
Aged 45 to 49	11.1	12.8	10.7	11.9	9.3	9.6	10.9	11.9
Aged 50 to 54	10.4	12.2	8.6	9.2	10.3	10.5	11.3	11.6
Aged 55 to 64	15.9	19.2	9.7	11.6	20.3	21.1	16.6	17.2
Aged 65 to 74	8.9	9.4	5.7	4.0	13.1	13.9	10.6	11.3
Aged 75 or older	6.6	4.5	4.5	4.2	13.8	15.3	6.2	6.9
PERCENT DISTRIBUTION BY HOUSEHOLD TYPE								
Total black households	**100.0%**	**29.1%**	**28.0%**	**6.4%**	**20.4%**	**18.3%**	**16.2%**	**13.5%**
Under age 25	100.0	6.3	44.8	13.5	18.2	12.7	17.1	11.6
Aged 25 to 29	100.0	19.5	36.4	6.9	19.8	14.6	17.4	13.3
Aged 30 to 34	100.0	29.8	37.5	6.5	11.9	10.4	14.1	10.7
Aged 35 to 39	100.0	34.5	32.6	7.9	10.9	8.9	14.2	11.6
Aged 40 to 44	100.0	33.3	32.8	6.7	13.0	11.6	14.2	12.0
Aged 45 to 49	100.0	33.3	27.0	6.8	17.1	15.7	15.9	14.5
Aged 50 to 54	100.0	33.9	22.9	5.6	20.1	18.4	17.5	15.0
Aged 55 to 64	100.0	35.2	17.2	4.6	26.1	24.3	16.9	14.7
Aged 65 to 74	100.0	30.5	17.7	2.9	29.8	28.5	19.1	17.1
Aged 75 or older	100.0	19.9	18.8	4.1	42.2	42.0	15.0	14.0

Note: Blacks are those who identify themselves as being of the race alone or the race in combination with other races.
Source: Bureau of the Census, Current Population Survey Annual Social and Economic Supplement, Internet site http://www
.census.gov/hhes/www/income/dinctabs.html; calculations by New Strategist

People Who Live Alone Account for Nearly One-Third of Black Households

The percentage of blacks who live alone rises with age.

Black households are only slightly larger than the average household, with 2.62 people on average in black households versus 2.59 people in households nationally. Although black households are larger than average, blacks are more likely to live alone. Thirty-two percent of black households are people who live alone versus 27 percent of households nationally. Blacks account for 15 percent of the nation's single-person households.

The percentage of blacks who live alone rises from just 4 percent of those under age 25 to 39 percent of those aged 75 or older. Older women are far more likely than older men to live alone. Among blacks aged 75 or older, 28 percent of men and 45 percent of women live by themselves.

■ Because many blacks are not married, the percentage of those who live alone in old age may rise.

Most black households are home to only one or two people

(percent distribution of black households, by size, 2010)

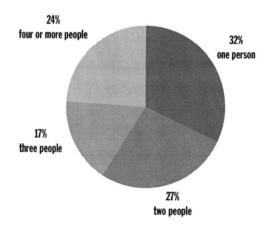

24%
four or more people

32%
one person

17%
three people

27%
two people

Table 7.4 Total and Black Households by Size, 2010

(number and percent distribution of total and black households and black share of total, by size, 2010; numbers in thousands)

	total		black		
	number	percent distribution	number	percent distribution	share of total
Total households	**117,538**	**100.0%**	**15,212**	**100.0%**	**12.9%**
One person	31,399	26.7	4,839	31.8	15.4
Two people	39,487	33.6	4,162	27.4	10.5
Three people	18,638	15.9	2,627	17.3	14.1
Four people	16,122	13.7	1,910	12.6	11.8
Five people	7,367	6.3	954	6.3	12.9
Six people	2,784	2.4	420	2.8	15.1
Seven or more people	1,740	1.5	299	2.0	17.2
Average number of persons per household	2.59	–	2.62	–	–

Note: Blacks are those who identify themselves as being of the race alone or the race in combination with other races. "–" means not applicable.
Source: Bureau of the Census, Current Population Survey Annual Social and Economic Supplement, Internet site http://www.census.gov/hhes/www/income/dinctabs.html; calculations by New Strategist

Table 7.5 Blacks Who Live Alone by Sex and Age, 2010

(total number of blacks aged 15 or older, number and percent who live alone, and percent distribution of blacks living alone, by sex and age, 2010; numbers in thousands)

| | | | living alone | |
| | | | | |
	total	number	percent distribution	share of total
Total blacks	**30,468**	**4,839**	**100.0%**	**15.9%**
Under age 25	6,766	261	5.4	3.9
Aged 25 to 34	5,800	718	14.8	12.4
Aged 35 to 44	5,250	691	14.3	13.2
Aged 45 to 54	5,464	1,041	21.5	19.1
Aged 55 to 64	3,782	940	19.4	24.9
Aged 65 to 74	1,955	620	12.8	31.7
Aged 75 or older	1,450	567	11.7	39.1
Black men	**13,830**	**2,060**	**100.0**	**14.9**
Under age 25	3,288	125	6.1	3.8
Aged 25 to 34	2,705	352	17.1	13.0
Aged 35 to 44	2,349	370	18.0	15.8
Aged 45 to 54	2,475	483	23.4	19.5
Aged 55 to 64	1,673	354	17.2	21.2
Aged 65 to 74	832	233	11.3	28.0
Aged 75 or older	507	142	6.9	28.0
Black women	**16,638**	**2,779**	**100.0**	**16.7**
Under age 25	3,478	136	4.9	3.9
Aged 25 to 34	3,095	366	13.2	11.8
Aged 35 to 44	2,902	321	11.6	11.1
Aged 45 to 54	2,989	558	20.1	18.7
Aged 55 to 64	2,109	586	21.1	27.8
Aged 65 to 74	1,123	387	13.9	34.5
Aged 75 or older	943	425	15.3	45.1

Note: Blacks are those who identify themselves as being of the race alone or in combination with other races.
Source: Bureau of the Census, 2010 Current Population Survey Annual Social and Economic Supplement, Internet site http://www.census.gov/hhes/www/income/data/incpovhlth/2009/dtables.html; calculations by New Strategist

Black Households Are More Likely to include Children

Many black children live with their mother only.

Thirty-three percent of black households include children under age 18, slightly greater than the 30 percent share among all U.S. households. Forty-five percent of black households include children of any age compared with 40 percent of all households. The majority of black householders ranging in age from 25 to 49 have children (of any age) under their roof.

Black children are much less likely than the average American child to live with married parents. Among black children under age 18, only 40 percent live with married parents. A larger 52 percent live with their mother only.

■ The poverty rate among black children is well above average because so many live in female-headed families—the poorest family type.

Forty-five percent of black households have children in the home

(percent of total and black households with children under age 18 and children of any age in the household, 2010)

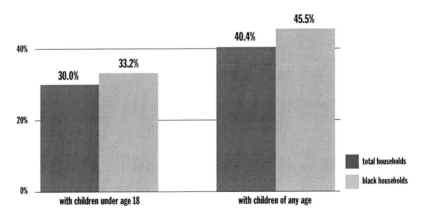

Table 7.6 Total and Black Households with Children under Age 18 by Age of Householder, 2010

(number of total and black households, number and percent with own children under age 18, and number and percent distribution of total and black households with children under age 18 by age of householder and black share of total, 2010; numbers in thousands)

	total		black		
	number	percent distribution	number	percent distribution	share of total
Total households	**117,538**	**100.0%**	**15,212**	**100.0%**	**12.9%**
Households with children under 18	35,218	30.0	5,046	33.2	14.3
Total households with children under 18	**35,218**	**100.0**	**5,046**	**100.0**	**14.3**
Under age 25	1,746	5.0	430	8.5	24.6
Aged 25 to 29	4,046	11.5	735	14.6	18.2
Aged 30 to 34	5,813	16.5	939	18.6	16.2
Aged 35 to 39	7,115	20.2	991	19.6	13.9
Aged 40 to 44	6,557	18.6	822	16.3	12.5
Aged 45 to 49	5,527	15.7	590	11.7	10.7
Aged 50 to 54	2,826	8.0	303	6.0	10.7
Aged 55 to 64	1,347	3.8	194	3.8	14.4
Aged 65 or older	241	0.7	42	0.8	17.4

Note: Blacks are those who identify themselves as being of the race alone or the race in combination with other races.
Source: Bureau of the Census, America's Families and Living Arrangements: 2010, Current Population Survey Annual Social and Economic Supplement, Internet site http://www.census.gov/population/www/socdemo/hh-fam/cps2010.html; calculations by New Strategist

Table 7.7 Total and Black Households with Children of Any Age by Age of Householder, 2010

(number of total and black households, number and percent with own children of any age, and number and percent distribution of total and black households with children of any age by age of householder and black share of total, 2010; numbers in thousands)

	total		black		
	number	percent distribution	number	percent distribution	share of total
Total households	**117,538**	**100.0%**	**15,212**	**100.0%**	**12.9%**
Households with children of any age	47,463	40.4	6,920	45.5	14.6
Households with children of any age	**47,463**	**100.0**	**6,920**	**100.0**	**14.6**
Under age 25	1,779	3.7	434	6.3	24.4
Aged 25 to 29	4,059	8.6	739	10.7	18.2
Aged 30 to 34	5,868	12.4	953	13.8	16.2
Aged 35 to 39	7,299	15.4	1,053	15.2	14.4
Aged 40 to 44	7,297	15.4	968	14.0	13.3
Aged 45 to 49	7,306	15.4	882	12.7	12.1
Aged 50 to 54	5,457	11.5	686	9.9	12.6
Aged 55 to 64	5,170	10.9	717	10.4	13.9
Aged 65 or older	3,228	6.8	489	7.1	15.1

Note: Blacks are those who identify themselves as being of the race alone or the race in combination with other races.
Source: Bureau of the Census, America's Families and Living Arrangements: 2010, Current Population Survey Annual Social and Economic Supplement, Internet site http://www.census.gov/population/www/socdemo/hh-fam/cps2010.html; calculations by New Strategist

Table 7.8 Total and Black Households with Children by Type of Household, 2010

(number and percent distribution of total and black households with own children under age 18 or of any age, and black share of total, by type of household, 2010; numbers in thousands)

	total		black		
	number	percent distribution	number	percent distribution	share of total
Total households with own children under 18	**35,218**	**100.0%**	**5,046**	**100.0%**	**14.3%**
Married couples	24,575	69.8	2,013	39.9	8.2
Female-headed families	8,419	23.9	2,617	51.9	31.1
Male-headed families	2,224	6.3	416	8.2	18.7
Total households with own children of any age	**47,463**	**100.0**	**6,920**	**100.0**	**14.6**
Married couples	31,514	66.4	2,710	39.2	8.6
Female-headed families	12,624	26.6	3,635	52.5	28.8
Male-headed families	3,325	7.0	575	8.3	17.3

Note: Blacks are those who identify themselves as being of the race alone or as being of the race in combination with other races.

Source: Bureau of the Census, America's Families and Living Arrangements: 2010, Current Population Survey Annual Social and Economic Supplement, Internet site http://www.census.gov/population/www/socdemo/hh-fam/cps2010.html; calculations by New Strategist

Table 7.9 Black Households by Age of Householder, Type of Household, and Presence of Children under Age 18, 2010

(number and percent distribution of black households by age of householder, type of household, and presence of own children under age 18, and average age of householder, 2010; numbers in thousands)

	total		married couples		female-headed families		male-headed families	
	total	with children <18	total	with children <18	total	with children <18	total	with children <18
Total black households	**15,212**	**5,046**	**4,427**	**2,013**	**4,257**	**2,617**	**968**	**416**
Under age 25	1,074	430	68	48	481	356	145	26
Aged 25 to 29	1,430	735	279	214	521	473	98	48
Aged 30 to 34	1,508	939	450	351	566	522	98	66
Aged 35 to 39	1,610	991	555	448	525	459	127	84
Aged 40 to 44	1,523	822	507	387	499	366	102	69
Aged 45 to 49	1,695	590	565	289	457	252	115	49
Aged 50 to 54	1,589	303	538	155	364	111	89	36
Aged 55 to 64	2,413	194	850	108	414	53	112	33
Aged 65 or older	2,370	42	615	12	431	25	80	5
Average age of householder	47.0	37.8	49.2	40.0	43.4	35.7	42.8	39.9

PERCENT OF HOUSEHOLDS WITH CHILDREN BY TYPE

	total		married couples		female-headed families		male-headed families	
Total black households	**100.0%**	**33.2%**	**100.0%**	**45.5%**	**100.0%**	**61.5%**	**100.0%**	**43.0%**
Under age 25	100.0	40.0	100.0	70.6	100.0	74.0	100.0	17.9
Aged 25 to 29	100.0	51.4	100.0	76.7	100.0	90.8	100.0	49.0
Aged 30 to 34	100.0	62.3	100.0	78.0	100.0	92.2	100.0	67.3
Aged 35 to 39	100.0	61.6	100.0	80.7	100.0	87.4	100.0	66.1
Aged 40 to 44	100.0	54.0	100.0	76.3	100.0	73.3	100.0	67.6
Aged 45 to 49	100.0	34.8	100.0	51.2	100.0	55.1	100.0	42.6
Aged 50 to 54	100.0	19.1	100.0	28.8	100.0	30.5	100.0	40.4
Aged 55 to 64	100.0	8.0	100.0	12.7	100.0	12.8	100.0	29.5
Aged 65 or older	100.0	1.8	100.0	2.0	100.0	5.8	100.0	6.3

Note: Blacks are those who identify themselves as being of the race alone or the race in combination with other races.
Source: Bureau of the Census, America's Families and Living Arrangements: 2010, Current Population Survey Annual Social and Economic Supplement, Internet site http://www.census.gov/population/www/socdemo/hh-fam/cps2010.html; calculations by New Strategist

Table 7.10 **Black Households by Age of Householder, Type of Household, and Presence of Children of Any Age, 2010**

(number and percent distribution of black households by age of householder, type of household, and presence of own children of any age, and average age of householder, 2010; numbers in thousands)

	total		married couples		female-headed families		male-headed families	
	total	with children of any age	total	with children of any age	total	with children of any age	total	with children of any age
Total black households	15,212	6,920	4,427	2,710	4,257	3,635	968	575
Under age 25	1,074	434	68	48	481	356	145	30
Aged 25 to 29	1,430	739	279	215	521	473	98	50
Aged 30 to 34	1,508	953	450	355	566	527	98	71
Aged 35 to 39	1,610	1,053	555	463	525	504	127	85
Aged 40 to 44	1,523	968	507	421	499	466	102	81
Aged 45 to 49	1,695	882	565	411	457	402	115	70
Aged 50 to 54	1,589	686	538	319	364	308	89	59
Aged 55 to 64	2,413	717	850	354	414	291	112	71
Aged 65 or older	2,370	489	615	122	431	309	80	57
Average age of householder	47.0	43.5	49.2	44.2	43.4	42.6	42.8	45.6

PERCENT OF HOUSEHOLDS WITH CHILDREN BY TYPE

	total		married couples		female-headed families		male-headed families	
Total black households	100.0%	45.5%	100.0%	61.2%	100.0%	85.4%	100.0%	59.4%
Under age 25	100.0	40.4	100.0	70.6	100.0	74.0	100.0	20.7
Aged 25 to 29	100.0	51.7	100.0	77.1	100.0	90.8	100.0	51.0
Aged 30 to 34	100.0	63.2	100.0	78.9	100.0	93.1	100.0	72.4
Aged 35 to 39	100.0	65.4	100.0	83.4	100.0	96.0	100.0	66.9
Aged 40 to 44	100.0	63.6	100.0	83.0	100.0	93.4	100.0	79.4
Aged 45 to 49	100.0	52.0	100.0	72.7	100.0	88.0	100.0	60.9
Aged 50 to 54	100.0	43.2	100.0	59.3	100.0	84.6	100.0	66.3
Aged 55 to 64	100.0	29.7	100.0	41.6	100.0	70.3	100.0	63.4
Aged 65 or older	100.0	20.6	100.0	19.8	100.0	71.7	100.0	71.3

Note: Blacks are those who identify themselves as being of the race alone or the race in combination with other races.
Source: Bureau of the Census, America's Families and Living Arrangements: 2010, Current Population Survey Annual Social and Economic Supplement, Internet site http://www.census.gov/population/www/socdemo/hh-fam/cps2010.html; calculations by New Strategist

Table 7.11 Living Arrangements of Total and Black Children, 2010

(number and percent distribution of total and black children under age 18 by living arrangement, and black share of total, 2010; numbers in thousands)

	total		black		
	number	percent distribution	number	percent distribution	share of total
TOTAL CHILDREN	**74,718**	**100.0%**	**12,653**	**100.0%**	**16.9%**
Living with two parents	**51,823**	**69.4**	**5,163**	**40.8**	**10.0**
Married parents	49,106	65.7	4,541	35.9	9.2
Unmarried parents	2,717	3.6	622	4.9	22.9
Biological mother and father	46,438	62.2	4,324	34.2	9.3
Married parents	44,099	59.0	3,765	29.8	8.5
Biological mother and stepfather	3,252	4.4	533	4.2	16.4
Biological father and stepmother	955	1.3	115	0.9	12.0
Biological mother and adoptive father	167	0.2	12	0.1	7.2
Biological father and adoptive mother	33	0.0	4	0.0	12.1
Adoptive mother and father	768	1.0	144	1.1	18.8
Other	210	0.3	31	0.2	14.8
Living with one parent	**19,857**	**26.6**	**6,573**	**51.9**	**33.1**
Mother only	17,285	23.1	6,135	48.5	35.5
Father only	2,572	3.4	439	3.5	17.1
Living with no parents	**3,038**	**4.1**	**917**	**7.2**	**30.2**
Grandparents	1,655	2.2	563	4.4	34.0
Other	1,383	1.9	354	2.8	25.6
At least one biological parent	**70,236**	**94.0**	**11,436**	**90.4**	**16.3**
At least one stepparent	**4,615**	**6.2**	**719**	**5.7**	**15.6**
At least one adoptive parent	**1,258**	**1.7**	**253**	**2.0**	**20.1**

Note: Blacks are those who identify themselves as being of the race alone and those who identify themselves as being of the race in combination with other races.
Source: Bureau of the Census, Current Population Survey Annual Social and Economic Supplement, America's Families and Living Arrangements: 2010, detailed tables, Internet site http://www.census.gov/population/www/socdemo/hh-fam/cps2010 .html; calculations by New Strategist

Table 7.12 Living Arrangements of Total and Black Adults, 2010

(number and percent distribution of total people and blacks aged 15 or older and black share of total, by relationship to householder, 2010; numbers in thousands)

	total		black		
	number	percent distribution	number	percent distribution	share of total
Total people	**242,168**	**100.0%**	**30,468**	**100.0%**	**12.6%**
Householder	78,867	32.6	9,660	31.7	12.2
Spouse of householder	58,428	24.1	4,425	14.5	7.6
Child of householder	36,605	15.1	6,110	20.1	16.7
Other relative of householder	14,476	6.0	2,836	9.3	19.6
Nonrelatives	53,791	22.2	7,437	24.4	13.8

Note: Blacks are those who identify themselves as being of the race alone or as being of the race in combination with other races.
Source: Bureau of the Census, Current Population Survey Annual Social and Economic Supplement, Internet site http://www .census.gov/hhes/www/income/dinctabs.html; calculations by New Strategist

Table 7.13 Living Arrangements of Blacks by Sex, 2010

(number and percent distribution of black men and women aged 15 or older by relationship to householder, 2010; numbers in thousands)

	men		women	
	number	percent distribution	number	percent distribution
Total blacks	**13,830**	**100.0%**	**16,638**	**100.0%**
Householder	3,623	26.2	6,037	36.3
Spouse of householder	1,920	13.9	2,505	15.1
Child of householder	3,419	24.7	2,691	16.2
Other relative of householder	1,341	9.7	1,495	9.0
Nonrelatives	3,527	25.5	3,910	23.5

Note: Blacks are those who identify themselves as being of the race alone or as being of the race in combination with other races.
Source: Bureau of the Census, Current Population Survey Annual Social and Economic Supplement, Internet site http://www .census.gov/hhes/www/income/dinctabs.html; calculations by New Strategist

Many Blacks Have Never Married

Only about one in three black adults is currently married.

Fewer than half of blacks are married. Among black men, only 37 percent are currently married and living with their spouse. The figure is a smaller 28 percent among black women. A larger share of both men and women has never married.

A study of marital history by the Census Bureau reveals that 30 percent of black men and 25 percent of black women have married once and are still married. From 18 to 19 percent of black men and women have ever divorced. The figure surpasses one-third among black men and women aged 50 to 69. Among black women aged 70 or older, 60 percent have been widowed.

■ Because many blacks are not married, and married couples are the most affluent household type, black household incomes are well below average .

Many blacks have yet to marry

(percent distribution of blacks aged 15 or older by marital history and sex, 2009)

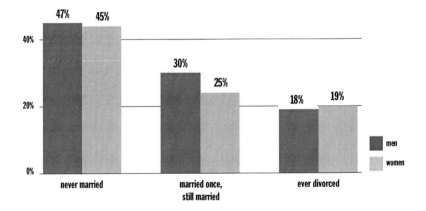

Table 7.14 Total and Black Marital Status, 2010

(number and percent distribution of total people and blacks aged 15 or older, and black share of total, by marital status, 2010; numbers in thousands)

	total		blacks		
	number	percent distribution	number	percent distribution	share of total
Total people	**242,047**	**100.0%**	**30,450**	**100.0%**	**12.6%**
Never married	74,243	30.7	14,326	47.0	19.3
Married, spouse present	120,768	49.9	9,145	30.0	7.6
Married, spouse absent	3,415	1.4	560	1.8	16.4
Separated	5,539	2.3	1,242	4.1	22.4
Divorced	23,742	9.8	3,325	10.9	14.0
Widowed	14,341	5.9	1,853	6.1	12.9

Note: Blacks are those who identify themselves as being of the race alone or of the race in combination with other races.
Source: Bureau of the Census, America's Families and Living Arrangements: 2010, Current Population Survey Annual Social and Economic Supplement, Internet site http://www.census.gov/population/www/socdemo/hh-fam/cps2010.html; calculations by New Strategist

Table 7.15 Marital Status of Black Men by Age, 2010

(number and percent distribution of black men aged 18 or older by age and current marital status, 2010; numbers in thousands)

	total	never married	married, spouse present	married, spouse absent	separated	divorced	widowed
Total black men	**12,695**	**5,650**	**4,725**	**210**	**476**	**1,271**	**363**
Aged 18 to 19	629	621	3	3	0	2	0
Aged 20 to 24	1,532	1,433	61	9	13	14	2
Aged 25 to 29	1,466	1,100	263	8	38	51	6
Aged 30 to 34	1,237	622	471	27	42	70	6
Aged 35 to 39	1,164	423	572	21	40	105	3
Aged 40 to 44	1,184	417	530	24	58	148	8
Aged 45 to 49	1,267	366	592	24	80	190	14
Aged 50 to 54	1,204	306	578	32	48	204	35
Aged 55 to 64	1,673	271	915	31	87	295	74
Aged 65 or older	1,338	90	739	31	69	193	215
Total black men	**100.0%**	**44.5%**	**37.2%**	**1.7%**	**3.7%**	**10.0%**	**2.9%**
Aged 18 to 19	100.0	98.7	0.5	0.5	0.0	0.3	0.0
Aged 20 to 24	100.0	93.5	4.0	0.6	0.8	0.9	0.1
Aged 25 to 29	100.0	75.0	17.9	0.5	2.6	3.5	0.4
Aged 30 to 34	100.0	50.3	38.1	2.2	3.4	5.7	0.5
Aged 35 to 39	100.0	36.3	49.1	1.8	3.4	9.0	0.3
Aged 40 to 44	100.0	35.2	44.8	2.0	4.9	12.5	0.7
Aged 45 to 49	100.0	28.9	46.7	1.9	6.3	15.0	1.1
Aged 50 to 54	100.0	25.4	48.0	2.7	4.0	16.9	2.9
Aged 55 to 64	100.0	16.2	54.7	1.9	5.2	17.6	4.4
Aged 65 or older	100.0	6.7	55.2	2.3	5.2	14.4	16.1

Note: Blacks are those who identify themselves as being of the race alone or of the race in combination with other races.
Source: Bureau of the Census, America's Families and Living Arrangements: 2010, Current Population Survey Annual Social and Economic Supplement, Internet site http://www.census.gov/population/www/socdemo/hh-fam/cps2010.html; calculations by New Strategist

Table 7.16 Marital Status of Black Women by Age, 2010

(number and percent distribution of black women aged 18 or older by age and current marital status, 2010; numbers in thousands)

	total	never married	married, spouse present	married, spouse absent	separated	divorced	widowed
Total black women	**15,508**	**6,454**	**4,415**	**349**	**752**	**2,052**	**1,486**
Aged 18 to 19	666	641	4	0	10	9	1
Aged 20 to 24	1,688	1,521	113	12	19	18	5
Aged 25 to 29	1,616	1,110	347	52	66	28	13
Aged 30 to 34	1,472	784	469	30	69	118	2
Aged 35 to 39	1,449	561	523	62	90	192	20
Aged 40 to 44	1,453	498	555	37	97	238	28
Aged 45 to 49	1,547	425	592	39	119	303	69
Aged 50 to 54	1,442	345	535	29	102	334	97
Aged 55 to 64	2,109	363	787	51	118	502	289
Aged 65 or older	2,066	205	490	36	62	311	962
Total black women	**100.0%**	**41.6%**	**28.5%**	**2.3%**	**4.8%**	**13.2%**	**9.6%**
Aged 18 to 19	100.0	96.2	0.6	0.0	1.5	1.4	0.2
Aged 20 to 24	100.0	90.1	6.7	0.7	1.1	1.1	0.3
Aged 25 to 29	100.0	68.7	21.5	3.2	4.1	1.7	0.8
Aged 30 to 34	100.0	53.3	31.9	2.0	4.7	8.0	0.1
Aged 35 to 39	100.0	38.7	36.1	4.3	6.2	13.3	1.4
Aged 40 to 44	100.0	34.3	38.2	2.5	6.7	16.4	1.9
Aged 45 to 49	100.0	27.5	38.3	2.5	7.7	19.6	4.5
Aged 50 to 54	100.0	23.9	37.1	2.0	7.1	23.2	6.7
Aged 55 to 64	100.0	17.2	37.3	2.4	5.6	23.8	13.7
Aged 65 or older	100.0	9.9	23.7	1.7	3.0	15.1	46.6

Note: Blacks are those who identify themselves as being of the race alone or of the race in combination with other races.
Source: Bureau of the Census, America's Families and Living Arrangements: 2010, Current Population Survey Annual Social and Economic Supplement, Internet site http://www.census.gov/population/www/socdemo/hh-fam/cps2010.html; calculations by New Strategist

Table 7.17 Marital History of Black Men by Age, 2009

(number of black men aged 15 or older and percent distribution by marital history and age, 2009; numbers in thousands)

	total	15–19	20–24	25–29	30–34	35–39	40–49	50–59	60–69	70+
Total black men, number	12,955	1,659	1,395	1,325	1,104	1,122	2,410	2,042	1,109	789
Total black men, percent	100.0%	100.0%	100.0%	100.0%	100.0%	100.0%	100.0%	100.0%	100.0%	100.0%
Never married	46.9	98.4	91.7	73.1	54.5	43.1	24.2	17.5	9.4	8.1
Ever married	53.1	1.6	8.3	26.9	45.5	56.9	75.8	82.5	90.6	91.9
Married once	41.9	1.6	8.3	26.3	42.9	51.0	62.1	57.6	61.4	68.1
Still married	29.9	0.7	7.2	22.0	35.5	39.0	43.6	37.3	43.7	43.6
Married twice	9.2	0.0	0.0	0.5	2.6	5.7	12.6	20.5	20.1	19.5
Still married	6.8	0.0	0.0	0.3	2.6	4.5	9.2	15.4	15.5	11.8
Married three or more times	2.0	0.0	0.0	0.0	0.0	0.2	1.1	4.5	9.0	4.4
Still married	1.4	0.0	0.0	0.0	0.0	0.2	1.0	3.2	6.6	2.5
Ever divorced	17.7	0.4	0.2	3.1	6.6	14.7	26.5	39.2	34.6	22.9
Currently divorced	9.2	0.4	0.2	2.8	4.1	10.0	15.5	20.3	12.5	7.7
Ever widowed	3.7	0.5	0.0	0.5	0.0	0.6	2.2	3.2	10.7	28.2
Currently widowed	2.8	0.5	0.0	0.5	0.0	0.3	1.9	2.4	6.7	22.7

Note: Blacks are those who identify themselves as being of the race alone.
Source: Bureau of the Census, Number, Timing, and Duration of Marriages and Divorces: 2009, Detailed Tables, Internet site http://www.census.gov/hhes/socdemo/marriage/data/sipp/index.html

Table 7.18 Marital History of Black Women by Age, 2009

(number of black women aged 15 or older and percent distribution by marital history and age, 2009; numbers in thousands)

	total	15–19	20–24	25–29	30–34	35–39	40–49	50–59	60–69	70+
Total black women, number	15,776	1,686	1,545	1,514	1,367	1,419	2,946	2,483	1,530	1,286
Total black women, percent	100.0%	100.0%	100.0%	100.0%	100.0%	100.0%	100.0%	100.0%	100.0%	100.0%
Never married	45.2	98.3	88.6	70.5	53.6	39.2	30.7	21.5	14.5	7.0
Ever married	54.8	1.7	11.4	29.5	46.4	60.8	69.3	78.5	85.5	93.0
Married once	44.6	1.5	11.1	29.0	42.4	52.5	59.2	58.8	62.8	71.0
Still married	24.8	1.3	9.0	23.1	30.2	33.7	37.0	30.4	30.8	14.6
Married twice	8.4	0.2	0.2	0.5	3.8	7.5	8.7	15.6	18.4	18.0
Still married	4.4	0.2	0.2	0.5	3.1	5.5	4.8	9.5	9.0	3.3
Married three or more times	1.7	0.0	0.0	0.0	0.2	0.8	1.4	4.1	4.3	3.9
Still married	0.8	0.0	0.0	0.0	0.0	0.4	0.9	1.7	2.4	0.8
Ever divorced	19.2	0.2	1.3	4.3	11.1	19.9	24.3	37.8	34.4	25.9
Currently divorced	12.3	0.0	1.1	3.8	7.9	13.8	17.3	24.7	18.5	12.0
Ever widowed	9.1	0.2	0.3	0.0	0.7	1.0	3.2	8.2	21.8	60.1
Currently widowed	8.3	0.2	0.3	0.0	0.3	0.6	2.6	6.5	19.9	58.2

Note: Blacks are those who identify themselves as being of the race alone.
Source: Bureau of the Census, Number, Timing, and Duration of Marriages and Divorces: 2009, Detailed Tables, Internet site http://www.census.gov/hhes/socdemo/marriage/data/sipp/index.html

8

Population

■ The number of blacks in the United States increased 13 percent between 2000 and 2010. The black growth rate greatly exceeded the 1.2 percent increase in the non-Hispanic white population.

■ The nation's 42 million blacks account for one in seven Americans. Seventeen percent of people under age 20 are black, a share that falls to 9 percent among people aged 65 or older.

■ The 55 percent majority of blacks live in the South, where they account for one in five residents.

■ Unlike Asians and Hispanics, blacks are not concentrated in just a handful of states. In fact, no single state is home to more than 8 percent of the black population. The broad distribution of blacks throughout most of the country boosts their cultural and political power.

■ Seven metropolitan areas are home to more than 1 million blacks: Atlanta, Chicago, Houston, Miami, New York, Philadelphia, and Washington, DC.

The Black Population Is Growing Slowly

The growth rate of the black population is well below that of Asians or Hispanics.

The number of blacks in the U.S. population grew 13 percent between 2000 and 2010, less than the 43 to 44 percent growth rate of Hispanics and Asians. But the black growth rate greatly exceeded the small 1.2 percent increase for non-Hispanic whites.

The count of blacks ranges from 39 million who identify themselves as black and no other race (called black alone) to 42 million who identify themselves as black alone or in combination with other races. Beginning in 2000, Americans could identify themselves as being of more than one race, which increases the complexity of racial identification. The single biggest mixed-race group is black and white, at 1.8 million in 2010. Another addition to the complexity is the fact that Hispanic is an ethnic identity rather than a race, meaning blacks can also be Hispanic. In 2010, 4.5 percent of the nation's blacks also identified themselves as Hispanic.

■ Unlike Hispanics and Asians, most of whom live in a handful of states, blacks are an important segment of the population throughout most of the country. This adds to their cultural influence and political power.

Blacks are outnumbered by Hispanics

(population by race and Hispanic origin, 2010)

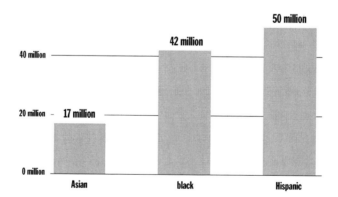

Table 8.1 Population by Race, 2000 and 2010

(number of people by race and Hispanic origin, 2000 and 2010; numerical and percent change, 2000–10)

	2010		2000		change	
	number	percent distribution	number	percent distribution	numerical	percent
Total population	**308,745,538**	**100.0%**	**281,421,906**	**100.0%**	**27,323,632**	**9.7%**
Race alone						
American Indian	2,932,248	0.9	2,475,956	0.9	456,292	18.4
Asian	14,674,252	4.8	10,242,998	3.6	4,431,254	43.3
Black	38,929,319	12.6	34,658,190	12.3	4,271,129	12.3
Native Hawaiian	540,013	0.2	398,835	0.1	141,178	35.4
White	223,553,265	72.4	211,460,626	75.1	12,092,639	5.7
Other race	19,107,368	6.2	15,359,073	5.5	3,748,295	24.4
Two or more races	**9,009,073**	**2.9**	**6,826,228**	**2.4**	**2,182,845**	**32.0**
Race alone or in combination						
American Indian	5,220,579	1.7	4,225,058	1.5	995,521	23.6
Asian	17,320,856	5.6	12,006,894	4.3	5,313,962	44.3
Black	42,020,743	13.6	37,104,248	13.2	4,916,495	13.3
Native Hawaiian	1,225,195	0.4	906,785	0.3	318,410	35.1
White	231,040,398	74.8	231,434,388	82.2	–393,990	–0.2
Hispanic	**50,477,594**	**16.3**	**35,305,818**	**12.5**	**15,171,776**	**43.0**
Non-Hispanic white	**196,817,552**	**63.7**	**194,552,774**	**69.1**	**2,264,778**	**1.2**

Note: Numbers by race in combination do not add to total because they include those who identify themselves as being of the race alone and those who identify themselves as being of the race in combination with other races. Hispanics may be of any race. Non-Hispanic whites are those who identify themselves as being white alone and not Hispanic. Numbers are for April 1 of each year.
Source: Bureau of the Census, An Overview: Race and Hispanic Origin and the 2010 Census, 2010 Census Briefs, Internet site http://2010.census.gov/2010census/data/; calculations by New Strategist

Table 8.2 Two-or-More-Races Population, 2010

(number and percent of people who identify themselves as being of two or more races, by racial identification, 2010)

	number	percent distribution
TOTAL POPULATION	308,745,538	100.0%
One race	**299,736,465**	**97.1**
White	223,553,265	72.4
Black	38,929,319	12.6
American Indian	2,932,248	0.9
Asian	14,674,252	4.8
Native Hawaiian	540,013	0.2
Other race	19,107,368	6.2
Two races	**8,265,318**	**2.7**
White and black	1,834,212	0.6
White and American Indian	1,432,309	0.5
White and Asian	1,623,234	0.5
White and Native Hawaiian	169,991	0.1
White and some other race	1,740,924	0.6
Black and American Indian	269,421	0.1
Black and Asian	185,595	0.1
Black and Native Hawaiian	50,308	0.0
Black and other race	314,571	0.1
American Indian and Asian	58,829	0.0
American Indian and Native Hawaiian	11,039	0.0
American Indian and other race	115,752	0.0
Asian and Native Hawaiian	165,690	0.1
Asian and other race	234,462	0.1
Native Hawaiian and other race	58,981	0.0
Three races	**676,469**	**0.2**
White, black, and American Indian	230,848	0.1
White, black, and Asian	61,511	0.0
White, black, and Native Hawaiian	9,245	0.0
White, black, and other race	46,641	0.0
White, American Indian, and Asian	45,960	0.0
White, American Indian, and Native Hawaiian	8,656	0.0
White, American Indian, and other race	30,941	0.0
White, Asian, and Native Hawaiian	143,126	0.0
White, Asian, and other race	35,786	0.0
White, Native Hawaiian, and other race	9,181	0.0
Black, American Indian, and Asian	9,460	0.0
Black, American Indian, and Native Hawaiian	2,142	0.0
Black, American Indian, and other race	8,236	0.0
Black, Asian, and Native Hawaiian	7,295	0.0
Black, Asian, and other race	8,122	0.0

	number	percent distribution
Black, Native Hawaiian, and other race	4,233	0.0%
American Indian, Asian, and Native Hawaiian	3,827	0.0
American Indian, Asian, and other race	3,785	0.0
American Indian, Native Hawaiian, and other race	2,000	0.0
Asian, Native Hawaiian, and other race	5,474	0.0
Four races	**57,875**	**0.0**
White, black, American Indian, and Asian	19,018	0.0
White, black, American Indian, and Native Hawaiian	2,673	0.0
White, black, American Indian, and other race	8,757	0.0
White, black, Asian, and Native Hawaiian	4,852	0.0
White, black, Asian, and other race	2,420	0.0
White, black, Native Hawaiian, and other race	560	0.0
White, American Indian, Asian, and Native Hawaiian	11,500	0.0
White, American Indian, Asian, and other race	1,535	0.0
White, American Indian, Native Hawaiian, and other race	454	0.0
White, Asian, Native Hawaiian, and other race	3,486	0.0
Black, American Indian, Asian, and Native Hawaiian	1,011	0.0
Black, American Indian, Asian, and other race	539	0.0
Black, American Indian, Native Hawaiian, and other race	212	0.0
Black, Asian, Native Hawaiian, and other race	574	0.0
American Indian, Asian, Native Hawaiian, and other race	284	0.0
Five races	**8,619**	**0.0**
White, black, American Indian, Asian, and Native Hawaiian	6,605	0.0
White, black, American Indian, Asian, and other race	1,023	0.0
White, black, American Indian, Native Hawaiian, and other race	182	0.0
White, black, Asian, Native Hawaiian, and other race	268	0.0
White, American Indian, Asian, Native Hawaiian, and other race	443	0.0
Black, American Indian, Asian, Native Hawaiian, and other race	98	0.0
Six races	**792**	**0.0**
White, black, American Indian, Asian, Native Hawaiian, and other race	792	0.0

Note: Most who identify themselves as "other race" are Hispanics who consider Hispanic a race rather than an ethnicity. Census racial categories are shown in the order provided by the Census Bureau. For readability, the names of some census racial categories have been shortened. Blacks include those who identify themselves as African American; American Indians include Alaska Natives; Native Hawaiians include other Pacific Islanders.

Source: Bureau of the Census, An Overview: Race and Hispanic Origin and the 2010 Census, 2010 Census Briefs, Internet site http://2010.census.gov/2010census/data/

Table 8.3 Blacks by Racial Identification, 2000 and 2010

(total number of people, and number and percent distribution of blacks by racial identification, 2000 and 2010 percent change, 2000–10)

	2010		2000		
	number	percent distribution	number	percent distribution	percent change 2000–10
Total people	**308,745,538**	**100.0%**	**281,421,906**	**100.0%**	**9.7%**
Black alone or in combination					
with one or more other races	42,020,743	13.6	37,104,248	13.2	13.3
Black alone	38,929,319	12.6	34,658,190	12.3	12.3
Black in combination	3,091,424	1.0	2,446,058	0.9	26.4

Source: Bureau of the Census, An Overview: Race and Hispanic Origin and the 2010 Census, 2010 Census Briefs, Internet site http://2010.census.gov/2010census/data/; calculations by New Strategist

Table 8.4 Blacks by Hispanic Origin, 2010

(number and percent distribution of blacks by Hispanic origin and racial identification, 2010)

	black alone or in combination		black alone	
	number	percent distribution	number	percent distribution
Total blacks	**42,020,743**	**100.0%**	**38,929,319**	**100.0%**
Not Hispanic	40,123,525	95.5	37,685,848	96.8
Hispanic	1,897,218	4.5	1,243,471	3.2

Source: Bureau of the Census, An Overview: Race and Hispanic Origin and the 2010 Census, 2010 Census Briefs, Internet site http://2010.census.gov/2010census/data/; calculations by New Strategist

The Black Population Is Younger than Average

Seventeen percent of the nation's children and young adults are black.

The nation's 42 million blacks account for one in seven Americans. The black share of the population is largest among children and young adults. Seventeen percent of Americans under age 20 are black. The share falls with age to just 9 percent of people aged 65 or older. The median age of the black population was 30 in 2009, according to Census Bureau estimates. This is much younger than the median age of 37 for Americans as a whole.

The black population, like the non-Hispanic white population, has been affected by baby boom and baby bust over the decades. Consequently, some age groups are growing while others are shrinking. The number of blacks aged 55 to 59 expanded by 57 percent between 2000 and 2010 as boomers entered the age group. But the number of blacks aged 35 to 39 fell 6 percent as the small generation X aged into its late thirties.

Black females outnumber black males beginning in the 25-to-29 age group. By age 65 or older, only 63 black males are left per 100 black females.

■ The diversity of older Americans will increase greatly as today's young adults become the nation's elderly.

The black share of the population declines with age

(black share of the total population for selected age groups, 2010)

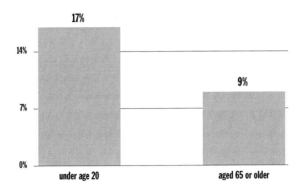

Table 8.5 Black Share of Total Population by Age, 2009

(total number of people, number and percent distribution of blacks, and black share of total, by age, 2009)

| | | black | | |
	total	number	percent distribution	share of total
Total people	**307,006,550**	**41,804,073**	**100.0%**	**13.6%**
Under age 5	21,299,656	3,665,743	8.8	17.2
Aged 5 to 9	20,609,634	3,360,097	8.0	16.3
Aged 10 to 14	19,973,564	3,336,589	8.0	16.7
Aged 15 to 19	21,537,837	3,693,533	8.8	17.1
Aged 20 to 24	21,539,559	3,424,321	8.2	15.9
Aged 25 to 29	21,677,719	3,233,759	7.7	14.9
Aged 30 to 34	19,888,603	2,817,172	6.7	14.2
Aged 35 to 39	20,538,351	2,806,264	6.7	13.7
Aged 40 to 44	20,991,605	2,782,519	6.7	13.3
Aged 45 to 49	22,831,092	2,895,949	6.9	12.7
Aged 50 to 54	21,761,391	2,625,762	6.3	12.1
Aged 55 to 59	18,975,026	2,135,788	5.1	11.3
Aged 60 to 64	15,811,923	1,572,724	3.8	9.9
Aged 65 to 69	11,784,320	1,112,353	2.7	9.4
Aged 70 to 74	9,007,747	858,233	2.1	9.5
Aged 75 to 79	7,325,528	655,403	1.6	8.9
Aged 80 to 84	5,822,334	458,899	1.1	7.9
Aged 85 or older	5,630,661	368,965	0.9	6.6
Aged 18 to 24	30,412,035	4,935,010	11.8	16.2
Aged 18 or older	232,458,335	29,258,800	70.0	12.6
Aged 65 or older	39,570,590	3,453,853	8.3	8.7
Median age (years)	36.8	30.3	–	–

Note: Blacks are those who identify themselves as being of the race alone or as being of the race in combination with other races. "–" means not applicable.
Source: Bureau of the Census, National Population Estimates, Internet site http://www.census.gov/popest/national/asrh/; calculations by New Strategist

Table 8.6 Blacks by Age, 2000 and 2009

(number of blacks by age, 2000 and 2009; percent change, 2000–09)

	2009	2000	percent change
Total blacks	**41,804,073**	**37,225,810**	**12.3%**
Under age 5	3,665,743	3,238,768	13.2
Aged 5 to 9	3,360,097	3,547,628	−5.3
Aged 10 to 14	3,336,589	3,423,180	−2.5
Aged 15 to 19	3,693,533	3,165,617	16.7
Aged 20 to 24	3,424,321	2,860,300	19.7
Aged 25 to 29	3,233,759	2,720,412	18.9
Aged 30 to 34	2,817,172	2,776,884	1.5
Aged 35 to 39	2,806,264	2,969,807	−5.5
Aged 40 to 44	2,782,519	2,841,390	−2.1
Aged 45 to 49	2,895,949	2,390,304	21.2
Aged 50 to 54	2,625,762	1,907,983	37.6
Aged 55 to 59	2,135,788	1,362,911	56.7
Aged 60 to 64	1,572,724	1,103,990	42.5
Aged 65 to 69	1,112,353	911,765	22.0
Aged 70 to 74	858,233	754,799	13.7
Aged 75 to 79	655,403	570,476	14.9
Aged 80 to 84	458,899	358,678	27.9
Aged 85 or older	368,965	320,918	15.0
Aged 18 to 24	4,935,010	4,125,974	19.6
Aged 18 or older	29,258,800	25,116,291	16.5
Aged 65 or older	3,453,853	2,916,636	18.4

Note: Blacks are those who identify themselves as being of the race alone or as being of the race in combination with other races. Numbers for 2000 and 2009 are July 1 estimates.
Source: Bureau of the Census, National Population Estimates, Internet site http://www.census.gov/popest/national/asrh/; calculations by New Strategist

Table 8.7 Blacks by Age and Sex, 2009

(number of blacks by age and sex, and sex ratio by age, 2009)

	total	females	males	sex ratio
Total blacks	**41,804,073**	**21,807,716**	**19,996,357**	**92**
Under age 5	3,665,743	1,803,212	1,862,531	103
Aged 5 to 9	3,360,097	1,656,060	1,704,037	103
Aged 10 to 14	3,336,589	1,644,304	1,692,285	103
Aged 15 to 19	3,693,533	1,822,253	1,871,280	103
Aged 20 to 24	3,424,321	1,691,193	1,733,128	102
Aged 25 to 29	3,233,759	1,621,895	1,611,864	99
Aged 30 to 34	2,817,172	1,465,218	1,351,954	92
Aged 35 to 39	2,806,264	1,480,673	1,325,591	90
Aged 40 to 44	2,782,519	1,476,543	1,305,976	88
Aged 45 to 49	2,895,949	1,552,077	1,343,872	87
Aged 50 to 54	2,625,762	1,419,710	1,206,052	85
Aged 55 to 59	2,135,788	1,174,699	961,089	82
Aged 60 to 64	1,572,724	880,819	691,905	79
Aged 65 to 69	1,112,353	641,184	471,169	73
Aged 70 to 74	858,233	506,052	352,181	70
Aged 75 to 79	655,403	403,109	252,294	63
Aged 80 to 84	458,899	300,626	158,273	53
Aged 85 or older	368,965	268,089	100,876	38
Aged 18 to 24	4,935,010	2,436,405	2,498,605	103
Aged 18 or older	29,258,800	15,627,099	13,631,701	87
Aged 65 or older	3,453,853	2,119,060	1,334,793	63

Note: Blacks are those who identify themselves as being of the race alone or as being of the race in combination with other races. The sex ratio is the number of males divided by the number of females multiplied by 100.
Source: Bureau of the Census, National Population Estimates, Internet site http://www.census.gov/popest/national/asrh/; calculations by New Strategist

Most Blacks Live in the South

Blacks account for one in five Southerners.

The 55 percent majority of blacks live in the South, where they account for a substantial 20 percent of the population. The Northeast is home to 17 percent of blacks and the Midwest to 18 percent. Only 10 percent of blacks live in the West.

Although most blacks live in the South, no single state is home to more than 8 percent of the black population. New York has the largest black population among the 50 states, but only 8 percent of blacks live in the state. Blacks account for the largest share of state populations in the South. They are more than 30 percent of the populations of Georgia, Louisiana, Maryland, and Mississippi.

Seven metropolitan areas are home to more than 1 million blacks: Atlanta, Chicago, Houston, Miami, New York, Philadelphia, and Washington, DC. In 10 metropolitan areas, blacks account for more than 40 percent of the population: Albany, GA; Columbus, GA–AL; Florence, SC; Jackson, MS; Macon, GA; Memphis, TN–MS–AR; Montgomery, AL; Pine Bluff, AR; Rocky Mount, NC; and Sumter, SC.

■ The number of blacks grew in every state between 2000 and 2010, but in Washington, D.C., the black population fell 10 percent during the decade.

Few blacks live in the West

(percent distribution of blacks by region, 2010)

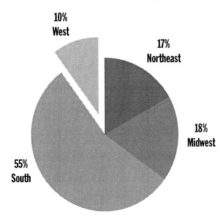

10%
West

17%
Northeast

18%
Midwest

55%
South

Table 8.8 Total and Black Population by Region, 2010

(total number of people, number and percent distribution of blacks, and black share of total, by region, 2010)

	total	black number	black percent distribution	black share of total
Total people	**308,745,538**	**42,020,743**	**100.0%**	**13.6%**
Northeast	55,317,240	7,187,488	17.1	13.0
Midwest	66,927,001	7,594,486	18.1	11.3
South	114,555,744	23,105,082	55.0	20.2
West	71,945,553	4,133,687	9.8	5.7

Note: Blacks are those who identify themselves as being of the race alone or as being of the race in combination with other races.
Source: Bureau of the Census, 2010 Census, American Factfinder, Internet site http://factfinder2.census.gov/faces/nav/jsf/pages/index.xhtml; calculations by New Strategist

Table 8.9 Blacks by Region, 2000 and 2010

(number of blacks by region, 2000 and 2010; percent change, 2000–10)

	2010	2000	percent change
Total blacks	**42,020,743**	**36,419,434**	**15.4%**
Northeast	7,187,488	6,556,909	9.6
Midwest	7,594,486	6,838,669	11.1
South	23,105,082	19,528,231	18.3
West	4,133,687	3,495,625	18.3

Note: Blacks are those who identify themselves as being of the race alone or as being of the race in combination with other races. Total number of blacks in 2000 differs from the total in previous tables of this chapter because these are unadjusted census counts from April 1, 2000.
Source: Bureau of the Census, 2010 Census, American Factfinder, Internet site http://factfinder2.census.gov/faces/nav/jsf/pages/index.xhtml; calculations by New Strategist

Table 8.10 Total and Black Population by State, 2010

(total number of people, number and percent distribution of blacks, and black share of total, by state, 2010)

		black		
	total	number	percent distribution	share of total
Total people	**308,745,538**	**42,020,743**	**100.0%**	**13.6%**
Alabama	4,779,736	1,281,118	3.0	26.8
Alaska	710,231	33,150	0.1	4.7
Arizona	6,392,017	318,665	0.8	5.0
Arkansas	2,915,918	468,710	1.1	16.1
California	37,253,956	2,683,914	6.4	7.2
Colorado	5,029,196	249,812	0.6	5.0
Connecticut	3,574,097	405,600	1.0	11.3
Delaware	897,934	205,923	0.5	22.9
District of Columbia	601,723	314,352	0.7	52.2
Florida	18,801,310	3,200,663	7.6	17.0
Georgia	9,687,653	3,054,098	7.3	31.5
Hawaii	1,360,301	38,820	0.1	2.9
Idaho	1,567,582	15,940	0.0	1.0
Illinois	12,830,632	1,974,113	4.7	15.4
Indiana	6,483,802	654,415	1.6	10.1
Iowa	3,046,355	113,225	0.3	3.7
Kansas	2,853,118	202,149	0.5	7.1
Kentucky	4,339,367	376,213	0.9	8.7
Louisiana	4,533,372	1,486,885	3.5	32.8
Maine	1,328,361	21,764	0.1	1.6
Maryland	5,773,552	1,783,899	4.2	30.9
Massachusetts	6,547,629	508,413	1.2	7.8
Michigan	9,883,640	1,505,514	3.6	15.2
Minnesota	5,303,925	327,548	0.8	6.2
Mississippi	2,967,297	1,115,801	2.7	37.6
Missouri	5,988,927	747,474	1.8	12.5
Montana	989,415	7,917	0.0	0.8
Nebraska	1,826,341	98,959	0.2	5.4
Nevada	2,700,551	254,452	0.6	9.4
New Hampshire	1,316,470	21,736	0.1	1.7
New Jersey	8,791,894	1,300,363	3.1	14.8
New Mexico	2,059,179	57,040	0.1	2.8
New York	19,378,102	3,334,550	7.9	17.2
North Carolina	9,535,483	2,151,456	5.1	22.6
North Dakota	672,591	11,086	0.0	1.6
Ohio	11,536,504	1,541,771	3.7	13.4
Oklahoma	3,751,351	327,621	0.8	8.7
Oregon	3,831,074	98,479	0.2	2.6
Pennsylvania	12,702,379	1,507,965	3.6	11.9
Rhode Island	1,052,567	77,754	0.2	7.4

	total	black		
		number	percent distribution	share of total
South Carolina	4,625,364	1,332,188	3.2%	28.8%
South Dakota	814,180	14,705	0.0	1.8
Tennessee	6,346,105	1,107,178	2.6	17.4
Texas	25,145,561	3,168,469	7.5	12.6
Utah	2,763,885	43,209	0.1	1.6
Vermont	625,741	9,343	0.0	1.5
Virginia	8,001,024	1,653,563	3.9	20.7
Washington	6,724,540	325,004	0.8	4.8
West Virginia	1,852,994	76,945	0.2	4.2
Wisconsin	5,686,986	403,527	1.0	7.1
Wyoming	563,626	7,285	0.0	1.3

Note: Blacks are those who identify themselves as being of the race alone and those who identify themselves as being of the race in combination with other races.
Source: Bureau of the Census, 2000 Census, The Black Population 2000, Internet site http://www.census.gov/population/www/ cen2000/briefs.html; and 2010 Census, American Factfinder, Internet site http://factfinder2.census.gov/faces/nav/jsf/pages/ index.xhtml; calculations by New Strategist

Table 8.11 Blacks by State, 2000 and 2010

(number of blacks by state, 2000 and 2010; percent change, 2000–10)

	2010	2000	percent change
Total blacks	**42,020,743**	**36,419,434**	**15.4%**
Alabama	1,281,118	1,168,998	9.6
Alaska	33,150	27,147	22.1
Arizona	318,665	185,599	71.7
Arkansas	468,710	427,152	9.7
California	2,683,914	2,513,041	6.8
Colorado	249,812	190,717	31.0
Connecticut	405,600	339,078	19.6
Delaware	205,923	157,152	31.0
District of Columbia	314,352	350,455	-10.3
Florida	3,200,663	2,471,730	29.5
Georgia	3,054,098	2,393,425	27.6
Hawaii	38,820	33,343	16.4
Idaho	15,940	8,127	96.1
Illinois	1,974,113	1,937,671	1.9
Indiana	654,415	538,015	21.6
Iowa	113,225	72,512	56.1
Kansas	202,149	170,610	18.5
Kentucky	376,213	311,878	20.6
Louisiana	1,486,885	1,468,317	1.3
Maine	21,764	9,553	127.8
Maryland	1,783,899	1,525,036	17.0
Massachusetts	508,413	398,479	27.6
Michigan	1,505,514	1,474,613	2.1
Minnesota	327,548	202,972	61.4
Mississippi	1,115,801	1,041,708	7.1
Missouri	747,474	655,377	14.1
Montana	7,917	4,441	78.3
Nebraska	98,959	75,833	30.5
Nevada	254,452	150,508	69.1
New Hampshire	21,736	12,218	77.9
New Jersey	1,300,363	1,211,750	7.3
New Mexico	57,040	42,412	34.5
New York	3,334,550	3,234,165	3.1
North Carolina	2,151,456	1,776,283	21.1
North Dakota	11,086	5,372	106.4
Ohio	1,541,771	1,372,501	12.3
Oklahoma	327,621	284,766	15.0
Oregon	98,479	72,647	35.6
Pennsylvania	1,507,965	1,289,123	17.0
Rhode Island	77,754	58,051	33.9
South Carolina	1,332,188	1,200,901	10.9
South Dakota	14,705	6,687	119.9

	2010	2000	percent change
Tennessee	1,107,178	953,349	16.1%
Texas	3,168,469	2,493,057	27.1
Utah	43,209	24,382	77.2
Vermont	9,343	4,492	108.0
Virginia	1,653,563	1,441,207	14.7
Washington	325,004	238,398	36.3
West Virginia	76,945	62,817	22.5
Wisconsin	403,527	326,506	23.6
Wyoming	7,285	4,863	49.8

Note: Blacks are those who identify themselves as being of the race alone or as being of the race in combination with other races. Total number of blacks in 2000 differs from the total in previous tables of this chapter because these are unadjusted census counts from April 1, 2000.

Source: Bureau of the Census, 2000 Census, The Black Population 2000, Internet site http://www.census.gov/population/www/cen2000/briefs.html; and 2010 Census, American Factfinder, Internet site http://factfinder2.census.gov/faces/nav/jsf/pages/index.xhtml; calculations by New Strategist

Table 8.12 Total and Black Population by Metropolitan Area, 2010

(total number of people, number of blacks, and black share of total, for metropolitan areas, 2010)

	total population	black number	black share of total
Abilene, TX	165,252	12,184	7.4%
Akron, OH	703,200	84,807	12.1
Albany–Schenectady–Troy, NY	870,716	67,361	7.7
Albany, GA	157,308	82,029	52.1
Albuquerque, NM	887,077	23,742	2.7
Alexandria, LA	153,922	45,583	29.6
Allentown–Bethlehem–Easton, PA–NJ	821,173	41,220	5.0
Altoona, PA	127,089	2,129	1.7
Amarillo, TX	249,881	15,278	6.1
Ames, IA	89,542	2,196	2.5
Anchorage, AK	380,821	17,082	4.5
Anderson, IN	131,636	10,963	8.3
Anderson, SC	187,126	30,020	16.0
Ann Arbor, MI	344,791	43,767	12.7
Anniston–Oxford, AL	118,572	24,382	20.6
Appleton, WI	225,666	1,982	0.9
Asheville, NC	424,858	19,299	4.5
Athens–Clarke County, GA	192,541	37,544	19.5
Atlanta–Sandy Springs–Marietta, GA	5,268,860	1,707,913	32.4
Atlantic City–Hammonton, NJ	274,549	44,138	16.1
Auburn–Opelika, AL	140,247	31,901	22.7
Augusta–Richmond County, GA–SC	556,877	196,695	35.3
Austin–Round Rock–San Marcos, TX	1,716,289	127,397	7.4
Bakersfield–Delano, CA	839,631	48,921	5.8
Baltimore–Towson, MD	2,710,489	778,879	28.7
Bangor, ME	153,923	1,159	0.8
Barnstable Town, MA	215,888	4,062	1.9
Baton Rouge, LA	802,484	285,911	35.6
Battle Creek, MI	136,146	14,872	10.9
Bay City, MI	107,771	1,702	1.6
Beaumont–Port Arthur, TX	388,745	95,463	24.6
Bellingham, WA	201,140	1,929	1.0
Bend, OR	157,733	568	0.4
Billings, MT	158,050	968	0.6
Binghamton, NY	251,725	9,989	4.0
Birmingham–Hoover, AL	1,128,047	318,373	28.2
Bismarck, ND	108,779	603	0.6
Blacksburg–Christiansburg–Radford, VA	162,958	7,013	4.3
Bloomington–Normal, IL	169,572	12,426	7.3
Bloomington, IN	192,714	4,605	2.4
Boise City–Nampa, ID	616,561	5,576	0.9
Boston–Cambridge–Quincy, MA–NH	4,552,402	331,292	7.3
Boulder, CO	294,567	2,532	0.9
Bowling Green, KY	125,953	10,480	8.3
Bremerton–Silverdale, WA	251,133	6,650	2.6

	total population	black	
		number	share of total
Bridgeport–Stamford–Norwalk, CT	916,829	99,317	10.8
Brownsville–Harlingen, TX	406,220	2,155	0.5
Brunswick, GA	112,370	26,413	23.5
Buffalo–Niagara Falls, NY	1,135,509	138,782	12.2
Burlington–South Burlington, VT	211,261	3,557	1.7
Burlington, NC	151,131	28,369	18.8
Canton–Massillon, OH	404,422	28,676	7.1
Cape Coral–Fort Myers, FL	618,754	51,069	8.3
Cape Girardeau–Jackson, MO–IL	96,275	8,277	8.6
Carson City, NV	55,274	1,054	1.9
Casper, WY	75,450	665	0.9
Cedar Rapids, IA	257,940	8,856	3.4
Champaign–Urbana, IL	231,891	25,089	10.8
Charleston–North Charleston–Summerville, SC	664,607	184,019	27.7
Charleston, WV	304,284	14,751	4.8
Charlotte–Gastonia–Rock Hill, NC–SC	1,758,038	421,105	24.0
Charlottesville, VA	201,559	25,109	12.5
Chattanooga, TN–GA	528,143	73,299	13.9
Cheyenne, WY	91,738	2,248	2.5
Chicago–Joliet–Naperville, IL–IN–WI	9,461,105	1,645,993	17.4
Chico, CA	220,000	3,415	1.6
Cincinnati–Middletown, OH–KY–IN	2,130,151	255,905	12.0
Clarksville, TN–KY	273,949	50,048	18.3
Cleveland–Elyria–Mentor, OH	2,077,240	416,528	20.1
Cleveland, TN	115,788	4,269	3.7
Coeur d'Alene, ID	138,494	416	0.3
College Station–Bryan, TX	228,660	27,098	11.9
Colorado Springs, CO	645,613	38,602	6.0
Columbia, MO	172,786	15,643	9.1
Columbia, SC	767,598	255,104	33.2
Columbus, GA–AL	294,865	119,023	40.4
Columbus, IN	76,794	1,420	1.8
Columbus, OH	1,836,536	273,560	14.9
Corpus Christi, TX	428,185	15,011	3.5
Corvallis, OR	85,579	759	0.9
Crestview–Fort Walton Beach–Destin, FL	180,822	16,797	9.3
Cumberland, MD–WV	103,299	6,810	6.6
Dallas–Fort Worth–Arlington, TX	6,371,773	961,871	15.1
Dalton, GA	142,227	4,090	2.9
Danville, IL	81,625	10,571	13.0
Danville, VA	106,561	34,813	32.7
Davenport–Moline–Rock Island, IA–IL	379,690	25,860	6.8
Dayton, OH	841,502	125,815	15.0
Decatur, AL	153,829	18,123	11.8
Decatur, IL	110,768	18,027	16.3
Deltona–Daytona Beach–Ormond Beach, FL	494,593	51,791	10.5
Denver–Aurora–Broomfield, CO	2,543,482	143,128	5.6
Des Moines–West Des Moines, IA	569,633	27,049	4.7
Detroit–Warren–Livonia, MI	4,296,250	980,451	22.8
Dothan, AL	145,639	33,657	23.1

	total population	black	
		number	share of total
Dover, DE	162,310	38,913	24.0%
Dubuque, IA	93,653	2,486	2.7
Duluth, MN–WI	279,771	3,723	1.3
Durham–Chapel Hill, NC	504,357	136,543	27.1
Eau Claire, WI	161,151	1,856	1.2
El Centro, CA	174,528	5,773	3.3
El Paso, TX	800,647	24,864	3.1
Elizabethtown, KY	119,736	12,719	10.6
Elkhart–Goshen, IN	197,559	11,307	5.7
Elmira, NY	88,830	5,828	6.6
Erie, PA	280,566	20,155	7.2
Eugene–Springfield, OR	351,715	3,369	1.0
Evansville, IN–KY	358,676	22,133	6.2
Fairbanks, AK	97,581	4,423	4.5
Fargo, ND–MN	208,777	4,270	2.0
Farmington, NM	130,044	756	0.6
Fayetteville–Springdale–Rogers, AR–MO	463,204	8,981	1.9
Fayetteville, NC	366,383	132,833	36.3
Flagstaff, AZ	134,421	1,629	1.2
Flint, MI	425,790	88,127	20.7
Florence–Muscle Shoals, AL	147,137	18,025	12.3
Florence, SC	205,566	85,079	41.4
Fond du Lac, WI	101,633	1,305	1.3
Fort Collins–Loveland, CO	299,630	2,500	0.8
Fort Smith, AR–OK	298,592	10,643	3.6
Fort Wayne, IN	416,257	41,813	10.0
Fresno, CA	930,450	49,523	5.3
Gadsden, AL	104,430	15,796	15.1
Gainesville, FL	264,275	51,179	19.4
Gainesville, GA	179,684	13,279	7.4
Glens Falls, NY	128,923	2,483	1.9
Goldsboro, NC	122,623	38,499	31.4
Grand Forks, ND–MN	98,461	1,631	1.7
Grand Junction, CO	146,723	935	0.6
Grand Rapids–Wyoming, MI	774,160	62,381	8.1
Great Falls, MT	81,327	1,010	1.2
Greeley, CO	252,825	2,473	1.0
Green Bay, WI	306,241	5,633	1.8
Greensboro–High Point, NC	723,801	184,730	25.5
Greenville–Mauldin–Easley, SC	636,986	106,284	16.7
Greenville, NC	189,510	65,221	34.4
Gulfport–Biloxi, MS	248,820	47,935	19.3
Hagerstown–Martinsburg, MD–WV	269,140	21,662	8.0
Hanford–Corcoran, CA	152,982	11,014	7.2
Harrisburg–Carlisle, PA	549,475	56,209	10.2
Harrisonburg, VA	125,228	4,385	3.5
Hartford–West Hartford–East Hartford, CT	1,212,381	131,929	10.9
Hattiesburg, MS	142,842	40,416	28.3
Hickory–Lenoir–Morganton, NC	365,497	25,182	6.9
Hinesville–Fort Stewart, GA	77,917	30,452	39.1

	total population	black	
		number	share of total
Holland–Grand Haven, MI	263,801	3,874	1.5%
Honolulu, HI	953,207	19,256	2.0
Hot Springs, AR	96,024	7,615	7.9
Houma–Bayou Cane–Thibodaux, LA	208,178	33,885	16.3
Houston–Sugar Land–Baytown, TX	5,946,800	1,025,775	17.2
Huntington–Ashland, WV–KY–OH	287,702	7,794	2.7
Huntsville, AL	417,593	90,805	21.7
Idaho Falls, ID	130,374	637	0.5
Indianapolis–Carmel, IN	1,756,241	263,376	15.0
Iowa City, IA	152,586	6,451	4.2
Ithaca, NY	101,564	4,020	4.0
Jackson, MI	160,248	12,739	7.9
Jackson, MS	539,057	257,021	47.7
Jackson, TN	115,425	37,205	32.2
Jacksonville, FL	1,345,596	292,881	21.8
Jacksonville, NC	177,772	27,672	15.6
Janesville, WI	160,331	7,978	5.0
Jefferson City, MO	149,807	11,153	7.4
Johnson City, TN	198,716	5,610	2.8
Johnstown, PA	143,679	5,222	3.6
Jonesboro, AR	121,026	14,415	11.9
Joplin, MO	175,518	2,705	1.5
Kalamazoo–Portage, MI	326,589	30,366	9.3
Kankakee–Bradley, IL	113,449	17,187	15.1
Kansas City, MO–KS	2,035,334	254,509	12.5
Kennewick–Pasco–Richland, WA	253,340	3,694	1.5
Killeen–Temple–Fort Hood, TX	405,300	79,275	19.6
Kingsport–Bristol–Bristol, TN–VA	309,544	5,903	1.9
Kingston, NY	182,493	10,982	6.0
Knoxville, TN	698,030	44,827	6.4
Kokomo, IN	98,688	5,709	5.8
La Crosse, WI–MN	133,665	1,711	1.3
Lafayette, IN	201,789	7,003	3.5
Lafayette, LA	273,738	73,112	26.7
Lake Charles, LA	199,607	47,901	24.0
Lake Havasu City–Kingman, AZ	200,186	1,882	0.9
Lakeland–Winter Haven, FL	602,095	88,833	14.8
Lancaster, PA	519,445	19,035	3.7
Lansing–East Lansing, MI	464,036	41,407	8.9
Laredo, TX	250,304	1,132	0.5
Las Cruces, NM	209,233	3,656	1.7
Las Vegas–Paradise, NV	1,951,269	204,379	10.5
Lawrence, KS	110,826	4,357	3.9
Lawton, OK	124,098	21,669	17.5
Lebanon, PA	133,568	2,885	2.2
Lewiston–Auburn, ME	107,702	3,931	3.6
Lewiston, ID–WA	60,888	209	0.3
Lexington–Fayette, KY	472,099	51,075	10.8
Lima, OH	106,331	12,639	11.9
Lincoln, NE	302,157	9,980	3.3

	total population	black number	black share of total
Little Rock–North Little Rock–Conway, AR	699,757	155,081	22.2%
Logan, UT–ID	125,442	725	0.6
Longview, TX	214,369	37,241	17.4
Longview, WA	102,410	642	0.6
Los Angeles–Long Beach–Santa Ana, CA	12,828,837	907,618	7.1
Louisville/Jefferson County, KY–IN	1,283,566	176,107	13.7
Lubbock, TX	284,890	21,161	7.4
Lynchburg, VA	252,634	44,260	17.5
Macon, GA	232,293	100,934	43.5
Madera–Chowchilla, CA	150,865	5,629	3.7
Madison, WI	568,593	26,151	4.6
Manchester–Nashua, NH	400,721	8,298	2.1
Manhattan, KS	127,081	11,076	8.7
Mankato–North Mankato, MN	96,740	2,408	2.5
Mansfield, OH	124,475	11,709	9.4
McAllen–Edinburg–Mission, TX	774,769	4,569	0.6
Medford, OR	203,206	1,372	0.7
Memphis, TN–MS–AR	1,316,100	601,043	45.7
Merced, CA	255,793	9,926	3.9
Miami–Fort Lauderdale–Pompano Beach, FL	5,564,635	1,169,185	21.0
Michigan City–La Porte, IN	111,467	12,001	10.8
Midland, TX	136,872	9,087	6.6
Milwaukee–Waukesha–West Allis, WI	1,555,908	261,010	16.8
Minneapolis–St. Paul–Bloomington, MN–WI	3,279,833	243,414	7.4
Missoula, MT	109,299	445	0.4
Mobile, AL	412,992	142,992	34.6
Modesto, CA	514,453	14,721	2.9
Monroe, LA	176,441	62,398	35.4
Monroe, MI	152,021	3,237	2.1
Montgomery, AL	374,536	159,330	42.5
Morgantown, WV	129,709	3,857	3.0
Morristown, TN	136,608	3,682	2.7
Mount Vernon–Anacortes, WA	116,901	774	0.7
Muncie, IN	117,671	8,146	6.9
Muskegon–Norton Shores, MI	172,188	24,882	14.5
Myrtle Beach–North Myrtle Beach–Conway, SC	269,291	36,202	13.4
Napa, CA	136,484	2,668	2.0
Naples–Marco Island, FL	321,520	21,087	6.6
Nashville–Davidson–Murfreesboro–Franklin, TN	1,589,934	242,264	15.2
New Haven–Milford, CT	862,477	109,850	12.7
New Orleans–Metairie–Kenner, LA	1,167,764	397,095	34.0
New York–Northern New Jersey–Long Island, NY–NJ–PA	18,897,109	3,362,616	17.8
Niles–Benton Harbor, MI	156,813	24,037	15.3
North Port–Bradenton–Sarasota, FL	702,281	46,045	6.6
Norwich–New London, CT	274,055	16,025	5.8
Ocala, FL	331,298	40,828	12.3
Ocean City, NJ	97,265	4,565	4.7
Odessa, TX	137,130	6,141	4.5

	total population	black number	share of total
		black	
Ogden–Clearfield, UT	547,184	6,854	1.3%
Oklahoma City, OK	1,252,987	130,597	10.4
Olympia, WA	252,264	6,752	2.7
Omaha–Council Bluffs, NE–IA	865,350	68,021	7.9
Orlando–Kissimmee–Sanford, FL	2,134,411	344,820	16.2
Oshkosh–Neenah, WI	166,994	2,975	1.8
Owensboro, KY	114,752	4,756	4.1
Oxnard–Thousand Oaks–Ventura, CA	823,318	15,163	1.8
Palm Bay–Melbourne–Titusville, FL	543,376	54,799	10.1
Palm Coast, FL	95,696	10,884	11.4
Panama City–Lynn Haven–Panama City Beach, FL	168,852	18,180	10.8
Parkersburg–Marietta–Vienna, WV–OH	162,056	1,731	1.1
Pascagoula, MS	162,246	31,863	19.6
Pensacola–Ferry Pass–Brent, FL	448,991	76,487	17.0
Peoria, IL	379,186	34,663	9.1
Philadelphia–Camden–Wilmington, PA–NJ–DE–MD	5,965,343	1,241,780	20.8
Phoenix–Mesa–Glendale, AZ	4,192,887	207,734	5.0
Pine Bluff, AR	100,258	47,921	47.8
Pittsburgh, PA	2,356,285	196,755	8.4
Pittsfield, MA	131,219	3,572	2.7
Pocatello, ID	90,656	647	0.7
Port St. Lucie, FL	424,107	60,878	14.4
Portland–South Portland–Biddeford, ME	514,098	8,143	1.6
Portland–Vancouver–Hillsboro, OR–WA	2,226,009	63,650	2.9
Poughkeepsie–Newburgh–Middletown, NY	670,301	67,464	10.1
Prescott, AZ	211,033	1,267	0.6
Providence–New Bedford–Fall River, RI–MA	1,600,852	78,021	4.9
Provo–Orem, UT	526,810	2,824	0.5
Pueblo, CO	159,063	3,222	2.0
Punta Gorda, FL	159,978	9,089	5.7
Racine, WI	195,408	21,767	11.1
Raleigh–Cary, NC	1,130,490	228,268	20.2
Rapid City, SD	126,382	1,369	1.1
Reading, PA	411,442	20,143	4.9
Redding, CA	177,223	1,548	0.9
Reno–Sparks, NV	425,417	9,854	2.3
Richmond, VA	1,258,251	375,427	29.8
Riverside–San Bernardino–Ontario, CA	4,224,851	322,405	7.6
Roanoke, VA	308,707	39,603	12.8
Rochester, MN	186,011	7,010	3.8
Rochester, NY	1,054,323	122,611	11.6
Rockford, IL	349,431	37,172	10.6
Rocky Mount, NC	152,392	68,085	44.7
Rome, GA	96,317	13,640	14.2
Sacramento—Arden–Arcade—Roseville, CA	2,149,127	158,426	7.4
Saginaw–Saginaw Township North, MI	200,169	38,114	19.0
Salem, OR	390,738	3,795	1.0
Salinas, CA	415,057	12,785	3.1
Salisbury, MD	125,203	35,065	28.0
Salt Lake City, UT	1,124,197	16,964	1.5

	total population	black number	black share of total
San Angelo, TX	111,823	4,456	4.0%
San Antonio–New Braunfels, TX	2,142,508	141,468	6.6
San Diego–Carlsbad–San Marcos, CA	3,095,313	158,213	5.1
San Francisco–Oakland–Fremont, CA	4,335,391	363,905	8.4
San Jose–Sunnyvale–Santa Clara, CA	1,836,911	46,911	2.6
San Luis Obispo–Paso Robles, CA	269,637	5,550	2.1
Sandusky, OH	77,079	6,644	8.6
Santa Barbara–Santa Maria–Goleta, CA	423,895	8,513	2.0
Santa Cruz–Watsonville, CA	262,382	2,766	1.1
Santa Fe, NM	144,170	1,239	0.9
Santa Rosa–Petaluma, CA	483,878	7,610	1.6
Savannah, GA	347,611	117,726	33.9
Scranton–Wilkes-Barre, PA	563,631	16,398	2.9
Seattle–Tacoma–Bellevue, WA	3,439,809	191,967	5.6
Sebastian–Vero Beach, FL	138,028	12,397	9.0
Sheboygan, WI	115,507	1,684	1.5
Sherman–Denison, TX	120,877	7,081	5.9
Shreveport–Bossier City, LA	398,604	155,174	38.9
Sioux City, IA–NE–SD	143,577	3,229	2.2
Sioux Falls, SD	228,261	6,755	3.0
South Bend–Mishawaka, IN–MI	319,224	36,779	11.5
Spartanburg, SC	284,307	58,565	20.6
Spokane, WA	471,221	8,056	1.7
Springfield, IL	210,170	23,411	11.1
Springfield, MA	692,942	46,365	6.7
Springfield, MO	436,712	8,937	2.0
Springfield, OH	138,333	12,128	8.8
St. Cloud, MN	189,093	5,407	2.9
St. George, UT	138,115	790	0.6
St. Joseph, MO–KS	127,329	6,436	5.1
St. Louis, MO–IL	2,812,896	516,446	18.4
State College, PA	153,990	4,638	3.0
Steubenville–Weirton, OH–WV	124,454	4,872	3.9
Stockton, CA	685,306	51,744	7.6
Sumter, SC	107,456	50,414	46.9
Syracuse, NY	662,577	53,542	8.1
Tallahassee, FL	367,413	119,320	32.5
Tampa–St. Petersburg–Clearwater, FL	2,783,243	329,334	11.8
Terre Haute, IN	172,425	8,509	4.9
Texarkana, TX–Texarkana, AR	136,027	33,054	24.3
Toledo, OH	651,429	87,455	13.4
Topeka, KS	233,870	15,534	6.6
Trenton–Ewing, NJ	366,513	74,318	20.3
Tucson, AZ	980,263	34,674	3.5
Tulsa, OK	937,478	78,928	8.4
Tuscaloosa, AL	219,461	74,282	33.8
Tyler, TX	209,714	37,629	17.9
Utica–Rome, NY	299,397	15,388	5.1
Valdosta, GA	139,588	47,432	34.0
Vallejo–Fairfield, CA	413,344	60,750	14.7

	total population	black number	black share of total
Victoria, TX	115,384	6,421	5.6
Vineland–Millville–Bridgeton, NJ	156,898	31,741	20.2%
Virginia Beach–Norfolk–Newport News, VA–NC	1,671,683	522,409	31.3
Visalia–Porterville, CA	442,179	7,196	1.6
Waco, TX	234,906	34,767	14.8
Warner Robins, GA	139,900	39,998	28.6
Washington–Arlington–Alexandria, DC–VA–MD–WV	5,582,170	1,438,436	25.8
Waterloo–Cedar Falls, IA	167,819	11,859	7.1
Wausau, WI	134,063	841	0.6
Wenatchee–East Wenatchee, WA	110,884	364	0.3
Wheeling, WV–OH	147,950	4,647	3.1
Wichita Falls, TX	151,306	13,908	9.2
Wichita, KS	623,061	48,057	7.7
Williamsport, PA	116,111	5,203	4.5
Wilmington, NC	362,315	51,467	14.2
Winchester, VA–WV	128,472	6,279	4.9
Winston-Salem, NC	477,717	96,928	20.3
Worcester, MA	798,552	33,314	4.2
Yakima, WA	243,231	2,320	1.0
York–Hanover, PA	434,972	24,344	5.6
Youngstown–Warren–Boardman, OH–PA	565,773	61,576	10.9
Yuba City, CA	166,892	4,280	2.6
Yuma, AZ	195,751	3,931	2.0

Note: Blacks are those who identify themselves as being of the race alone.
Source: Bureau of the Census, 2010 Census, Internet site, http://factfinder2.census.gov/faces/nav/jsf/pages/index.xhtml; calculations by New Strategist

9

Spending

■ The nation's 14.7 million black households spent an average of $35,311 in 2009, less than the $49,067 spent by the average household.

■ The spending of blacks is below average because married couples—the most affluent household-ers—head relatively few black households. Nevertheless, blacks spend more than average on such items as pork, poultry, fish, noncarbonated fruit-flavored drinks, clothes, shoes, phone service, and mass transit.

■ Because homeownership is relatively low among blacks, they spend less than average on mortgage interest, but more on rent.

Black Households Spend Less than the Average Household

On some products and services, however, they spend more.

The nation's 14.7 million black households spent an average of $35,311 in 2009, according to the Bureau of Labor Statistics' Consumer Expenditure Survey. While the annual spending of black households (called consumer units by the Bureau of Labor Statistics) is less than the $49,067 spent by the average household, on some items blacks spend more.

One reason for the lower spending of blacks is that married couples head relatively few black households, and married couples are the most affluent household type. Despite this fact, blacks spend more than average on pork, poultry, and fish. They spend 33 percent more than the average household on shoes, and 5 percent more on telephone service.

■ Black spending will remain below average until married couples become a larger share of black households.

Black households spend 28 percent less than the average household

(average annual spending of total and black consumer units, 2009)

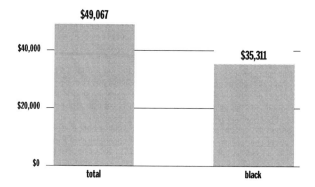

Table 9.1 Average Spending by Race and Hispanic Origin of Householder, 2009

(average annual spending of households by product and service category and by race and Hispanic origin of householder, 2009)

	total households	Asian	black	Hispanic	non-Hispanic white and other
Number of households (in 000s)	120,847	4,584	14,659	14,295	92,119
Average number of persons per household	2.5	2.7	2.6	3.3	2.4
Average annual household spending	$49,067	$56,308	$35,311	$41,981	$52,320
FOOD	6,372	7,565	4,524	6,094	6,696
Food at home	3,753	3,905	2,880	3,784	3,882
Cereals and bakery products	506	520	390	479	529
Cereals and cereal products	173	215	149	184	174
Bakery products	334	305	241	294	354
Meats, poultry, fish, and eggs	841	966	845	955	823
Beef	226	186	191	252	227
Pork	168	172	193	202	160
Other meats	114	82	91	110	118
Poultry	154	184	183	192	144
Fish and seafood	135	274	144	141	133
Eggs	44	67	42	58	42
Dairy products	406	346	258	403	429
Fresh milk and cream	144	152	105	171	146
Other dairy products	262	195	153	232	283
Fruits and vegetables	656	903	484	734	671
Fresh fruits	220	310	151	256	225
Fresh vegetables	209	385	136	240	216
Processed fruits	118	117	105	121	120
Processed vegetables	110	91	92	117	111
Other food at home	1,343	1,169	903	1,213	1,430
Sugar and other sweets	141	106	88	109	153
Fats and oils	102	99	82	105	105
Miscellaneous foods	715	646	462	617	768
Nonalcoholic beverages	337	267	253	348	348
Food prepared by consumer unit on trips	49	52	17	33	56
Restaurants and other food away from home	2,619	3,660	1,645	2,310	2,814
ALCOHOLIC BEVERAGES	435	350	201	267	496
HOUSING	16,895	20,395	13,503	15,983	17,579
Shelter	10,075	13,571	7,919	10,043	10,429
Owned dwellings	6,543	8,543	3,632	5,298	7,198
Mortgage interest and charges	3,594	5,349	2,220	3,454	3,837
Property taxes	1,811	2,334	912	1,368	2,021
Maintenance, repair, insurance, other expenses	1,138	860	500	476	1,340
Rented dwellings	2,860	4,411	4,046	4,415	2,437
Other lodging	672	616	241	330	794

	total households	Asian	black	Hispanic	non-Hispanic white and other
Utilities, fuels, and public services	**$3,645**	**$3,270**	**$3,668**	**$3,532**	**$3,660**
Natural gas	483	499	517	389	493
Electricity	1,377	1,056	1,462	1,339	1,369
Fuel oil and other fuels	141	48	50	47	171
Telephone services	1,162	1,123	1,224	1,272	1,135
Water and other public services	481	544	415	485	492
Household services	**1,011**	**1,347**	**633**	**714**	**1,119**
Personal services	389	688	281	334	417
Other household services	622	659	352	380	702
Housekeeping supplies	**659**	**536**	**429**	**517**	**714**
Laundry and cleaning supplies	156	130	124	194	155
Other household products	360	292	224	233	399
Postage and stationery	143	113	81	91	160
Household furnishings and equipment	**1,506**	**1,671**	**854**	**1,177**	**1,657**
Household textiles	124	187	79	101	134
Furniture	343	304	271	331	357
Floor coverings	30	13	7	7	37
Major appliances	194	183	127	146	212
Small appliances and miscellaneous housewares	93	134	51	80	102
Miscellaneous household equipment	721	848	319	513	814
APPAREL AND RELATED SERVICES	**1,725**	**2,150**	**1,755**	**2,002**	**1,678**
Men and boys	**383**	**427**	**388**	**432**	**375**
Men, aged 16 or older	304	335	303	323	302
Boys, aged 2 to 15	79	91	86	109	73
Women and girls	**678**	**913**	**629**	**693**	**682**
Women, aged 16 or older	561	789	504	509	576
Girls, aged 2 to 15	118	124	126	185	106
Children under age 2	**91**	**122**	**75**	**147**	**85**
Footwear	**323**	**344**	**430**	**472**	**285**
Other apparel products and services	**249**	**344**	**231**	**258**	**251**
TRANSPORTATION	**7,658**	**8,784**	**5,302**	**7,156**	**8,109**
Vehicle purchases	**2,657**	**2,582**	**1,489**	**2,333**	**2,897**
Cars and trucks, new	1,297	1,131	568	1,010	1,460
Cars and trucks, used	1,304	1,451	910	1,293	1,371
Gasoline and motor oil	**1,986**	**1,871**	**1,618**	**2,104**	**2,026**
Other vehicle expenses	**2,536**	**3,153**	**1,876**	**2,309**	**2,670**
Vehicle finance charges	281	208	242	278	288
Maintenance and repairs	733	713	504	584	791
Vehicle insurance	1,075	1,610	859	1,049	1,109
Vehicle rentals, leases, licenses, other charges	447	623	270	398	482
Public transportation	**479**	**1,178**	**319**	**410**	**516**
HEALTH CARE	**3,126**	**2,498**	**1,763**	**1,568**	**3,581**
Health insurance	1,785	1,509	1,133	848	2,033
Medical services	736	575	294	418	855
Drugs	486	307	279	241	556
Medical supplies	119	107	57	61	137

	total households	Asian	black	Hispanic	non-Hispanic white and other
ENTERTAINMENT	**$2,693**	**$2,270**	**$1,404**	**$1,664**	**$3,050**
Fees and admissions	628	848	223	302	742
Audio and visual equipment and services	975	924	840	818	1,020
Pets, toys, and playground equipment	690	295	242	391	804
Other entertainment products and services	400	202	99	153	485
PERSONAL CARE PRODUCTS, SERVICES	**596**	**557**	**536**	**532**	**614**
READING	**110**	**111**	**46**	**36**	**131**
EDUCATION	**1,068**	**2,327**	**591**	**707**	**1,197**
TOBACCO PRODUCTS AND SMOKING SUPPLIES	**380**	**122**	**230**	**182**	**434**
MISCELLANEOUS	**816**	**611**	**626**	**544**	**887**
CASH CONTRIBUTIONS	**1,723**	**1,452**	**1,280**	**1,015**	**1,903**
PERSONAL INSURANCE AND PENSIONS	**5,471**	**7,117**	**3,550**	**4,230**	**5,966**
Life and other personal insurance	309	283	235	119	350
Pensions and Social Security	5,162	6,834	3,315	4,111	5,616
PERSONAL TAXES	**2,104**	**3,526**	**743**	**745**	**2,525**
Federal income taxes	1,404	2,541	378	421	1,716
State and local income taxes	524	787	291	230	605
Other taxes	177	198	74	95	205
GIFTS FOR PEOPLE IN OTHER HOUSEHOLDS	**1,067**	**1,153**	**570**	**743**	**1,193**

Note: "Asian" and "black" include Hispanics and non-Hispanics who identify themselves as being of the respective race alone. "Hispanic" includes people of any race who identify themselves as Hispanic. "Other" includes people who identify themselves as non-Hispanic and as Alaska Native, American Indian, Asian (who are also included in the Asian column), Native Hawaiian or other Pacific Islander, as well as non-Hispanics reporting more than one race. Spending by category does not add to total spending because gift spending is also included in the preceding product and service categories and personal taxes are not included in the total.
Source: Bureau of Labor Statistics, 2009 Consumer Expenditure Survey, Internet site http://www.bls.gov/cex/

Table 9.2 Indexed Spending by Race and Hispanic Origin of Householder, 2009

(indexed average annual spending of households by product and service category and by race and Hispanic origin of householder, 2009; index definition: an index of 100 is the average for all households; an index of 150 means that spending by households in that group is 50 percent above the average for all households; an index of 50 indicates spending that is 50 percent below the average for all households)

	total households	Asian	black	Hispanic	non-Hispanic white and other
Average household spending, total	$49,067	$56,308	$35,311	$41,981	$52,320
Average household spending, index	100	115	72	86	107
FOOD	100	119	71	96	105
Food at home	100	104	77	101	103
Cereals and bakery products	100	103	77	95	105
Cereals and cereal products	100	124	86	106	101
Bakery products	100	91	72	88	106
Meats, poultry, fish, and eggs	100	115	100	114	98
Beef	100	82	85	112	100
Pork	100	102	115	120	95
Other meats	100	72	80	96	104
Poultry	100	119	119	125	94
Fish and seafood	100	203	107	104	99
Eggs	100	152	95	132	95
Dairy products	100	85	64	99	106
Fresh milk and cream	100	106	73	119	101
Other dairy products	100	74	58	89	108
Fruits and vegetables	100	138	74	112	102
Fresh fruits	100	141	69	116	102
Fresh vegetables	100	184	65	115	103
Processed fruits	100	99	89	103	102
Processed vegetables	100	83	84	106	101
Other food at home	100	87	67	90	106
Sugar and other sweets	100	75	62	77	109
Fats and oils	100	97	80	103	103
Miscellaneous foods	100	90	65	86	107
Nonalcoholic beverages	100	79	75	103	103
Food prepared by consumer unit on trips	100	106	35	67	114
Restaurants and other food away from home	100	140	63	88	107
ALCOHOLIC BEVERAGES	100	80	46	61	114
HOUSING	100	121	80	95	104
Shelter	100	135	79	100	104
Owned dwellings	100	131	56	81	110
Mortgage interest and charges	100	149	62	96	107
Property taxes	100	129	50	76	112
Maintenance, repair, insurance, other expenses	100	76	44	42	118
Rented dwellings	100	154	141	154	85
Other lodging	100	92	36	49	118

	total households	Asian	black	Hispanic	non-Hispanic white and other
Utilities, fuels, and public services	**100**	**90**	**101**	**97**	**100**
Natural gas	100	103	107	81	102
Electricity	100	77	106	97	99
Fuel oil and other fuels	100	34	35	33	121
Telephone services	100	97	105	109	98
Water and other public services	100	113	86	101	102
Household services	**100**	**133**	**63**	**71**	**111**
Personal services	100	177	72	86	107
Other household services	100	106	57	61	113
Housekeeping supplies	**100**	**81**	**65**	**78**	**108**
Laundry and cleaning supplies	100	83	79	124	99
Other household products	100	81	62	65	111
Postage and stationery	100	79	57	64	112
Household furnishings and equipment	**100**	**111**	**57**	**78**	**110**
Household textiles	100	151	64	81	108
Furniture	100	89	79	97	104
Floor coverings	100	43	23	23	123
Major appliances	100	94	65	75	109
Small appliances and miscellaneous housewares	100	144	55	86	110
Miscellaneous household equipment	100	118	44	71	113
APPAREL AND RELATED SERVICES	**100**	**125**	**102**	**116**	**97**
Men and boys	**100**	**111**	**101**	**113**	**98**
Men, aged 16 or older	100	110	100	106	99
Boys, aged 2 to 15	100	115	109	138	92
Women and girls	**100**	**135**	**93**	**102**	**101**
Women, aged 16 or older	100	141	90	91	103
Girls, aged 2 to 15	100	105	107	157	90
Children under age 2	**100**	**134**	**82**	**162**	**93**
Footwear	**100**	**107**	**133**	**146**	**88**
Other apparel products and services	**100**	**138**	**93**	**104**	**101**
TRANSPORTATION	**100**	**115**	**69**	**93**	**106**
Vehicle purchases	**100**	**97**	**56**	**88**	**109**
Cars and trucks, new	100	87	44	78	113
Cars and trucks, used	100	111	70	99	105
Gasoline and motor oil	**100**	**94**	**81**	**106**	**102**
Other vehicle expenses	**100**	**124**	**74**	**91**	**105**
Vehicle finance charges	100	74	86	99	102
Maintenance and repairs	100	97	69	80	108
Vehicle insurance	100	150	80	98	103
Vehicle rentals, leases, licenses, other charges	100	139	60	89	108
Public transportation	**100**	**246**	**67**	**86**	**108**
HEALTH CARE	**100**	**80**	**56**	**50**	**115**
Health insurance	100	85	63	48	114
Medical services	100	78	40	57	116
Drugs	100	63	57	50	114
Medical supplies	100	90	48	51	115

	total households	Asian	black	Hispanic	non-Hispanic white and other
ENTERTAINMENT	100	84	52	62	113
Fees and admissions	100	135	36	48	118
Audio and visual equipment and services	100	95	86	84	105
Pets, toys, and playground equipment	100	43	35	57	117
Other entertainment products and services	100	51	25	38	121
PERSONAL CARE PRODUCTS, SERVICES	100	93	90	89	103
READING	100	101	42	33	119
EDUCATION	100	218	55	66	112
TOBACCO PRODUCTS AND SMOKING SUPPLIES	100	32	61	48	114
MISCELLANEOUS	100	75	77	67	109
CASH CONTRIBUTIONS	100	84	74	59	110
PERSONAL INSURANCE AND PENSIONS	100	130	65	77	109
Life and other personal insurance	100	92	76	39	113
Pensions and Social Security	100	132	64	80	109
PERSONAL TAXES	100	168	35	35	120
Federal income taxes	100	181	27	30	122
State and local income taxes	100	150	56	44	115
Other taxes	100	112	42	54	116
GIFTS FOR PEOPLE IN OTHER HOUSEHOLDS	100	108	53	70	112

Note: "Asian" and "black" include Hispanics and non-Hispanics who identify themselves as being of the respective race alone. "Hispanic" includes people of any race who identify themselves as Hispanic. "Other" includes people who identify themselves as non-Hispanic and as Alaska Native, American Indian, Asian (who are also included in the Asian column), Native Hawaiian or other Pacific Islander, as well as non-Hispanics reporting more than one race.
Source: Calculations by New Strategist based on the Bureau of Labor Statistics' 2009 Consumer Expenditure Survey

Table 9.3 Total Spending by Race and Hispanic Origin of Householder, 2009

(total annual spending by race and Hispanic origin groups, 2009; households and dollars in thousands)

	total households	Asian	black	Hispanic	non-Hispanic white and other
Number of households	120,847	4,584	14,659	14,295	92,119
Total spending of all households	$5,929,599,749	$258,115,872	$517,623,949	$600,118,395	$4,819,666,080
FOOD	770,037,084	34,677,960	66,317,316	87,113,730	616,828,824
Groceries	453,538,791	17,900,520	42,217,920	54,092,280	357,605,958
Cereals and bakery products	61,148,582	2,383,680	5,717,010	6,847,305	48,730,951
Cereals and cereal products	20,906,531	985,560	2,184,191	2,630,280	16,028,706
Bakery products	40,362,898	1,398,120	3,532,819	4,202,730	32,610,126
Meats, poultry, fish, and eggs	101,632,327	4,428,144	12,386,855	13,651,725	75,813,937
Beef	27,311,422	852,624	2,799,869	3,602,340	20,911,013
Pork	20,302,296	788,448	2,829,187	2,887,590	14,739,040
Other meats	13,776,558	375,888	1,333,969	1,572,450	10,870,042
Poultry	18,610,438	843,456	2,682,597	2,744,640	13,265,136
Fish and seafood	16,314,345	1,256,016	2,110,896	2,015,595	12,251,827
Eggs	5,317,268	307,128	615,678	829,110	3,868,998
Dairy products	49,063,882	1,586,064	3,782,022	5,760,885	39,519,051
Fresh milk and cream	17,401,968	696,768	1,539,195	2,444,445	13,449,374
Other dairy products	31,661,914	893,880	2,242,827	3,316,440	26,069,677
Fruits and vegetables	79,275,632	4,139,352	7,094,956	10,492,530	61,811,849
Fresh fruits	26,586,340	1,421,040	2,213,509	3,659,520	20,726,775
Fresh vegetables	25,257,023	1,764,840	1,993,624	3,430,800	19,897,704
Processed fruits	14,259,946	536,328	1,539,195	1,729,695	11,054,280
Processed vegetables	13,293,170	417,144	1,348,628	1,672,515	10,225,209
Other food at home	162,297,521	5,358,696	13,237,077	17,339,835	131,730,170
Sugar and other sweets	17,039,427	485,904	1,289,992	1,558,155	14,094,207
Fats and oils	12,326,394	453,816	1,202,038	1,500,975	9,672,495
Miscellaneous foods	86,405,605	2,961,264	6,772,458	8,820,015	70,747,392
Nonalcoholic beverages	40,725,439	1,223,928	3,708,727	4,974,660	32,057,412
Food prepared by consumer unit on trips	5,921,503	238,368	249,203	471,735	5,158,664
Restaurants and other food away from home	316,498,293	16,777,440	24,114,055	33,021,450	259,222,866
ALCOHOLIC BEVERAGES	52,568,445	1,604,400	2,946,459	3,816,765	45,691,024
HOUSING	2,041,710,065	93,490,680	197,940,477	228,476,985	1,619,359,901
Shelter	1,217,533,525	62,209,464	116,084,621	143,564,685	960,709,051
Owned dwellings	790,701,921	39,161,112	53,241,488	75,734,910	663,072,562
Mortgage interest and charges	434,324,118	24,519,816	32,542,980	49,374,930	353,460,603
Property taxes	218,853,917	10,699,056	13,369,008	19,555,560	186,172,499
Maintenance, repair, insurance, other expenses	137,523,886	3,942,240	7,329,500	6,804,420	123,439,460
Rented dwellings	345,622,420	20,220,024	59,310,314	63,112,425	224,494,003
Other lodging	81,209,184	2,823,744	3,532,819	4,717,350	73,142,486

	total households	Asian	black	Hispanic	non-Hispanic white and other
Utilities, fuels, and public services	$440,487,315	$14,989,680	$53,769,212	$50,489,940	$337,155,540
Natural gas	58,369,101	2,287,416	7,578,703	5,560,755	45,414,667
Electricity	166,406,319	4,840,704	21,431,458	19,141,005	126,110,911
Fuel oil and other fuels	17,039,427	220,032	732,950	671,865	15,752,349
Telephone	140,424,214	5,147,832	17,942,616	18,183,240	104,555,065
Water and other public services	58,127,407	2,493,696	6,083,485	6,933,075	45,322,548
Household services	**122,176,317**	**6,174,648**	**9,279,147**	**10,206,630**	**103,081,161**
Personal services	47,009,483	3,153,792	4,119,179	4,774,530	38,413,623
Other household services	75,166,834	3,020,856	5,159,968	5,432,100	64,667,538
Housekeeping supplies	**79,638,173**	**2,457,024**	**6,288,711**	**7,390,515**	**65,772,966**
Laundry and cleaning supplies	18,852,132	595,920	1,817,716	2,773,230	14,278,445
Other household products	43,504,920	1,338,528	3,283,616	3,330,735	36,755,481
Postage and stationery	17,281,121	517,992	1,187,379	1,300,845	14,739,040
Household furnishings, equipment	**181,995,582**	**7,659,864**	**12,518,786**	**16,825,215**	**152,641,183**
Household textiles	14,985,028	857,208	1,158,061	1,443,795	12,343,946
Furniture	41,450,521	1,393,536	3,972,589	4,731,645	32,886,483
Floor coverings	3,625,410	59,592	102,613	100,065	3,408,403
Major appliances	23,444,318	838,872	1,861,693	2,087,070	19,529,228
Small appliances and misc. housewares	11,238,771	614,256	747,609	1,143,600	9,396,138
Miscellaneous household equipment	87,130,687	3,887,232	4,676,221	7,333,335	74,984,866
APPAREL, RELATED SERVICES	**208,461,075**	**9,855,600**	**25,726,545**	**28,618,590**	**154,575,682**
Men and boys	**46,284,401**	**1,957,368**	**5,687,692**	**6,175,440**	**34,544,625**
Men, aged 16 or older	36,737,488	1,535,640	4,441,677	4,617,285	27,819,938
Boys, aged 2 to 15	9,546,913	417,144	1,260,674	1,558,155	6,724,687
Women and girls	**81,934,266**	**4,185,192**	**9,220,511**	**9,906,435**	**62,825,158**
Women, aged 16 or older	67,795,167	3,616,776	7,388,136	7,276,155	53,060,544
Girls, aged 2 to 15	14,259,946	568,416	1,847,034	2,644,575	9,764,614
Children under age 2	**10,997,077**	**559,248**	**1,099,425**	**2,101,365**	**7,830,115**
Footwear	**39,033,581**	**1,576,896**	**6,303,370**	**6,747,240**	**26,253,915**
Other apparel products and services	**30,090,903**	**1,576,896**	**3,386,229**	**3,688,110**	**23,121,869**
TRANSPORTATION	**925,446,326**	**40,265,856**	**77,722,018**	**102,295,020**	**746,992,971**
Vehicle purchases	**321,090,479**	**11,835,888**	**21,827,251**	**33,350,235**	**266,868,743**
Cars and trucks, new	156,738,559	5,184,504	8,326,312	14,437,950	134,493,740
Cars and trucks, used	157,584,488	6,651,384	13,339,690	18,483,435	126,295,149
Gasoline and motor oil	**240,002,142**	**8,576,664**	**23,718,262**	**30,076,680**	**186,633,094**
Other vehicle expenses	**306,467,992**	**14,453,352**	**27,500,284**	**33,007,155**	**245,957,730**
Vehicle finance charges	33,958,007	953,472	3,547,478	3,974,010	26,530,272
Maintenance and repairs	88,580,851	3,268,392	7,388,136	8,348,280	72,866,129
Vehicle insurance	129,910,525	7,380,240	12,592,081	14,995,455	102,159,971
Vehicle rentals, leases, licenses, other charges	54,018,609	2,855,832	3,957,930	5,689,410	44,401,358
Public transportation	**57,885,713**	**5,399,952**	**4,676,221**	**5,860,950**	**47,533,404**
HEALTH CARE	**377,767,722**	**11,450,832**	**25,843,817**	**22,414,560**	**329,878,139**
Health insurance	215,711,895	6,917,256	16,608,647	12,122,160	187,277,927
Medical services	88,943,392	2,635,800	4,309,746	5,975,310	78,761,745
Drugs	58,731,642	1,407,288	4,089,861	3,445,095	51,218,164
Medical supplies	14,380,793	490,488	835,563	871,995	12,620,303

	total households	Asian	black	Hispanic	non-Hispanic white and other
ENTERTAINMENT	**$325,440,971**	**$10,405,680**	**$20,581,236**	**$23,786,880**	**$280,962,950**
Fees and admissions	75,891,916	3,887,232	3,268,957	4,317,090	68,352,298
Audio and visual equipment, services	117,825,825	4,235,616	12,313,560	11,693,310	93,961,380
Pets, toys, hobbies, and playground equipment	83,384,430	1,352,280	3,547,478	5,589,345	74,063,676
Other entertainment products and services	48,338,800	925,968	1,451,241	2,187,135	44,677,715
PERSONAL CARE PRODUCTS AND SERVICES	**72,024,812**	**2,553,288**	**7,857,224**	**7,604,940**	**56,561,066**
READING	**13,293,170**	**508,824**	**674,314**	**514,620**	**12,067,589**
EDUCATION	**129,064,596**	**10,666,968**	**8,663,469**	**10,106,565**	**110,266,443**
TOBACCO PRODUCTS AND SMOKING SUPPLIES	**45,921,860**	**559,248**	**3,371,570**	**2,601,690**	**39,979,646**
MISCELLANEOUS	**98,611,152**	**2,800,824**	**9,176,534**	**7,776,480**	**81,709,553**
CASH CONTRIBUTIONS	**208,219,381**	**6,655,968**	**18,763,520**	**14,509,425**	**175,302,457**
PERSONAL INSURANCE AND PENSIONS	**661,153,937**	**32,624,328**	**52,039,450**	**60,467,850**	**549,581,954**
Life and other personal insurance	37,341,723	1,297,272	3,444,865	1,701,105	32,241,650
Pensions and Social Security	623,812,214	31,327,056	48,594,585	58,766,745	517,340,304
PERSONAL TAXES	**254,262,088**	**16,163,184**	**10,891,637**	**10,649,775**	**232,600,475**
Federal income taxes	169,669,188	11,647,944	5,541,102	6,018,195	158,076,204
State and local income taxes	63,323,828	3,607,608	4,265,769	3,287,850	55,731,995
Other taxes	21,389,919	907,632	1,084,766	1,358,025	18,884,395
GIFTS FOR PEOPLE IN OTHER HOUSEHOLDS	**128,943,749**	**5,285,352**	**8,355,630**	**10,621,185**	**109,897,967**

Note: "Asian" and "black" include Hispanics and non-Hispanics who identify themselves as being of the respective race alone. "Hispanic" includes people of any race who identify themselves as Hispanic. "Other" includes people who identify themselves as non-Hispanic and as Alaska Native, American Indian, Asian (who are also included in the Asian column), Native Hawaiian or other Pacific Islander, as well as non-Hispanics reporting more than one race. Spending by category does not add to total spending because gift spending is also included in the preceding product and service categories and personal taxes are not included in the total.
Source: Calculations by New Strategist based on the Bureau of Labor Statistics' 2009 Consumer Expenditure Survey

Table 9.4 Market Shares by Race and Hispanic Origin of Householder, 2009

(percentage of total annual spending accounted for by race and Hispanic origin groups, 2009)

	total households	Asian	black	Hispanic	non-Hispanic white and other
Share of total households	100.0%	3.8%	12.1%	11.8%	76.2%
Share of total spending	100.0	4.4	8.7	10.1	81.3
FOOD	100.0	4.5	8.6	11.3	80.1
Groceries	100.0	3.9	9.3	11.9	78.8
Cereals and bakery products	100.0	3.9	9.3	11.2	79.7
Cereals and cereal products	100.0	4.7	10.4	12.6	76.7
Bakery products	100.0	3.5	8.8	10.4	80.8
Meats, poultry, fish, and eggs	100.0	4.4	12.2	13.4	74.6
Beef	100.0	3.1	10.3	13.2	76.6
Pork	100.0	3.9	13.9	14.2	72.6
Other meats	100.0	2.7	9.7	11.4	78.9
Poultry	100.0	4.5	14.4	14.7	71.3
Fish and seafood	100.0	7.7	12.9	12.4	75.1
Eggs	100.0	5.8	11.6	15.6	72.8
Dairy products	100.0	3.2	7.7	11.7	80.5
Fresh milk and cream	100.0	4.0	8.8	14.0	77.3
Other dairy products	100.0	2.8	7.1	10.5	82.3
Fruits and vegetables	100.0	5.2	8.9	13.2	78.0
Fresh fruits	100.0	5.3	8.3	13.8	78.0
Fresh vegetables	100.0	7.0	7.9	13.6	78.8
Processed fruits	100.0	3.8	10.8	12.1	77.5
Processed vegetables	100.0	3.1	10.1	12.6	76.9
Other food at home	100.0	3.3	8.2	10.7	81.2
Sugar and other sweets	100.0	2.9	7.6	9.1	82.7
Fats and oils	100.0	3.7	9.8	12.2	78.5
Miscellaneous foods	100.0	3.4	7.8	10.2	81.9
Nonalcoholic beverages	100.0	3.0	9.1	12.2	78.7
Food prepared by consumer unit on trips	100.0	4.0	4.2	8.0	87.1
Restaurants and other food away from home	100.0	5.3	7.6	10.4	81.9
ALCOHOLIC BEVERAGES	100.0	3.1	5.6	7.3	86.9
HOUSING	100.0	4.6	9.7	11.2	79.3
Shelter	100.0	5.1	9.5	11.8	78.9
Owned dwellings	100.0	5.0	6.7	9.6	83.9
Mortgage interest and charges	100.0	5.6	7.5	11.4	81.4
Property taxes	100.0	4.9	6.1	8.9	85.1
Maintenance, repair, insurance, other expenses	100.0	2.9	5.3	4.9	89.8
Rented dwellings	100.0	5.9	17.2	18.3	65.0
Other lodging	100.0	3.5	4.4	5.8	90.1

	total households	Asian	black	Hispanic	non-Hispanic white and other
Utilities, fuels, and public services	**100.0%**	**3.4%**	**12.2%**	**11.5%**	**76.5%**
Natural gas	100.0	3.9	13.0	9.5	77.8
Electricity	100.0	2.9	12.9	11.5	75.8
Fuel oil and other fuels	100.0	1.3	4.3	3.9	92.4
Telephone	100.0	3.7	12.8	12.9	74.5
Water and other public services	**100.0**	**4.3**	**10.5**	**11.9**	**78.0**
Household services	100.0	5.1	7.6	8.4	84.4
Personal services	100.0	6.7	8.8	10.2	81.7
Other household services	100.0	4.0	6.9	7.2	86.0
Housekeeping supplies	**100.0**	**3.1**	**7.9**	**9.3**	**82.6**
Laundry and cleaning supplies	100.0	3.2	9.6	14.7	75.7
Other household products	100.0	3.1	7.5	7.7	84.5
Postage and stationery	100.0	3.0	6.9	7.5	85.3
Household furnishings and equipment	**100.0**	**4.2**	**6.9**	**9.2**	**83.9**
Household textiles	100.0	5.7	7.7	9.6	82.4
Furniture	100.0	3.4	9.6	11.4	79.3
Floor coverings	100.0	1.6	2.8	2.8	94.0
Major appliances	100.0	3.6	7.9	8.9	83.3
Small appliances and miscellaneous housewares	100.0	5.5	6.7	10.2	83.6
Miscellaneous household equipment	100.0	4.5	5.4	8.4	86.1
APPAREL AND RELATED SERVICES	**100.0**	**4.7**	**12.3**	**13.7**	**74.2**
Men and boys	**100.0**	**4.2**	**12.3**	**13.3**	**74.6**
Men, aged 16 or older	100.0	4.2	12.1	12.6	75.7
Boys, aged 2 to 15	100.0	4.4	13.2	16.3	70.4
Women and girls	**100.0**	**5.1**	**11.3**	**12.1**	**76.7**
Women, aged 16 or older	100.0	5.3	10.9	10.7	78.3
Girls, aged 2 to 15	100.0	4.0	13.0	18.5	68.5
Children under age 2	**100.0**	**5.1**	**10.0**	**19.1**	**71.2**
Footwear	**100.0**	**4.0**	**16.1**	**17.3**	**67.3**
Other apparel products and services	**100.0**	**5.2**	**11.3**	**12.3**	**76.8**
TRANSPORTATION	**100.0**	**4.4**	**8.4**	**11.1**	**80.7**
Vehicle purchases	**100.0**	**3.7**	**6.8**	**10.4**	**83.1**
Cars and trucks, new	100.0	3.3	5.3	9.2	85.8
Cars and trucks, used	100.0	4.2	8.5	11.7	80.1
Gasoline and motor oil	**100.0**	**3.6**	**9.9**	**12.5**	**77.8**
Other vehicle expenses	**100.0**	**4.7**	**9.0**	**10.8**	**80.3**
Vehicle finance charges	100.0	2.8	10.4	11.7	78.1
Maintenance and repairs	100.0	3.7	8.3	9.4	82.3
Vehicle insurance	100.0	5.7	9.7	11.5	78.6
Vehicle rentals, leases, licenses, other charges	100.0	5.3	7.3	10.5	82.2
Public transportation	**100.0**	**9.3**	**8.1**	**10.1**	**82.1**
HEALTH CARE	**100.0**	**3.0**	**6.8**	**5.9**	**87.3**
Health insurance	100.0	3.2	7.7	5.6	86.8
Medical services	100.0	3.0	4.8	6.7	88.6
Drugs	100.0	2.4	7.0	5.9	87.2
Medical supplies	100.0	3.4	5.8	6.1	87.8

	total households	Asian	black	Hispanic	non-Hispanic white and other
ENTERTAINMENT	**100.0%**	**3.2%**	**6.3%**	**7.3%**	**86.3%**
Fees and admissions	100.0	5.1	4.3	5.7	90.1
Audio and visual equipment and services	100.0	3.6	10.5	9.9	79.7
Pets, toys, hobbies, and playground equipment	100.0	1.6	4.3	6.7	88.8
Other entertainment products and services	100.0	1.9	3.0	4.5	92.4
PERSONAL CARE PRODUCTS, SERVICES	**100.0**	**3.5**	**10.9**	**10.6**	**78.5**
READING	**100.0**	**3.8**	**5.1**	**3.9**	**90.8**
EDUCATION	**100.0**	**8.3**	**6.7**	**7.8**	**85.4**
TOBACCO PRODUCTS AND SMOKING SUPPLIES	**100.0**	**1.2**	**7.3**	**5.7**	**87.1**
MISCELLANEOUS	**100.0**	**2.8**	**9.3**	**7.9**	**82.9**
CASH CONTRIBUTIONS	**100.0**	**3.2**	**9.0**	**7.0**	**84.2**
PERSONAL INSURANCE AND PENSIONS	**100.0**	**4.9**	**7.9**	**9.1**	**83.1**
Life and other personal insurance	100.0	3.5	9.2	4.6	86.3
Pensions and Social Security	100.0	5.0	7.8	9.4	82.9
PERSONAL TAXES	**100.0**	**6.4**	**4.3**	**4.2**	**91.5**
Federal income taxes	100.0	6.9	3.3	3.5	93.2
State and local income taxes	100.0	5.7	6.7	5.2	88.0
Other taxes	100.0	4.2	5.1	6.3	88.3
GIFTS FOR PEOPLE IN OTHER HOUSEHOLDS	**100.0**	**4.1**	**6.5**	**8.2**	**85.2**

Note: "Asian" and "black" include Hispanics and non-Hispanics who identify themselves as being of the respective race alone. "Hispanic" includes people of any race who identify themselves as Hispanic. "Other" includes people who identify themselves as non-Hispanic and as Alaska Native, American Indian, Asian (who are also included in the Asian column), Native Hawaiian or other Pacific Islander, as well as non-Hispanics reporting more than one race.
Source: Calculations by New Strategist based on the Bureau of Labor Statistics' 2009 Consumer Expenditure Survey

Blacks Are Big Spenders on Residential Phone Service

Black spending is below average on a variety of items because so many housheolds are female-headed families.

Although black households spend less than the average household on many products and services, they are big spenders on a number of items. Black households spend 2 percent more than the average household on clothes, with spending on shoes a substantial 33 percent above average. Blacks control 24 percent of the market for boys' shoes.

Black households spend 13 percent less than the average household on groceries overall, but they spend 19 percent more than average on poultry. They also spend more than average on fish and pork. Consistently over the years blacks have spent more than the average household on noncarbonated fruit-flavored drinks.

Because homeownership is relatively low among blacks, they spend less than average on mortgage interest, but their spending is 39 percent above average on rent. They spend 10 percent more than the average household on residential phone service and 3 percent more on cell phone service.

Blacks spend less than average on new cars and trucks, but they spend 67 percent more than the average household on mass transit.

■ Blacks spend much less than the average household on pets.

Blacks spend more than average on cell phone service

(indexed spending of black households on selected items, 2009)

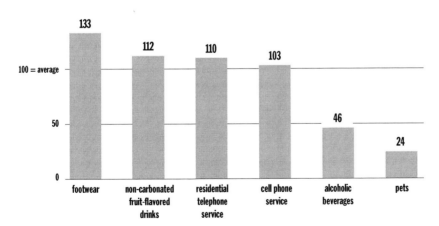

Table 9.5 Spending on Alcoholic Beverages by Black Households, 2009

(average annual, indexed, aggregate, and market share of spending by black households on alcoholic beverages, 2009)

	black average	index	aggregate (in 000s)	market share
ALCOHOLIC BEVERAGES, TOTAL	**$201.00**	**46**	**$2,946,459**	**5.6%**
At home	**130.04**	**53**	**1,906,256**	**6.4**
Beer and ale	84.21	73	1,234,434	8.9
Whiskey	2.48	24	36,354	3.0
Wine	30.69	30	449,885	3.7
Other alcoholic beverages	12.66	65	185,583	7.9
Away from home	**70.96**	**38**	**1,040,203**	**4.6**
Beer and ale	17.14	25	251,255	3.0
Wine	12.16	39	178,253	4.8
Other alcoholic beverages	29.05	63	425,844	7.6
Alcoholic beverages purchased on trips	12.62	30	184,997	3.7

Note: The index is calculated by dividing black spending on each item by average household spending on the item and multiplying by 100. Subcategories may not add to total because some are not shown.
Source: Bureau of Labor Statistics, unpublished data from the 2009 Consumer Expenditure Survey; calculations by New Strategist

Table 9.6 Spending on Apparel by Black Households, 2009

(average annual, indexed, aggregate, and market share of spending by black households on apparel, accessories, and related services, 2009)

	black average	index	aggregate (in 000s)	market share
APPAREL, TOTAL	**$1,754.85**	**102**	**$25,724,346**	**12.3%**
Men's apparel	**302.82**	**100**	**4,439,038**	**12.1**
Suits	14.58	82	213,728	9.9
Sport coats and tailored jackets	4.42	65	64,793	7.9
Coats and jackets	56.01	160	821,051	19.4
Underwear	8.26	52	121,083	6.3
Hosiery	9.33	78	136,768	9.5
Nightwear	1.89	111	27,706	13.5
Accessories	32.13	113	470,994	13.7
Sweaters and vests	23.12	160	338,916	19.4
Active sportswear	4.52	27	66,259	3.2
Shirts	68.76	81	1,007,953	9.9
Pants and shorts	77.48	115	1,135,779	13.9
Uniforms	2.23	82	32,690	9.9
Costumes	0.10	14	1,466	1.7
Boys' (aged 2 to 15) apparel	**85.58**	**109**	**1,254,517**	**13.2**
Coats and jackets	5.04	116	73,881	14.1
Sweaters	2.42	130	35,475	15.8
Shirts	20.57	85	301,536	10.4
Underwear	3.39	56	49,694	6.8
Nightwear	0.84	78	12,314	9.4
Hosiery	8.16	170	119,617	20.6
Accessories	4.62	107	67,725	13.0
Suits, sport coats, and vests	1.80	194	26,386	23.5
Pants and shorts	33.55	130	491,809	15.8
Uniforms	4.37	130	64,060	15.8
Active sportswear	0.38	32	5,570	3.9
Costumes	0.44	59	6,450	7.2
Women's apparel	**503.88**	**90**	**7,386,377**	**10.9**
Coats and jackets	50.04	119	733,536	14.5
Dresses	75.68	105	1,109,393	12.7
Sport coats and tailored jackets	1.96	41	28,732	5.0
Sweaters and vests	25.04	57	367,061	6.9
Shirts, blouses, and tops	78.21	70	1,146,480	8.5
Skirts	4.12	45	60,395	5.4
Pants and shorts	88.39	96	1,295,709	11.7
Active sportswear	12.86	47	188,515	5.7
Nightwear	28.27	131	414,410	15.9
Undergarments	39.45	109	578,298	13.2
Hosiery	16.75	95	245,538	11.5
Suits	15.24	135	223,403	16.3
Accessories	59.70	94	875,142	11.4
Uniforms	7.70	121	112,874	14.7
Costumes	0.47	29	6,890	3.5

	black average	index	aggregate (in 000s)	market share
Girls' (aged 2 to 15) apparel	**$125.59**	**107**	**$1,841,024**	**12.9%**
Coats and jackets	6.86	97	100,561	11.7
Dresses and suits	10.76	83	157,731	10.0
Shirts, blouses, and sweaters	34.74	112	509,254	13.5
Skirts, pants, and shorts	34.56	130	506,615	15.7
Active sportswear	6.53	56	95,723	6.8
Underwear and nightwear	13.78	122	202,001	14.8
Hosiery	5.95	113	87,221	13.7
Accessories	5.20	81	76,227	9.9
Uniforms	5.44	166	79,745	20.1
Costumes	1.77	97	25,946	11.7
Children (under age 2) apparel	**75.22**	**83**	**1,102,650**	**10.0**
Coats, jackets, and snowsuits	3.10	114	45,443	13.9
Outerwear including dresses	25.17	119	368,967	14.5
Underwear	36.04	65	528,310	7.9
Nightwear and loungewear	6.31	131	92,498	15.9
Accessories	4.60	62	67,431	7.5
Footwear	**430.47**	**133**	**6,310,260**	**16.2**
Men's	142.99	153	2,096,090	18.6
Boys'	86.45	202	1,267,271	24.4
Women's	136.57	91	2,001,980	11.0
Girls'	64.46	177	944,919	21.5
Other apparel products and services	**231.29**	**93**	**3,390,480**	**11.2**
Material for making clothes	1.36	14	19,936	1.7
Sewing patterns and notions	2.52	45	36,941	5.5
Watches	39.52	158	579,324	19.1
Jewelry	43.21	44	633,415	5.4
Shoe repair and other shoe services	0.75	63	10,994	7.6
Coin-operated apparel laundry, dry cleaning	64.79	157	949,757	19.0
Apparel alteration, repair, tailoring services	4.52	79	66,259	9.6
Clothing rental	0.62	26	9,089	3.2
Watch and jewelry repair	3.07	86	45,003	10.5
Professional laundry, dry cleaning	65.26	118	956,646	14.3
Clothing storage	5.68	351	83,263	42.5

Note: The index is calculated by dividing black spending on each item by average household spending on the item and multiplying by 100. Subcategories may not add to total because some are not shown.
Source: Bureau of Labor Statistics, unpublished data from the 2009 Consumer Expenditure Survey; calculations by New Strategist

Table 9.7 Spending on Entertainment by Black Households, 2009

(average annual, indexed, aggregate, and market share of spending by black households on entertainment, 2009)

	black average	index	aggregate (in 000s)	market share
ENTERTAINMENT, TOTAL	$1,404.15	52	$20,583,435	6.3%
Fees and admissions	**223.24**	**36**	**3,272,475**	**4.3**
Recreation expenses on trips	8.31	42	121,816	5.1
Social, recreation, civic club membership	38.33	33	561,879	4.0
Fees for participant sports	19.50	16	285,851	1.9
Participant sports on trips	6.93	32	101,587	3.8
Movie, theater, amusement park, and other admissions	57.91	48	848,903	5.8
Movie, other admissions on trips	20.51	50	300,656	6.1
Admission to sports events	20.70	41	303,441	4.9
Admission to sports events on trips	6.84	50	100,268	6.1
Fees for recreational lessons	35.92	35	526,551	4.3
Other entertainment services on trips	8.31	42	121,816	5.1
Audio and visual equipment and services	**839.79**	**86**	**12,310,482**	**10.4**
Radios	1.91	85	27,999	10.3
Television sets	94.83	68	1,390,113	8.2
Tape recorders and players	0.81	123	11,874	14.9
Cable and satellite television services	598.28	100	8,770,187	12.1
Miscellaneous sound equipment	0.36	33	5,277	4.0
Miscellaneous video equipment	0.36	10	5,277	1.2
Satellite radio service	9.71	69	142,339	8.4
Sound equipment accessories	10.88	102	159,490	12.4
Online gaming services	0.50	23	7,330	2.8
VCRs and video disc players	7.60	61	111,408	7.4
Video game hardware and software	39.46	74	578,444	9.0
Video cassettes, tapes, and discs	21.60	72	316,634	8.7
Streaming and downloading video	0.84	60	12,314	7.3
Repair of TV, radio, and sound equipment	1.95	59	28,585	7.1
Rental of television sets	3.25	478	47,642	58.0
Personal digital audio players	7.11	55	104,225	6.6
Sound components and component systems	2.90	25	42,511	3.0
Satellite dishes	0.75	71	10,994	8.6
Compact discs, records, and audio tapes	17.44	94	255,653	11.5
Streaming and downloading audio	2.64	47	38,700	5.7
Rental of VCR, radio, and sound equipment	0.07	44	1,026	5.3
Musical instruments and accessories	3.66	16	53,652	1.9
Rental and repair of musical instruments	0.36	23	5,277	2.7
Rental of video cassettes, tapes, discs, films	12.47	49	182,798	5.9
Rental of computer and video game hardware and software	0.04	17	586	2.1
Installation of television sets	–	–	–	–

	black average	index	aggregate (in 000s)	market share
Pets, toys, hobbies, playground equipment	**$241.89**	**35**	**$3,545,866**	**4.3%**
Pets	130.02	24	1,905,963	2.9
Pet food	54.53	32	799,355	3.9
Pet purchase, supplies, and medicines	59.42	36	871,038	4.3
Pet services	8.44	19	123,722	2.4
Veterinarian services	7.63	5	111,848	0.6
Toys, games, hobbies, and tricycles	111.15	80	1,629,348	9.7
Stamp and coin collecting	0.53	10	7,769	1.2
Playground equipment	0.20	8	2,932	1.0
Other entertainment supplies, equipment, services	**99.23**	**25**	**1,454,613**	**3.0**
Unmotored recreational vehicles	–	–	–	–
Motorized recreational vehicles	–	–	–	–
Rental of recreational vehicles	2.92	45	42,804	5.4
Docking and landing fees	0.67	9	9,822	1.0
Sports, recreation, exercise equipment	44.71	34	655,404	4.2
Athletic gear, game tables, exercise equip.	30.09	58	441,089	7.1
Bicycles	6.99	51	102,466	6.2
Camping equipment	1.31	12	19,203	1.5
Hunting and fishing equipment	3.62	12	53,066	1.4
Winter sports equipment	–	–	–	–
Water sports equipment	0.07	2	1,026	0.3
Other sports equipment	2.43	41	35,621	4.9
Global positioning system devices	–	–	–	–
Rental and repair of misc. sports equipment	0.18	7	2,639	0.8
Photographic equipment and supplies	29.93	51	438,744	6.1
Film	1.06	61	15,539	7.4
Photo processing	6.95	54	101,880	6.6
Repair and rental of photographic equipment	0.60	102	8,795	12.3
Photographic equipment	10.13	37	148,496	4.5
Photographer fees	11.19	78	164,034	9.5
Fireworks	2.59	41	37,967	4.9
Souvenirs	3.46	135	50,720	16.3
Visual goods	0.44	31	6,450	3.8
Pinball, electronic video games	3.13	120	45,883	14.5
Live entertainment at catered affairs	1.55	18	22,721	2.2
Rental of party supplies for catered affairs	9.82	70	143,951	8.5

Note: The index is calculated by dividing black spending on each item by average household spending on the item and multiplying by 100. Subcategories may not add to total because some are not shown. "–" means sample is too small to make a reliable estimate.
Source: Bureau of Labor Statistics, unpublished data from the 2009 Consumer Expenditure Survey; calculations by New Strategist

Table 9.8 Spending on Financial Products and Services by Black Households, 2009

(average annual, indexed, aggregate, and market share of spending by black households on financial products and services, cash contributions, insurance, pensions, and taxes, 2009)

	black average	index	aggregate (in 000s)	market share
FINANCIAL PRODUCTS, SERVICES, TOTAL	**$625.65**	**77**	**$9,171,403**	**9.3%**
Lottery and gambling losses	106.23	142	1,557,226	17.2
Legal fees	91.93	57	1,347,602	6.9
Funeral expenses	41.81	88	612,893	10.7
Safe deposit box rental	1.38	36	20,229	4.4
Checking accounts, other bank service charges	24.13	103	353,722	12.4
Cemetery lots, vaults, and maintenance fees	20.36	145	298,457	17.6
Accounting fees	21.56	37	316,048	4.5
Miscellaneous personal services	69.43	168	1,017,774	20.4
Dating services	0.05	13	733	1.6
Finance charges, except mortgage, vehicles	141.98	70	2,081,285	8.5
Occupational expenses	31.50	55	461,759	6.7
Expenses for other properties	68.57	64	1,005,168	7.7
Credit card memberships	0.72	38	10,554	4.6
Shopping club membership fees	4.10	43	60,102	5.3
Vacation clubs	1.46	24	21,402	2.9
CASH CONTRIBUTIONS, TOTAL	**1,279.57**	**74**	**18,757,217**	**9.0**
Support for college students	44.65	41	654,524	5.0
Alimony expenditures	11.36	25	166,526	3.0
Child support expenditures	264.27	123	3,873,934	14.9
Gifts of stocks, bonds, and mutual funds for people in other households	5.46	44	80,038	5.3
Cash contributions to charities and other organizations	51.40	25	753,473	3.0
Cash contributions to church, religious organizations	720.75	99	10,565,474	12.1
Cash contributions to educational institutions	14.66	48	214,901	5.8
Cash contributions to political organizations	1.31	18	19,203	2.2
Other cash gifts	165.72	45	2,429,289	5.4
PERSONAL INSURANCE AND PENSIONS, TOTAL	**3,550.04**	**65**	**52,040,036**	**7.9**
Life and other personal insurance	**235.16**	**76**	**3,447,210**	**9.2**
Life, endowment, annuity, other personal insurance	224.68	77	3,293,584	9.3
Other nonhealth insurance	10.48	62	153,626	7.5
Pensions and Social Security	**3,314.89**	**64**	**48,592,973**	**7.8**
Deductions for government retirement	58.69	73	860,337	8.9
Deductions for private pensions	280.38	45	4,110,090	5.4
Nonpayroll deposit to retirement plans	151.21	33	2,216,587	4.0
Deductions for Social Security	2,824.51	71	41,404,492	8.6

	black average	index	aggregate (in 000s)	market share
PERSONAL TAXES, TOTAL	**$742.88**	**35**	**$10,889,878**	**4.3%**
Federal income taxes	378.46	27	5,547,845	3.3
State and local income taxes	291.10	56	4,267,235	6.7
Other taxes	73.84	42	1,082,421	5.1

Note: The index is calculated by dividing black spending on each item by average household spending on the item and multiplying by 100. Subcategories may not add to total because some are not shown.
Source: Bureau of Labor Statistics, unpublished data from the 2009 Consumer Expenditure Survey; calculations by New Strategist

Table 9.9 Spending on Gifts for People in Other Households by Black Households, 2009

(average annual, indexed, aggregate, and market share of spending by black households on gifts for people in other households, 2009)

	black average	index	aggregate (in 000s)	market share
GIFTS, TOTAL	$569.75	53	$8,351,965	6.5%
Food	47.43	49	695,276	6.0
Candy and chewing gum	0.64	9	9,382	1.0
Alcoholic beverages	0.80	9	11,727	1.1
Housing	119.79	59	1,756,002	7.2
Housekeeping supplies	9.10	30	133,397	3.6
Postage and stationery	4.58	22	67,138	2.7
Household textiles	0.25	3	3,665	0.3
Appliances and miscellaneous housewares	10.00	65	146,590	7.9
Major appliances	6.51	146	95,430	17.7
Small appliances and misc. housewares	3.49	32	51,160	3.9
Miscellaneous household equipment	14.00	34	205,226	4.1
Decorative items for the home	–	–	–	–
Plants and fresh flowers, indoor	4.28	49	62,741	5.9
Other housing	86.44	82	1,267,124	9.9
Apparel and services	217.16	92	3,183,348	11.1
Males, aged 2 and over	26.44	50	387,584	6.1
Females, aged 2 and over	84.51	98	1,238,832	11.9
Children under age 2	38.62	80	566,131	9.7
Other apparel products and services	67.59	137	990,802	16.6
Jewelry	12.77	97	187,195	11.8
Transportation	22.61	26	331,440	3.2
Airline fares	9.82	101	143,951	12.2
Ship fares	1.69	22	24,774	2.6
Health care	11.66	42	170,924	5.1
Entertainment	54.00	59	791,586	7.2
Toys and games, arts and crafts, tricycles	18.41	54	269,872	6.6
Other entertainment	35.60	62	521,860	7.5
Personal care products and services	2.32	19	34,009	2.3
Cosmetics, perfume, and bath products	1.87	22	27,412	2.6
Education	52.53	23	770,037	2.8
College tuition	34.37	18	503,830	2.2
All other gifts	41.30	54	605,417	6.6
Gift of trip expenses	23.74	52	348,005	6.3

Note: The index is calculated by dividing black spending on each item by average household spending on the item and multiplying by 100. Spending on gifts is also included in the product and service categories in other tables. Subcategories may not add to total because some are not shown.
Source: Bureau of Labor Statistics, unpublished data from the 2009 Consumer Expenditure Survey; calculations by New Strategist

Table 9.10 Spending on Groceries by Black Households, 2009

(average annual, indexed, aggregate, and market share of spending by black households on groceries, 2009)

	black average	index	aggregate (in 000s)	market share
GROCERIES, TOTAL	**$2,879.83**	**77**	**$42,215,428**	**9.3%**
Cereals and bakery products	**389.64**	**77**	**5,711,733**	**9.3**
Cereals and cereal products	148.82	86	2,181,552	10.5
Flour	6.11	70	89,566	8.5
Prepared flour mixes	12.42	86	182,065	10.5
Ready-to-eat and cooked cereals	84.86	91	1,243,963	11.0
Rice	24.57	102	360,172	12.4
Pasta, cornmeal, and other cereal products	20.86	65	305,787	7.9
Bakery products	240.81	72	3,530,034	8.8
Bread	72.85	77	1,067,908	9.3
White bread	31.21	92	457,507	11.2
Bread, other than white	41.64	68	610,401	8.3
Cookies and crackers	55.79	66	817,826	8.0
Cookies	32.31	68	473,632	8.3
Crackers	23.47	64	344,047	7.7
Frozen and refrigerated bakery products	24.84	90	364,130	10.9
Other bakery products	87.34	69	1,280,317	8.3
Biscuits and rolls	29.52	60	432,734	7.3
Cakes and cupcakes	30.99	83	454,282	10.1
Bread and cracker products	3.18	60	46,616	7.3
Sweetrolls, coffee cakes, doughnuts	14.63	67	214,461	8.2
Pies, tarts, turnovers	9.02	64	132,224	7.7
Meats, poultry, fish, and eggs	**844.98**	**100**	**12,386,562**	**12.2**
Beef	191.19	85	2,802,654	10.3
Ground beef	93.09	105	1,364,606	12.7
Roast	26.68	77	391,102	9.3
Chuck roast	7.88	84	115,513	10.2
Round roast	5.72	104	83,849	12.6
Other roast	13.09	66	191,886	8.0
Steak	47.60	57	697,768	7.0
Round steak	5.57	52	81,651	6.4
Sirloin steak	13.63	61	199,802	7.4
Other steak	28.40	57	416,316	6.9
Other beef	23.81	122	349,031	14.9
Pork	193.12	115	2,830,946	13.9
Bacon	35.87	111	525,818	13.5
Pork chops	38.90	132	570,235	16.1
Ham	30.43	80	446,073	9.7
Ham, not canned	29.57	80	433,467	9.7
Canned ham	0.86	83	12,607	10.0
Sausage	41.08	147	602,192	17.9
Other pork	46.85	115	686,774	13.9
Other meats	91.14	80	1,336,021	9.7
Frankfurters	22.69	100	332,613	12.2
Lunch meats (cold cuts)	57.67	72	845,385	8.7
Bologna, liverwurst, salami	14.62	77	214,315	9.3
Other lunch meats	43.05	70	631,070	8.5
Lamb, organ meats, and others	10.78	102	158,024	12.4

	black average	index	aggregate (in 000s)	market share
Poultry	$183.04	119	$2,683,183	14.4%
Fresh and frozen chicken	145.66	121	2,135,230	14.6
Fresh and frozen whole chicken	32.71	107	479,496	13.0
Fresh and frozen chicken parts	112.95	125	1,655,734	15.2
Other poultry	37.38	112	547,953	13.6
Fish and seafood	144.06	107	2,111,776	12.9
Canned fish and seafood	20.08	109	294,353	13.3
Fresh fish and shellfish	75.60	106	1,108,220	12.9
Frozen fish and shellfish	48.38	107	709,202	12.9
Eggs	42.42	97	621,835	11.7
Dairy products	**258.10**	**64**	**3,783,488**	**7.7**
Fresh milk and cream	104.80	73	1,536,263	8.8
Fresh milk, all types	97.59	77	1,430,572	9.3
Cream	7.21	42	105,691	5.1
Other dairy products	153.29	58	2,247,078	7.1
Butter	14.81	68	217,100	8.3
Cheese	68.72	52	1,007,366	6.3
Ice cream and related products	40.86	66	598,967	7.9
Miscellaneous dairy products	28.90	64	423,645	7.8
Fruits and vegetables	**484.18**	**74**	**7,097,595**	**8.9**
Fresh fruits	150.99	69	2,213,362	8.3
Apples	24.85	68	364,276	8.2
Bananas	26.98	81	395,500	9.8
Oranges	19.50	80	285,851	9.8
Citrus fruits, excluding oranges	11.70	60	171,510	7.3
Other fresh fruits	67.96	64	996,226	7.8
Fresh vegetables	135.76	65	1,990,106	7.9
Potatoes	30.58	83	448,272	10.0
Lettuce	17.98	68	263,569	8.2
Tomatoes	22.99	64	337,010	7.7
Other fresh vegetables	64.20	59	941,108	7.1
Processed fruits	105.17	89	1,541,687	10.8
Frozen fruits and fruit juices	5.91	51	86,635	6.2
Frozen orange juice	2.26	80	33,129	9.8
Frozen fruits	2.20	36	32,250	4.4
Frozen fruit juices, excluding orange	1.45	54	21,256	6.5
Canned fruits	17.33	85	254,040	10.3
Dried fruits	5.89	69	86,342	8.4
Fresh fruit juice	18.87	97	276,615	11.8
Canned and bottled fruit juice	57.16	98	837,908	11.9
Processed vegetables	92.26	84	1,352,439	10.2
Frozen vegetables	29.63	84	434,346	10.2
Canned and dried vegetables and juices	62.63	84	918,093	10.2
Canned beans	15.36	97	225,162	11.8
Canned corn	7.08	109	103,786	13.2
Canned miscellaneous vegetables	15.69	67	230,000	8.1
Dried peas	0.19	44	2,785	5.4
Dried beans	4.25	109	62,301	13.2
Dried miscellaneous vegetables	7.70	83	112,874	10.1
Fresh and canned vegetable juices	12.16	83	178,253	10.0

	black average	index	aggregate (in 000s)	market share
Sugar and other sweets	**$87.99**	**63**	**$1,289,845**	**7.6%**
Candy and chewing gum	42.41	49	621,688	6.0
Sugar	23.94	127	350,936	15.4
Artificial sweeteners	4.66	78	68,311	9.5
Jams, preserves, other sweets	16.97	57	248,763	7.0
Fats and oils	**82.26**	**80**	**1,205,849**	**9.8**
Margarine	7.62	94	111,702	11.4
Fats and oils	39.28	110	575,806	13.4
Salad dressings	19.88	70	291,421	8.5
Nondairy cream and imitation milk	8.20	51	120,204	6.2
Peanut butter	7.28	52	106,718	6.4
Miscellaneous foods	**462.49**	**65**	**6,779,641**	**7.8**
Frozen prepared foods	106.79	72	1,565,435	8.8
Frozen meals	50.78	74	744,384	8.9
Other frozen prepared foods	56.02	71	821,197	8.6
Canned and packaged soups	30.86	66	452,377	8.0
Potato chips, nuts, and other snacks	88.86	60	1,302,599	7.3
Potato chips and other snacks	67.91	63	995,493	7.6
Nuts	20.95	53	307,106	6.5
Condiments and seasonings	91.24	70	1,337,487	8.5
Salt, spices, and other seasonings	24.61	79	360,758	9.5
Olives, pickles, relishes	10.52	67	154,213	8.1
Sauces and gravies	38.81	70	568,916	8.5
Baking needs and miscellaneous products	17.31	63	253,747	7.6
Other canned or packaged prepared foods	144.75	60	2,121,890	7.2
Prepared salads	20.62	62	302,269	7.5
Prepared desserts	9.35	68	137,062	8.3
Baby food	20.20	61	296,112	7.4
Miscellaneous prepared foods	93.64	58	1,372,669	7.1
Nonalcoholic beverages	**252.83**	**75**	**3,706,235**	**9.1**
Cola	62.14	71	910,910	8.6
Other carbonated drinks	38.80	78	568,769	9.5
Tea	25.63	87	375,710	10.6
Coffee	26.31	46	385,678	5.5
Roasted coffee	17.21	45	252,281	5.4
Instant and freeze-dried coffee	9.10	47	133,397	5.8
Noncarbonated fruit-flavored drinks	27.56	112	404,002	13.6
Other nonalcoholic beverages and ice	8.55	67	125,334	8.1
Bottled water	51.53	91	755,378	11.0
Sports drinks	12.31	69	180,452	8.3
Groceries purchased on trips	**17.37**	**36**	**254,627**	**4.3**

Note: The index is calculated by dividing black spending on each item by average household spending on the item and multiplying by 100. Subcategories may not add to total because some are not shown.
Source: Bureau of Labor Statistics, unpublished data from the 2009 Consumer Expenditure Survey; calculations by New Strategist

Table 9.11 Out-of-Pocket Spending on Health Care by Black Households, 2009

(average annual, indexed, aggregate, and market share of spending by black households on out-of-pocket health care costs, 2009)

	black average	index	aggregate (in 000s)	market share
HEALTH CARE, TOTAL	**$1,763.25**	**56**	**$25,847,482**	**6.8%**
Health insurance	**1,132.52**	**63**	**16,601,611**	**7.7**
Commercial health insurance	183.30	53	2,686,995	6.5
Traditional fee-for-service health plan (not BCBS)	51.41	61	753,619	7.3
Preferred-provider health plan (not BCBS)	131.88	51	1,933,229	6.2
Blue Cross, Blue Shield	320.20	61	4,693,812	7.4
Traditional fee-for-service health plan	41.49	48	608,202	5.8
Preferred-provider health plan	102.63	48	1,504,453	5.8
Health maintenance organization	145.87	86	2,138,308	10.4
Commercial Medicare supplement	27.39	60	401,510	7.2
Other BCBS health insurance	2.82	30	41,338	3.6
Health maintenance plans (HMOs)	235.05	82	3,445,598	10.0
Medicare payments	258.14	74	3,784,074	9.0
Medicare prescription drug premium	54.54	88	799,502	10.6
Commercial Medicare supplements and other health insurance	67.21	44	985,231	5.3
Commercial Medicare supplement (not BCBS)	41.89	41	614,066	5.0
Other health insurance (not BCBS)	25.32	49	371,166	5.9
Long-term care insurance	14.08	22	206,399	2.7
Medical services	**294.43**	**40**	**4,316,049**	**4.9**
Physician's services	68.66	37	1,006,487	4.5
Dental services	112.72	42	1,652,362	5.1
Eye care services	57.16	143	837,908	17.4
Service by professionals other than physician	7.19	15	105,398	1.8
Lab tests, X-rays	8.28	17	121,377	2.1
Hospital room and services	23.11	22	338,769	2.7
Care in convalescent or nursing home	2.38	15	34,888	1.8
Other medical services	14.92	68	218,712	8.3
Drugs	**278.82**	**57**	**4,087,222**	**7.0**
Nonprescription drugs	40.01	49	586,507	5.9
Nonprescription vitamins	17.01	40	249,350	4.8
Prescription drugs	221.80	61	3,251,366	7.4
Medical supplies	**57.48**	**48**	**842,599**	**5.9**
Eyeglasses and contact lenses	29.82	50	437,131	6.0
Hearing aids	5.91	37	86,635	4.5
Topicals and dressings	13.76	43	201,708	5.2
Medical equipment for general use	0.86	31	12,607	3.8
Supportive and convalescent medical equipment	0.89	18	13,047	2.2
Rental of medical equipment	0.07	6	1,026	0.8
Rental of supportive, convalescent medical equip.	6.17	264	90,446	32.0

Note: The index is calculated by dividing black spending on each item by average household spending on the item and multiplying by 100. Subcategories may not add to total because some are not shown.
Source: Bureau of Labor Statistics, unpublished data from the 2009 Consumer Expenditure Survey; calculations by New Strategist

Table 9.12 Spending on Household Operations by Black Households, 2009

(average annual, indexed, aggregate, and market share of spending by black households on household services, supplies, furnishings, and equipment, 2009)

	black average	index	aggregate (in 000s)	market share
HOUSEHOLD SERVICES, TOTAL	$633.17	63	$9,281,639	7.6%
Personal services	281.22	72	4,122,404	8.8
Babysitting and child care in own home	18.74	40	274,710	4.8
Babysitting and child care in someone else's home	25.61	79	375,417	9.6
Care for elderly, invalids, handicapped, etc.	–	–	–	–
Day care centers, nurseries, preschools	236.76	91	3,470,665	11.1
Other household services	351.95	57	5,159,235	6.9
Housekeeping services	14.65	13	214,754	1.6
Gardening, lawn care service	47.59	44	697,622	5.4
Water-softening service	2.36	60	34,595	7.2
Nonclothing laundry, dry cleaning, sent out	0.66	64	9,675	7.8
Nonclothing laundry and dry cleaning, coin-operated	6.55	182	96,016	22.1
Termite and pest control services	11.06	60	162,129	7.2
Home security system service fee	28.98	138	424,818	16.7
Other home services	8.26	42	121,083	5.1
Termite and pest control products	1.92	67	28,145	8.1
Moving, storage, and freight express	20.29	55	297,431	6.7
Appliance repair, including at service center	7.81	47	114,487	5.7
Reupholstering and furniture repair	0.96	22	14,073	2.7
Repairs and rentals of lawn and garden equipment, hand and power tools, etc.	3.65	62	53,505	7.5
Appliance rental	2.07	152	30,344	18.5
Repair of office equipment for nonbusiness use	0.59	78	8,649	9.4
Repair of misc. household equip., furnishings	0.96	18	14,073	2.2
Repair of computer systems, nonbusiness use	5.17	77	75,787	9.3
Computer information services	188.42	74	2,762,049	9.0
HOUSEKEEPING SUPPLIES, TOTAL	428.97	65	6,288,271	7.9
Laundry and cleaning supplies	123.69	79	1,813,172	9.6
Soaps and detergents	73.74	86	1,080,955	10.4
Other laundry cleaning products	49.95	71	732,217	8.6
Other household products	223.81	62	3,280,831	7.5
Cleansing and toilet tissue, paper towels, and napkins	104.64	95	1,533,918	11.5
Miscellaneous household products	80.79	59	1,184,301	7.1
Lawn and garden supplies	38.38	34	562,612	4.2
Postage and stationery	81.47	57	1,194,269	6.9
Stationery, stationery supplies, giftwrap	32.84	44	481,402	5.3
Postage	46.86	73	686,921	8.8
Delivery services	1.77	45	25,946	5.4

	black average	index	aggregate (in 000s)	market share
HOUSEHOLD FURNISHINGS AND EQUIPMENT, TOTAL	**$854.48**	**57**	**$12,525,822**	**6.9%**
Household textiles	**79.22**	**64**	**1,161,286**	**7.7**
Bathroom linens	18.81	102	275,736	12.4
Bedroom linens	43.44	64	636,787	7.7
Kitchen and dining room linens	2.20	36	32,250	4.4
Curtains and draperies	9.75	57	142,925	6.9
Slipcovers and decorative pillows	2.12	61	31,077	7.4
Sewing materials for household items	1.82	19	26,679	2.3
Other linens	1.08	94	15,832	11.4
Furniture	**271.23**	**79**	**3,975,961**	**9.6**
Mattresses and springs	40.76	73	597,501	8.8
Other bedroom furniture	65.68	107	962,803	13.0
Sofas	51.74	62	758,457	7.5
Living room chairs	33.69	98	493,862	11.8
Living room tables	10.94	94	160,369	11.5
Kitchen and dining room furniture	25.50	80	373,805	9.7
Infants' furniture	7.15	89	104,812	10.8
Outdoor furniture	11.95	64	175,175	7.8
Wall units, cabinets, and other furniture	23.83	63	349,324	7.7
Floor coverings	**7.26**	**24**	**106,424**	**2.9**
Wall-to-wall carpeting	1.96	14	28,732	1.7
Floor coverings, nonpermanent	5.30	32	77,693	3.9
Major appliances	**126.84**	**65**	**1,859,348**	**7.9**
Dishwashers (built-in), garbage disposals, range hoods	0.93	7	13,633	0.8
Refrigerators and freezers	38.68	69	567,010	8.3
Washing machines	24.00	75	351,816	9.1
Clothes dryers	18.05	76	264,595	9.3
Cooking stoves, ovens	16.41	60	240,554	7.3
Microwave ovens	9.62	98	141,020	11.9
Window air conditioners	4.18	128	61,275	15.5
Electric floor-cleaning equipment	8.77	62	128,559	7.5
Sewing machines	0.36	4	5,277	0.5
Small appliances and misc. housewares	**50.51**	**54**	**740,426**	**6.6**
Housewares	28.21	44	413,530	5.4
Plastic dinnerware	2.75	110	40,312	13.4
China and other dinnerware	2.57	53	37,674	6.4
Flatware	3.23	88	47,349	10.7
Glassware	1.15	10	16,858	1.2
Silver serving pieces	2.86	100	41,925	12.1
Other serving pieces	0.44	25	6,450	3.0
Nonelectric cookware	7.58	57	111,115	6.9
Tableware, nonelectric kitchenware	7.64	32	111,995	3.9
Small appliances	22.29	76	326,749	9.2
Small electric kitchen appliances	13.37	65	195,991	7.9
Portable heating and cooling equipment	8.92	101	130,758	12.2

Miscellaneous household equipment	black average $319.43	index 44	aggregate (in 000s) $4,682,524	market share 5.4%
Window coverings	5.43	26	79,598	3.2
Infants' equipment	3.72	27	54,531	3.2
Laundry and cleaning equipment	10.38	63	152,160	7.6
Outdoor equipment	1.68	10	24,627	1.2
Lamps and lighting fixtures	10.70	37	156,851	4.5
Household decorative items (including clocks)	32.72	25	479,642	3.1
Telephones and accessories	42.07	89	616,704	10.8
Lawn and garden equipment	5.00	9	73,295	1.1
Power tools	27.69	78	405,908	9.5
Office furniture for home use	1.43	19	20,962	2.3
Hand tools	1.03	8	15,099	0.9
Indoor plants and fresh flowers	25.66	51	376,150	6.2
Closet and storage items	7.96	54	116,686	6.5
Rental of furniture	9.82	474	143,951	57.5
Luggage	5.52	51	80,918	6.1
Computers and computer hardware for nonbusiness use	75.70	48	1,109,686	5.9
Portable memory	5.06	66	74,175	8.0
Computer software and accessories for nonbusiness use	12.26	60	179,719	7.2
Personal digital assistants	2.97	107	43,537	13.0
Internet services away from home	2.24	102	32,836	12.4
Telephone answering devices	0.34	76	4,984	9.2
Business equipment for home use	2.29	81	33,569	9.9
Other hardware	10.86	83	159,197	10.1
Smoke alarms	0.77	58	11,287	7.1
Other household appliances	3.46	39	50,720	4.8
Miscellaneous household equipment and parts	12.69	30	186,023	3.7

Note: The index is calculated by dividing black spending on each item by average household spending on the item and multiplying by 100. Subcategories may not add to total because some are not shown. "–" means sample is too small to make a reliable estimate.

Source: Bureau of Labor Statistics, unpublished data from the 2009 Consumer Expenditure Survey; calculations by New Strategist

Table 9.13 **Spending on Personal Care, Reading, Education, and Tobacco by Black Households, 2009**

(average annual, indexed, aggregate, and market share of spending by black households on personal care, reading, education, and tobacco products, 2009)

	black average	index	aggregate (in 000s)	market share
PERSONAL CARE PRODUCTS AND SERVICES, TOTAL	**$535.95**	**90**	**$7,856,491**	**10.9%**
Personal care products	**212.62**	**70**	**3,116,797**	**8.5**
Hair care products	44.10	68	646,462	8.2
Hair accessories	6.48	102	94,990	12.3
Wigs and hairpieces	16.86	572	247,151	69.3
Oral hygiene products	19.31	66	283,065	8.0
Shaving products	10.61	66	155,532	8.0
Cosmetics, perfume, and bath products	82.20	57	1,204,970	7.0
Deodorants, feminine hygiene, misc. products	27.21	83	398,871	10.1
Electric personal care appliances	5.86	68	85,902	8.2
Personal care services	**323.32**	**111**	**4,739,548**	**13.5**
READING, TOTAL	**46.19**	**42**	**677,099**	**5.1**
Newspaper and magazine subscriptions	13.51	31	198,043	3.8
Newspapers and magazines, nonsubscription	13.43	90	196,870	10.9
Books	18.91	38	277,202	4.6
EDUCATION, TOTAL	**590.63**	**55**	**8,658,045**	**6.7**
College tuition	408.39	58	5,986,589	7.0
Elementary and high school tuition	53.93	33	790,560	4.0
Technical and vocational school tuition	13.43	102	196,870	12.4
Test preparation and tutoring services	4.55	52	66,698	6.4
Other school tuition	4.75	58	69,630	7.1
Other school expenses including rentals	16.56	47	242,753	5.7
Books, supplies for college	41.74	63	611,867	7.6
Books, supplies for elementary, high school	14.72	79	215,780	9.6
Books, supplies for technical and vocational school	0.54	95	7,916	11.5
Books, supplies for day care, nursery school	0.17	121	2,492	14.7
Books, supplies for others schools	0.25	17	3,665	2.0
Miscellaneous school expenses and supplies	31.59	64	463,078	7.8
TOBACCO PRODUCTS AND SMOKING SUPPLIES, TOTAL	**229.80**	**61**	**3,368,638**	**7.3**
Cigarettes	214.58	62	3,145,528	7.5
Other tobacco products	14.42	48	211,383	5.8
Smoking accessories	0.80	41	11,727	5.0

Note: The index is calculated by dividing black spending on each item by average household spending on the item and multiplying by 100. Subcategories may not add to total because some are not shown.
Source: Bureau of Labor Statistics, unpublished data from the 2009 Consumer Expenditure Survey; calculations by New Strategist

Table 9.14 Spending on Restaurant Meals by Black Households, 2009

(average annual, indexed, aggregate, and market share of spending by black households on restaurant meals and other food away from home, 2009)

	black average	index	aggregate (in 000s)	market share
FOOD AWAY FROM HOME, TOTAL	**$1,644.62**	**63**	**$24,108,485**	**7.6%**
Meals at restaurants	**1,444.69**	**66**	**21,177,711**	**8.0**
Lunch	512.96	70	7,519,481	8.5
At fast-food restaurants*	318.60	90	4,670,357	10.9
At full-service restaurants	126.99	44	1,861,546	5.3
At vending machines, mobile vendors	6.79	79	99,535	9.6
At employer and school cafeterias	60.57	75	887,896	9.2
Dinner	662.13	62	9,706,164	7.6
At fast-food restaurants*	343.72	98	5,038,591	11.9
At full-service restaurants	316.79	45	4,643,825	5.5
At vending machines, mobile vendors	0.49	17	7,183	2.1
At employer and school cafeterias	1.13	16	16,565	2.0
Snacks and nonalcoholic beverages	106.24	63	1,557,372	7.7
At fast-food restaurants*	70.41	64	1,032,140	7.8
At full-service restaurants	11.37	37	166,673	4.5
At vending machines, mobile vendors	17.97	85	263,422	10.3
At employer and school cafeterias	6.49	118	95,137	14.3
Breakfast and brunch	163.36	72	2,394,694	8.7
At fast-food restaurants*	110.80	95	1,624,217	11.5
At full-service restaurants	45.77	48	670,942	5.8
At vending machines, mobile vendors	1.01	37	14,806	4.5
At employer and school cafeterias	5.79	50	84,876	6.1
Board (including at school)	**25.67**	**57**	**376,297**	**6.9**
Catered affairs	**31.91**	**45**	**467,769**	**5.5**
Restaurant meals on trips	**81.59**	**37**	**1,196,028**	**4.4**
School lunches	**47.09**	**73**	**690,292**	**8.8**
Meals as pay	**13.67**	**51**	**200,389**	**6.2**

* The category fast-food restaurants also includes take-out, delivery, concession stands, buffets, and cafeterias other than employer and school.

Note: The index is calculated by dividing black spending on each item by average household spending on the item and multiplying by 100. Subcategories may not add to total because some are not shown.

Source: Bureau of Labor Statistics, unpublished data from the 2009 Consumer Expenditure Survey; calculations by New Strategist

Table 9.15 Spending on Shelter and Utilities by Black Households, 2009

(average annual, indexed, aggregate, and market share of spending by black households on shelter and utilities, 2009)

	black average	index	aggregate (in 000s)	market share
SHELTER, TOTAL	**$7,918.77**	**79**	**$116,081,249**	**9.5%**
Owned dwellings*	**3,632.07**	**56**	**53,242,514**	**6.7**
Mortgage interest and charges	2,219.93	62	32,541,954	7.5
Mortgage interest	2,165.88	64	31,749,635	7.8
Interest paid, home equity loan	29.60	37	433,906	4.5
Interest paid, home equity line of credit	24.45	19	358,413	2.3
Property taxes	911.82	50	13,366,369	6.1
Maintenance, repairs, insurance, other expenses	500.32	44	7,334,191	5.3
Homeowner's insurance	204.69	60	3,000,551	7.3
Ground rent	16.65	33	244,072	4.0
Maintenance and repair services	211.89	35	3,106,096	4.2
Painting and papering	20.53	26	300,949	3.2
Plumbing and water heating	36.03	62	528,164	7.5
Heat, air conditioning, electrical work	41.08	36	602,192	4.4
Roofing and gutters	44.08	38	646,169	4.7
Other repair and maintenance services	63.28	33	927,622	4.0
Repair, replacement of hard-surface flooring	5.28	10	77,400	1.2
Repair of built-in appliances	1.61	76	23,601	9.2
Maintenance and repair materials	38.87	53	569,795	6.4
Paints, wallpaper, and supplies	7.72	60	113,167	7.2
Tools, equipment for painting, wallpapering	0.83	60	12,167	7.2
Plumbing supplies and equipment	2.02	37	29,611	4.4
Electrical supplies, heating, cooling equipment	2.11	34	30,930	4.1
Hard-surface flooring, repair and replacement	4.22	61	61,861	7.3
Roofing and gutters	12.75	165	186,902	20.0
Plaster, paneling, siding, windows, doors, screens, awnings	5.14	37	75,347	4.5
Patio, walk, fence, driveway, masonry, brick, and stucco materials	0.09	13	1,319	1.6
Miscellaneous supplies and equipment	3.99	22	58,489	2.6
Property management and security	25.47	44	373,365	5.4
Property management	22.99	46	337,010	5.6
Management and upkeep services for security	2.48	31	36,354	3.7
Parking	2.75	44	40,312	5.3
Rented dwellings	**4,045.55**	**141**	**59,303,717**	**17.2**
Rent	3,818.95	139	55,981,988	16.9
Rent as pay	189.44	239	2,777,001	29.0
Maintenance, insurance, and other expenses	37.16	88	544,728	10.7
Tenant's insurance	10.76	87	157,731	10.5
Maintenance and repair services	19.22	97	281,746	11.8
Maintenance and repair materials	7.18	72	105,252	8.8

	black average	index	aggregate (in 000s)	market share
Other lodging	**$241.15**	**36**	**$3,535,018**	**4.4%**
Owned vacation homes	82.16	27	1,204,383	3.3
Mortgage interest and charges	37.54	27	550,299	3.3
Property taxes	26.13	25	383,040	3.0
Maintenance, insurance, and other expenses	18.49	31	271,045	3.7
Housing while attending school	47.06	69	689,853	8.3
Lodging on trips	111.93	37	1,640,782	4.5
UTILITIES, FUELS, AND PUBLIC SERVICES, TOTAL	**3,667.91**	**101**	**53,767,893**	**12.2**
Natural gas	**517.04**	**107**	**7,579,289**	**13.0**
Electricity	**1,462.06**	**106**	**21,432,338**	**12.9**
Fuel oil and other fuels	**50.45**	**36**	**739,547**	**4.3**
Fuel oil	35.62	46	522,154	5.6
Coal, wood, and other fuels	4.34	40	63,620	4.9
Bottled gas	10.49	19	153,773	2.4
Telephone services	**1,223.55**	**105**	**17,936,019**	**12.8**
Residential telephone and pay phones	478.01	110	7,007,149	13.4
Cellular phone service	730.09	103	10,702,389	12.4
Phone cards	8.31	87	121,816	10.5
Voice over IP	7.15	101	104,812	12.3
Water and other public services	**414.81**	**86**	**6,080,700**	**10.5**
Water and sewerage maintenance	344.61	98	5,051,638	11.9
Trash and garbage collection	70.05	55	1,026,863	6.7
Septic tank cleaning	0.16	4	2,345	0.4

* The amount paid in mortgage principal is not shown here because it is considered an asset.
Note: The index is calculated by dividing black spending on each item by average household spending on the item and multiplying by 100. Subcategories may not add to total because some are not shown.
Source: Bureau of Labor Statistics, unpublished data from the 2009 Consumer Expenditure Survey; calculations by New Strategist

Table 9.16 Spending on Transportation by Black Households, 2009

(average annual, indexed, aggregate, and market share of spending by black households on transportation, 2009)

	black average	index	aggregate (in 000s)	market share
TRANSPORTATION, TOTAL	$5,302.11	69	$77,723,630	8.4%
Vehicle purchases	1,488.69	56	21,822,707	6.8
Cars and trucks, new	568.07	44	8,327,338	5.3
New cars	290.49	42	4,258,293	5.0
New trucks	277.57	46	4,068,899	5.6
Cars and trucks, used	909.65	70	13,334,559	8.5
Used cars	600.08	87	8,796,573	10.5
Used trucks	309.56	51	4,537,840	6.1
Other vehicles	10.98	20	160,956	2.4
New motorcycles	–	–	–	–
Used motorcycles	10.98	33	160,956	4.0
Gasoline and motor oil	1,617.57	81	23,711,959	9.9
Gasoline	1,557.16	85	22,826,408	10.3
Diesel fuel	5.80	16	85,022	2.0
Gasoline on trips	48.49	45	710,815	5.4
Motor oil	5.63	58	82,530	7.0
Motor oil on trips	0.49	45	7,183	5.4
Other vehicle expenses	1,876.45	74	27,506,881	9.0
Vehicle finance charges	242.48	86	3,554,514	10.5
Automobile finance charges	149.60	125	2,192,986	15.1
Truck finance charges	91.40	67	1,339,833	8.1
Motorcycle and plane finance charges	1.21	25	17,737	3.0
Other vehicle finance charges	0.27	1	3,958	0.2
Maintenance and repairs	504.21	69	7,391,214	8.3
Coolant, additives, brake, transmission fluids	3.37	86	49,401	10.5
Tires—purchased, replaced, installed	66.95	56	981,420	6.8
Parts, equipment, and accessories	20.92	48	306,666	5.8
Vehicle audio equipment	0.36	16	5,277	1.9
Vehicle products and cleaning services	1.69	34	24,774	4.1
Vehicle video equipment	0.92	46	13,486	5.6
Miscellaneous auto repair, servicing	48.53	87	711,401	10.6
Body work and painting	11.64	43	170,631	5.2
Clutch and transmission repair	24.73	72	362,517	8.7
Drive shaft and rear-end repair	1.83	35	26,826	4.3
Brake work	53.78	82	788,361	10.0
Repair to steering or front-end	9.14	52	133,983	6.3
Repair to engine cooling system	20.78	92	304,614	11.2
Motor tune-up	36.51	79	535,200	9.6
Lube, oil change, and oil filters	55.32	74	810,936	9.0
Front-end alignment, wheel balance, rotation	6.50	51	95,284	6.1
Shock absorber replacement	5.38	95	78,865	11.5

	black average	index	aggregate (in 000s)	market share
Tire repair and other repair work	$32.80	67	$480,815	8.1%
Vehicle air conditioning repair	6.71	54	98,362	6.5
Exhaust system repair	10.62	102	155,679	12.3
Electrical system repair	29.52	96	432,734	11.6
Motor repair, replacement	43.47	63	637,227	7.7
Auto repair service policy	12.75	70	186,902	8.5
Vehicle insurance	859.47	80	12,598,971	9.7
Vehicle rental, leases, licenses, other charges	270.29	61	3,962,181	7.3
Leased and rented vehicles	147.49	63	2,162,056	7.7
Rented vehicles	29.18	88	427,750	10.7
Auto rental	9.18	184	134,570	22.4
Auto rental on trips	16.67	70	244,366	8.5
Truck rental	1.60	70	23,454	8.5
Truck rental on trips	1.73	105	25,360	12.7
Leased vehicles	118.31	59	1,734,306	7.2
Car lease payments	53.79	50	788,508	6.1
Truck lease payments	51.24	62	751,127	7.5
Vehicle registration, state	42.61	45	624,620	5.4
Vehicle registration, local	6.64	82	97,336	9.9
Driver's license	5.19	66	76,080	8.0
Vehicle inspection	6.24	55	91,472	6.7
Parking fees	25.00	63	366,475	7.6
Parking fees in home city, excl. residence	22.70	69	332,759	8.4
Parking fees on trips	2.30	33	33,716	4.0
Tolls	17.52	78	256,826	9.5
Tolls on trips	1.89	42	27,706	5.1
Towing charges	5.23	113	76,667	13.7
Global positioning services	1.47	77	21,549	9.3
Automobile service clubs	11.02	63	161,542	7.6
Public transportation	**319.39**	**67**	**4,681,938**	**8.1**
Airline fares	142.29	47	2,085,829	5.7
Intercity bus fares	5.38	58	78,865	7.1
Intracity mass transit fares	108.97	167	1,597,391	20.3
Local transportation on trips	4.85	45	71,096	5.5
Taxi fares and limousine service on trips	2.85	45	41,778	5.5
Taxi fares and limousine service	30.68	130	449,738	15.8
Intercity train fares	7.87	53	115,366	6.4
Ship fares	15.61	32	228,827	3.9
School bus	0.88	267	12,900	32.3

Note: The index is calculated by dividing black spending on each item by average household spending on the item and multiplying by 100. Subcategories may not add to total because some are not shown. "–" means sample is too small to make a reliable estimate.
Source: Bureau of Labor Statistics, unpublished data from the 2009 Consumer Expenditure Survey; calculations by New Strategist

10

Time Use

■ On an average day in 2009, 41 percent of blacks aged 15 or older worked or participated in work-related activities. Those who worked spent 7.23 hours on the job.

■ Blacks spend 87 percent more time than the average person involved in religious and spiritual activities on an average day. They spend 73 percent more time on the telephone.

■ Only 8 percent of blacks spend leisure time using a computer on an average day compared with 11 percent of all Americans. Thirty-nine percent shop on an average day, slightly below average.

Work Ranks Third in Time Use among Blacks

Watching television is second.

We know how blacks prioritize their time thanks to the American Time Use Survey (ATUS), first introduced by the Bureau of Labor Statistics in 2003. The survey collects data on how Americans spend their time during an average day. ATUS data are published annually, allowing social scientists to better understand our economy, our lifestyles, and the way policy decisions affect our lives. Through telephone interviews with a nationally representative sample of Americans aged 15 or older, ATUS asks survey respondents what they did minute by minute during the previous 24 hours—or diary day.

The following pages show how blacks aged 15 or older prioritize their time. Everyone spends more time sleeping than doing any other activity. Among blacks aged 15 or older, sleep consumes 8.97 hours a day, on average. After sleep, watching television is the most time consuming activity for blacks, with the average black watching TV for 3.66 hours a day. Work ranks third, with the average black adult spending 2.94 hours a day engaged in work or work-related activities. This figure appears low because it includes weekdays and weekends, people of working age and retirees. Blacks who worked on diary day spent 7.23 hours on the job.

■ Eight percent of blacks aged 15 or older are involved in educational activities on an average day.

More than one in eight blacks participate in religious activities on an average day

(percent of blacks aged 15 or older who participated in selected primary activities on an average day, 2009)

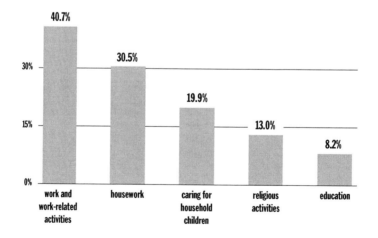

Table 10.1 Time Use of Total Blacks, 2009

(number and percent of total blacks aged 15 or older participating in primary activities on an average day, hours spent doing activity by the average black aged 15 or older and by blacks aged 15 or older who participated in the activity, 2009; numbers of participants in thousands)

	total blacks participating		time spent doing activity (hours)	
	number	percent	average black	black participants
Total, all activities	**28,754**	**100.0%**	**24.00**	**24.00**
Personal care	28,734	99.9	9.90	9.91
Sleeping	28,672	99.7	8.97	9.00
Grooming	23,410	81.4	0.83	1.02
Household activities	20,846	72.5	1.26	1.74
Housework	8,783	30.5	0.46	1.52
Food preparation and cleanup	14,743	51.3	0.47	0.92
Household management	6,696	23.3	0.13	0.55
Caring for and helping household members	6,777	23.6	0.39	1.67
Caring for and helping household children	5,728	19.9	0.32	1.60
Work and work-related activities	11,697	40.7	2.94	7.23
Working	10,666	37.1	2.84	7.66
Education	2,348	8.2	0.42	5.15
Consumer purchases (store, telephone, Internet)	11,261	39.2	0.31	0.80
Eating and drinking	26,981	93.8	0.84	0.89
Socializing, relaxing, and leisure	27,440	95.4	5.50	5.76
Socializing and communicating	10,735	37.3	0.68	1.82
Watching television	24,071	83.7	3.66	4.37
Computer use for leisure (excluding games)	2,403	8.4	0.13	1.61
Reading for personal interest	3,642	12.7	0.14	1.08
Sports, exercise, recreation	4,283	14.9	0.27	1.82
Religious and spiritual activities	3,728	13.0	0.28	2.15
Volunteer activities	1,666	5.8	0.13	2.32
Telephone calls	5,618	19.5	0.19	0.98
Traveling	24,191	84.1	1.14	1.35

Note: Primary activities are those respondents identified as their main activity. Other activities done simultaneously, such as eating while watching TV, are not included. Numbers may not add to total because not all categories are shown. Blacks are those who identify themselves as being of the race alone.
Source: Bureau of Labor Statistics, unpublished tables from the 2009 American Time Use Survey, Internet site http://www.bls .gov/tus/home.htm; calculations by New Strategist

Table 10.2 Time Use of Black Men, 2009

(number and percent of black men aged 15 or older participating in primary activities on an average day, hours spent doing activity by the average black man aged 15 or older and by black men aged 15 or older who participated in the activity, 2009; numbers of participants in thousands)

	black men participating		time spent doing activity (hours)	
	number	percent	average black man	black men participating
Total, all activities	**13,095**	**100.0%**	**24.00**	**24.00**
Personal care	13,075	99.8	9.86	9.87
Sleeping	13,013	99.4	9.10	9.16
Grooming	10,129	77.4	0.69	0.89
Household activities	8,608	65.7	1.05	1.59
Housework	2,940	22.5	0.30	1.35
Food preparation and cleanup	5,242	40.0	0.31	0.76
Household management	2,899	22.1	0.11	0.48
Caring for and helping household members	2,286	17.5	0.25	1.42
Caring for and helping household children	1,785	13.6	0.19	–
Work and work-related activities	5,234	40.0	3.01	7.54
Working	4,673	35.7	2.90	8.13
Education	817	6.2	0.35	–
Consumer purchases (store, telephone, Internet)	4,827	36.9	0.24	0.65
Eating and drinking	12,288	93.8	0.81	0.87
Socializing, relaxing, and leisure	12,509	95.5	5.94	6.22
Socializing and communicating	4,462	34.1	0.64	1.89
Watching television	11,115	84.9	3.97	4.68
Computer use for leisure (excluding games)	1,238	9.5	0.15	–
Reading for personal interest	1,471	11.2	0.11	0.97
Sports, exercise, recreation	2,658	20.3	0.40	1.97
Religious and spiritual activities	1,323	10.1	0.25	2.45
Volunteer activities	925	7.1	0.14	–
Telephone calls	2,009	15.3	0.15	0.96
Traveling	11,075	84.6	1.14	1.34

Note: Primary activities are those respondents identified as their main activity. Other activities done simultaneously, such as eating while watching TV, are not included. Numbers may not add to total because not all categories are shown. "–" means data are not available. Blacks are those who identify themselves as being of the race alone.
Source: Bureau of Labor Statistics, unpublished tables from the 2009 American Time Use Survey, Internet site http://www.bls .gov/tus/home.htm; calculations by New Strategist

Table 10.3 Time Use of Black Women, 2009

(number and percent of black women aged 15 or older participating in primary activities on an average day, hours spent doing activity by the average black woman aged 15 or older and by black women aged 15 or older who participated in the activity, 2009; numbers of participants in thousands)

	black women participating		time spent doing activity (hours)	
	number	percent	average black woman	black women participating
Total, all activities	**15,659**	**100.0%**	**24.00**	**24.00**
Personal care	15,659	100.0	9.93	9.93
Sleeping	15,659	100.0	8.87	8.87
Grooming	13,282	84.8	0.95	1.12
Household activities	12,238	78.2	1.44	1.84
Housework	5,843	37.3	0.60	1.60
Food preparation and cleanup	9,502	60.7	0.61	1.00
Household management	3,797	24.2	0.15	0.61
Caring for and helping household members	4,491	28.7	0.51	1.79
Caring for and helping household children	3,943	25.2	0.43	1.69
Work and work-related activities	6,463	41.3	2.88	6.97
Working	5,994	38.3	2.79	7.30
Education	1,531	9.8	0.48	4.86
Consumer purchases (store, telephone, Internet)	6,434	41.1	0.37	0.91
Eating and drinking	14,692	93.8	0.86	0.91
Socializing, relaxing, and leisure	14,931	95.4	5.13	5.38
Socializing and communicating	6,272	40.1	0.71	1.77
Watching television	12,956	82.7	3.39	4.10
Computer use for leisure (excluding games)	1,165	7.4	0.12	1.64
Reading for personal interest	2,171	13.9	0.16	1.16
Sports, exercise, recreation	1,625	10.4	0.16	1.56
Religious and spiritual activities	2,405	15.4	0.31	1.99
Volunteer activities	742	4.7	0.13	2.73
Telephone calls	3,609	23.0	0.23	0.98
Traveling	13,116	83.8	1.14	1.36

Note: Primary activities are those respondents identified as their main activity. Other activities done simultaneously, such as eating while watching TV, are not included. Numbers may not add to total because not all categories are shown. "–" means data are not available. Blacks are those who identify themselves as being of the race alone.
Source: Bureau of Labor Statistics, unpublished tables from the 2009 American Time Use Survey, Internet site http://www.bls .gov/tus/home.htm; calculations by New Strategist

Blacks Spend More Time Participating in Religious Activities

Black women spend the most time in religious activities.

Black time use is close to the average for most activities. They spend more time doing a few activities however. The biggest difference is in the amount of time devoted to religious activities. On an average day, blacks spend 87 percent more time than the average person engaged in religious activities. They spend 30 percent more time watching television and 73 percent more time on the telephone.

Black men spend 28 percent more time grooming than the average man and 28 percent more time watching television. Black women spend more time than the average woman working. They spend 20 percent more time grooming and 32 percent more time watching television.

■ Black women spend more than twice as much time as black men doing housework and caring for household children.

Black women spend more time reading than black men

(index of black women to black men in time spent doing selected primary activities on an average day, 2009)

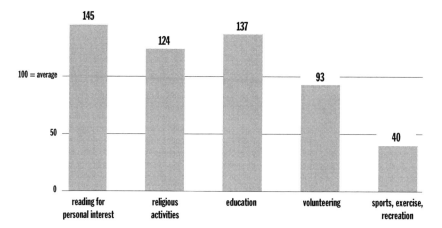

Table 10.4 Indexed Time Use of Total Blacks, 2009

(hours spent doing primary activities on an average day by total people and blacks aged 15 or older, and index of time spent by blacks to total people, 2009)

	average hours		index, blacks to total people
	total	blacks	
Total, all activities	**24.00**	**24.00**	**100**
Personal care	9.43	9.90	105
Sleeping	8.67	8.97	103
Grooming	0.67	0.83	124
Household activities	1.83	1.26	69
Housework	0.60	0.46	77
Food preparation and cleanup	0.54	0.47	87
Household management	0.21	0.13	62
Caring for and helping household members	0.46	0.39	85
Caring for and helping household children	0.38	0.32	84
Work and work-related activities	3.25	2.94	90
Working	3.18	2.84	89
Education	0.44	0.42	95
Consumer purchases (store, telephone, Internet)	0.38	0.31	82
Eating and drinking	1.11	0.84	76
Socializing, relaxing, and leisure	4.69	5.50	117
Socializing and communicating	0.63	0.68	108
Watching television	2.82	3.66	130
Computer use for leisure (excluding games)	0.16	0.13	81
Reading for personal interest	0.34	0.14	41
Sports, exercise, recreation	0.33	0.27	82
Religious and spiritual activities	0.15	0.28	187
Volunteer activities	0.15	0.13	87
Telephone calls	0.11	0.19	173
Traveling	1.20	1.14	95

Note: The index is calculated by dividing the average time spent by blacks doing primary activity by average time spent by total people doing primary activity and multiplying by 100. Primary activities are those respondents identified as their main activity. Other activities done simultaneously, such as eating while watching TV, are not included. Numbers may not add to total because not all subcategories are shown. Blacks are those who identify themselves as being of the race alone.
Source: Bureau of Labor Statistics, unpublished tables from the 2009 American Time Use Survey, Internet site http://www.bls .gov/tus/home.htm; calculations by New Strategist

Table 10.5 Indexed Time Use of Black Men, 2009

(hours spent doing primary activities on an average day by total and black men aged 15 or older, and index of time spent by black men to total men, 2009)

	average hours		index, black men to total men
	total men	black men	
Total, all activities	**24.00**	**24.00**	**100**
Personal care	9.24	9.86	107
Sleeping	8.62	9.10	106
Grooming	0.54	0.69	128
Household activities	1.35	1.05	78
Housework	0.26	0.30	115
Food preparation and cleanup	0.29	0.31	107
Household management	0.21	0.11	52
Caring for and helping household members	0.31	0.25	81
Caring for and helping household children	0.26	0.19	73
Work and work-related activities	3.90	3.01	77
Working	3.81	2.90	76
Education	0.40	0.35	88
Consumer purchases (store, telephone, Internet)	0.30	0.24	80
Eating and drinking	1.13	0.81	72
Socializing, relaxing, and leisure	4.91	5.94	121
Socializing and communicating	0.56	0.64	114
Watching television	3.09	3.97	128
Computer use for leisure (excluding games)	0.20	0.15	75
Reading for personal interest	0.27	0.11	41
Sports, exercise, recreation	0.44	0.40	91
Religious and spiritual activities	0.12	0.25	208
Volunteer activities	0.15	0.14	93
Telephone calls	0.07	0.15	214
Traveling	1.24	1.14	92

Note: The index is calculated by dividing the average time spent by black men doing primary activity by average time spent by total men doing primary activity and multiplying by 100. Primary activities are those respondents identified as their main activity. Other activities done simultaneously, such as eating while watching TV, are not included. Numbers may not add to total because not all subcategories are shown. Blacks are those who identify themselves as being of the race alone.
Source: Bureau of Labor Statistics, unpublished tables from the 2009 American Time Use Survey, Internet site http://www.bls .gov/tus/home.htm; calculations by New Strategist

Table 10.6 Indexed Time Use of Black Women, 2009

(hours spent doing primary activities on an average day by total and black women aged 15 or older, and index of time spent by black women to total women, 2009)

	average hours		index, black women
	total women	black women	to total women
Total, all activities	**24.00**	**24.00**	**100**
Personal care	9.61	9.93	103
Sleeping	8.73	8.87	102
Grooming	0.79	0.95	120
Household activities	2.28	1.44	63
Housework	0.92	0.60	65
Food preparation and cleanup	0.77	0.61	79
Household management	0.25	0.15	60
Caring for and helping household members	0.60	0.51	85
Caring for and helping household children	0.50	0.43	86
Work and work-related activities	2.65	2.88	109
Working	2.58	2.79	108
Education	0.47	0.48	102
Consumer purchases (store, telephone, Internet)	0.46	0.37	80
Eating and drinking	1.08	0.86	80
Socializing, relaxing, and leisure	4.48	5.13	115
Socializing and communicating	0.69	0.71	103
Watching television	2.56	3.39	132
Computer use for leisure (excluding games)	0.13	0.12	92
Reading for personal interest	0.42	0.16	38
Sports, exercise, recreation	0.23	0.16	70
Religious and spiritual activities	0.17	0.31	182
Volunteer activities	0.15	0.13	87
Telephone calls	0.15	0.23	153
Traveling	1.17	1.14	97

Note: The index is calculated by dividing the average time spent by black women doing primary activity by average time spent by total women doing primary activity and multiplying by 100. Primary activities are those respondents identified as their main activity. Other activities done simultaneously, such as eating while watching TV, are not included. Numbers may not add to total because not all subcategories are shown. Blacks are those who identify themselves as being of the race alone.
Source: Bureau of Labor Statistics, unpublished tables from the 2009 American Time Use Survey, Internet site http://www.bls .gov/tus/home.htm; calculations by New Strategist

Table 10.7 Indexed Time Use of Blacks by Sex, 2009

(average hours spent by blacks aged 15 or older doing primary activities on an average day by sex, and index of black women's time to black men's, 2009)

	blacks aged 15 or older, average hours		index of women to men
	black men	black women	
Total, all activities	**24.00**	**24.00**	**100**
Personal care	9.86	9.93	101
Sleeping	9.10	8.87	97
Grooming	0.69	0.95	138
Household activities	1.05	1.44	137
Housework	0.30	0.60	200
Food preparation and cleanup	0.31	0.61	197
Household management	0.11	0.15	136
Caring for and helping household members	0.25	0.51	204
Caring for and helping household children	0.19	0.43	226
Work and work-related activities	3.01	2.88	96
Working	2.90	2.79	96
Education	0.35	0.48	137
Consumer purchases (store, telephone, Internet)	0.24	0.37	154
Eating and drinking	0.81	0.86	106
Socializing, relaxing, and leisure	5.94	5.13	86
Socializing and communicating	0.64	0.71	111
Watching television	3.97	3.39	85
Computer use for leisure (excluding games)	0.15	0.12	80
Reading for personal interest	0.11	0.16	145
Sports, exercise, recreation	0.40	0.16	40
Religious and spiritual activities	0.25	0.31	124
Volunteer activities	0.14	0.13	93
Telephone calls	0.15	0.23	153
Traveling	1.14	1.14	100

Note: The index is calculated by dividing women's time by men's and multiplying by 100. Primary activities are those respondents identified as their main activity. Other activities done simultaneously, such as eating while watching TV, are not included. Numbers may not add to total because not all subcategories are shown. Blacks are those who identify themselves as being of the race alone.
Source: Bureau of Labor Statistics, unpublished tables from the 2009 American Time Use Survey, Internet site http://www.bls .gov/tus/home.htm; calculations by New Strategist

Blacks Spend More Time on the Phone

The percentage of blacks who watch television is close to the average.

Black participation in some activities is below average. Only 8 percent of blacks spend leisure time using a computer on an average day compared with 11 percent of all Americans aged 15 or older. Blacks are 21 percent less likely than the average person to participate in sports and exercise. They are much more likely to participate in religious activities. On an average day, 13 percent of blacks participate in religious or spiritual activities. Twenty percent of blacks are on the telephone as a primary activity on an average day versus 15 percent of all Americans.

Black men's participation in most activities is close to that of the average man, but their participation in religious activities is 45 percent above average. Black women are 10 percent more likely than the average woman to participate in educational activities and 42 percent more likely to participate in religious activities. They are much less likely than the average woman to read for personal interest.

■ Thirty-seven percent of black women and 22 percent of black men participate in housework on an average day.

Black participation is close to the average for most activities

(index of black to total people aged 15 or older who participated in selected primary activities on an average day, 2009)

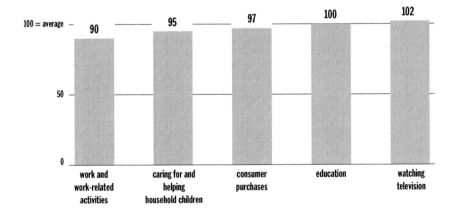

Table 10.8 Indexed Participation in Primary Activities: Total Blacks, 2009

(percent of total people and blacks aged 15 or older participating in primary activities on an average day, and index of participation by blacks to total people, 2009)

	percent participating		index, blacks
	total	blacks	to total people
Total, all activities	**100.0%**	**100.0%**	**100**
Personal care	100.0	99.9	100
Sleeping	99.9	99.7	100
Grooming	78.4	81.4	104
Household activities	78.2	72.5	93
Housework	36.3	30.5	84
Food preparation and cleanup	54.6	51.3	94
Household management	28.9	23.3	81
Caring for and helping household members	25.2	23.6	94
Caring for and helping household children	21.1	19.9	95
Work and work-related activities	45.3	40.7	90
Working	42.7	37.1	87
Education	8.2	8.2	100
Consumer purchases (store, telephone, Internet)	40.2	39.2	97
Eating and drinking	96.4	93.8	97
Socializing, relaxing, and leisure	95.1	95.4	100
Socializing and communicating	37.7	37.3	99
Watching television	81.8	83.7	102
Computer use for leisure (excluding games)	10.9	8.4	76
Reading for personal interest	24.2	12.7	52
Sports, exercise, recreation	18.9	14.9	79
Religious and spiritual activities	9.0	13.0	145
Volunteer activities	7.0	5.8	82
Telephone calls	15.4	19.5	127
Traveling	87.0	84.1	97

Note: The index is calculated by dividing percent of blacks doing primary activity by percent of total people doing primary activity and multiplying by 100. Primary activities are those respondents identified as their main activity. Other activities done simultaneously, such as eating while watching TV, are not included. Blacks are those who identify themselves as being of the race alone.
Source: Bureau of Labor Statistics, unpublished tables from the 2009 American Time Use Survey, Internet site http://www.bls.gov/tus/home.htm; calculations by New Strategist

Table 10.9 Indexed Participation in Primary Activities: Black Men, 2009

(percent of total and black men aged 15 or older participating in primary activities on an average day, and index of participation by black men to total men, 2009)

	percent participating		index, black men to total men
	total men	black men	
Total, all activities	**100.0%**	**100.0%**	**100**
Personal care	100.0	99.8	100
Sleeping	99.8	99.4	100
Grooming	74.6	77.4	104
Household activities	69.0	65.7	95
Housework	20.2	22.5	111
Food preparation and cleanup	39.9	40.0	100
Household management	25.1	22.1	88
Caring for and helping household members	20.2	17.5	86
Caring for and helping household children	15.9	13.6	86
Work and work-related activities	51.8	40.0	77
Working	48.4	35.7	74
Education	7.4	6.2	85
Consumer purchases (store, telephone, Internet)	35.8	36.9	103
Eating and drinking	96.1	93.8	98
Socializing, relaxing, and leisure	94.6	95.5	101
Socializing and communicating	33.4	34.1	102
Watching television	82.7	84.9	103
Computer use for leisure (excluding games)	11.9	9.5	79
Reading for personal interest	20.8	11.2	54
Sports, exercise, recreation	21.7	20.3	94
Religious and spiritual activities	7.0	10.1	145
Volunteer activities	7.0	7.1	101
Telephone calls	10.4	15.3	148
Traveling	88.4	84.6	96

Note: The index is calculated by dividing percent of black men doing primary activity by percent of total men doing primary activity and multiplying by 100. Primary activities are those respondents identified as their main activity. Other activities done simultaneously, such as eating while watching TV, are not included. Blacks are those who identify themselves as being of the race alone.
Source: Bureau of Labor Statistics, unpublished tables from the 2009 American Time Use Survey, Internet site http://www.bls .gov/tus/home.htm; calculations by New Strategist

Table 10.10 Indexed Participation in Primary Activities: Black Women, 2009

(percent of total and black women aged 15 or older participating in primary activities on an average day, and index of participation by black women to total women, 2009)

	percent participating		index, black women
	total women	black women	to total women
Total, all activities	**100.0%**	**100.0%**	**100**
Personal care	100.0	100.0	100
Sleeping	100.0	100.0	100
Grooming	82.1	84.8	103
Household activities	86.7	78.2	90
Housework	51.3	37.3	73
Food preparation and cleanup	68.3	60.7	89
Household management	32.5	24.2	75
Caring for and helping household members	29.9	28.7	96
Caring for and helping household children	25.9	25.2	97
Work and work-related activities	39.2	41.3	105
Working	37.3	38.3	103
Education	8.9	9.8	110
Consumer purchases (store, telephone, Internet)	44.4	41.1	93
Eating and drinking	96.7	93.8	97
Socializing, relaxing, and leisure	95.6	95.4	100
Socializing and communicating	41.8	40.1	96
Watching television	80.9	82.7	102
Computer use for leisure (excluding games)	10.1	7.4	74
Reading for personal interest	27.3	13.9	51
Sports, exercise, recreation	16.3	10.4	64
Religious and spiritual activities	10.8	15.4	142
Volunteer activities	7.1	4.7	67
Telephone calls	20.0	23.0	115
Traveling	85.6	83.8	98

Note: The index is calculated by dividing percent of black women doing primary activity by percent of total women doing primary activity and multiplying by 100. Primary activities are those respondents identified as their main activity. Other activities done simultaneously, such as eating while watching TV, are not included. Blacks are those who identify themselves as being of the race alone.
Source: Bureau of Labor Statistics, unpublished tables from the 2009 American Time Use Survey, Internet site http://www.bls .gov/tus/home.htm; calculations by New Strategist

Table 10.11 Indexed Participation in Primary Activities: Blacks by Sex, 2009

(percent of blacks aged 15 or older participating in primary activities on an average day by sex, and index of women's participation to men's, 2009)

	blacks aged 15 or older, percent participating		index of women to men
	men	women	
Total, all activities	**100.0%**	**100.0%**	**100**
Personal care	99.8	100.0	100
Sleeping	99.4	100.0	101
Grooming	77.4	84.8	110
Household activities	65.7	78.2	119
Housework	22.5	37.3	166
Food preparation and cleanup	40.0	60.7	152
Household management	22.1	24.2	110
Caring for and helping household members	17.5	28.7	164
Caring for and helping household children	13.6	25.2	185
Work and work-related activities	40.0	41.3	103
Working	35.7	38.3	107
Education	6.2	9.8	157
Consumer purchases (store, telephone, Internet)	36.9	41.1	111
Eating and drinking	93.8	93.8	100
Socializing, relaxing, and leisure	95.5	95.4	100
Socializing and communicating	34.1	40.1	118
Watching television	84.9	82.7	97
Computer use for leisure (excluding games)	9.5	7.4	79
Reading for personal interest	11.2	13.9	123
Sports, exercise, recreation	20.3	10.4	51
Religious and spiritual activities	10.1	15.4	152
Volunteer activities	7.1	4.7	67
Telephone calls	15.3	23.0	150
Traveling	84.6	83.8	99

Note: The index is calculated by dividing percent of women participating in primary activity by percent of men participating in primary activity and multiplying by 100. Primary activities are those respondents identified as their main activity. Other activities done simultaneously, such as eating while watching TV, are not included. Blacks are those who identify themselves as being of the race alone.
Source: Bureau of Labor Statistics, unpublished tables from the 2009 American Time Use Survey, Internet site http://www.bls.gov/tus/home.htm; calculations by New Strategist

11

Wealth

■ Between 2007 and 2009, the median net worth of nonwhite or Hispanic households fell by a substantial 29 percent after adjusting for inflation, to $23,300.

■ Eighty-nine percent of nonwhite or Hispanic households owned financial assets in 2009, which include checking and savings accounts, stocks, and retirement accounts.

■ The median value of the financial assets owned by nonwhite or Hispanic households fell 17 percent between 2007 and 2009 after adjusting for inflation, to $8,500.

■ Eighty-six percent of nonwhite or Hispanic households owned nonfinancial assets in 2009, which include vehicles, houses, and businesses.

■ The median value of the nonfinancial assets owned by nonwhite or Hispanic households fell 10 percent between 2007 and 2009 after adjusting for inflation, to $90,200.

■ Eighty percent of nonwhite or Hispanic households had debts in 2009, owing a median of $44,000. This was 3 percent less than they owed in 2007, after adjusting for inflation.

■ Social Security is the major source of income for blacks aged 65 or older, 85 percent of whom receive Social Security income.

Blacks Have Little Wealth

Their net worth fell sharply during the Great Recession.

The median net worth (assets minus debts) of nonwhite or Hispanic households amounted to just $23,300 in 2009. This figure was far below the $96,000 net worth of the average American household. (Note: The Federal Reserve collects wealth data for only two racial and ethnic categories: non-Hispanic whites and nonwhites or Hispanics. The nonwhite or Hispanic category includes primarily blacks and Hispanics, but also Asians and American Indians.)

On every measure of wealth, nonwhites or Hispanics have less than the average household. Their median financial assets are just 29 percent as high as the average, and their median nonfinancial assets are only 44 percent of the average. Fortunately for them, their median debts are also lower, amounting to 58 percent of the average.

Between 2007 and 2009, the net worth of nonwhite or Hispanic households fell by a substantial 29 percent, after adjusting for inflation. This loss was much greater than the 16 percent decline in net worth experienced by non-Hispanic white households during those years.

■ The net worth of nonwhite or Hispanic households is below average largely because blacks and Hispanics are less likely than the average household to own a home.

The net worth of blacks is well below average

(median net worth of total and nonwhite or Hispanic households, 2009)

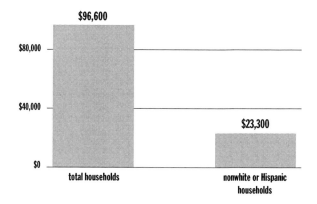

Table 11.1 Net Worth, Assets, and Debt of Total and Nonwhite or Hispanic Households, 2009

(median net worth, median value of assets for owners, and median amount of debt for debtors, for total and non-white or Hispanic households, and index of nonwhite or Hispanic to total, 2009)

	total households	nonwhite or Hispanic households	
		median	index
Median net worth	$96,000	$23,300	24
Median value of financial assets	29,600	8,500	29
Median value of nonfinancial assets	204,000	90,200	44
Median amount of debt	75,600	44,000	58

Note: The index is calculated by dividing the nonwhite or Hispanic figure by the total figure and multiplying by 100.
Source: Federal Reserve Board, Surveying the Aftermath of the Storm: Changes in Family Finances from 2007 to 2009, Jesse Bricker, Brian Bucks, Arthur Kennickell, Traci Mach, and Kevin Moore, Finance and Economics Discussion Series, 2011-17, Appendix tables, Internet site http://www.federalreserve.gov/pubs/oss/oss2/2009p/scf2009phome.html; calculations by New Strategist

Table 11.2 Net Worth of Households by Race and Hispanic Origin, 2007 and 2009

(median net worth of households by race and Hispanic origin of householder, 2007 and 2009; percent change, 2007–09; in 2009 dollars)

	2009	2007	percent change
Total households	**$96,000**	**$125,400**	**–23.4%**
Non-Hispanic white	149,900	178,800	–16.2
Nonwhite or Hispanic	23,300	32,800	–29.0

Source: Federal Reserve Board, Surveying the Aftermath of the Storm: Changes in Family Finances from 2007 to 2009, Jesse Bricker, Brian Bucks, Arthur Kennickell, Traci Mach, and Kevin Moore, Finance and Economics Discussion Series, 2011-17, Appendix tables, Internet site http://www.federalreserve.gov/pubs/oss/oss2/2009p/scf2009phome.html; calculations by New Strategist

Most Nonwhite Households Have Financial Assets

The median value of the financial assets owned by nonwhite or Hispanic households fell sharply between 2007 and 2009.

In 2009, 95 percent of all households owned financial assets, which include checking and savings accounts, stocks, and retirement accounts. Among non-Hispanic white households, the ownership rate was a nearly universal 97 percent. Among nonwhite or Hispanic households, the figure was a smaller 89 percent.

The median value of financial assets fell between 2007 and 2009 because of the Great Recession and the decline in the stock market. Non-Hispanic white households experienced a 5 percent loss in the value of their financial assets during those years, while the drop for nonwhite or Hispanic households was a much larger 17 percent, after adjusting for inflation. In 2009, the median value of the financial assets owned by nonwhite or Hispanic households was just $8,500, down from $10,200 in 2007.

A transaction account (checking and savings) is the most widely owned financial asset among nonwhite or Hispanic households, 85 percent having such an account. The median value of the transaction accounts owned by nonwhites or Hispanics was just $1,800. Forty-two percent of nonwhite or Hispanic households own a retirement account. The median value of their retirement accounts was $26,000 in 2009—12 percent less than their value in 2007. Twenty-one percent of nonwhite or Hispanic households own a life insurance policy with a median cash value of $5,000.

■ The retirement accounts of nonwhite and Hispanic households were hit hard by the Great Recession.

Only three types of financial assets are owned by more than 10 percent of nonwhite or Hispanic households

(percent of nonwhite or Hispanic households that own selected financial assets, 2009)

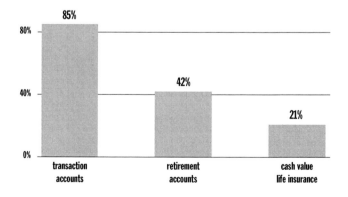

Table 11.3 Ownership and Value of Financial Assets by Race and Hispanic Origin, 2007 and 2009

(percentage of households that own any financial asset and median value of financial assets for owners, by race and Hispanic origin of householder, 2007 and 2009; percentage point change in ownership and percent change in value, 2007–09; in 2009 dollars)

	percent owning any financial asset			median value of financial assets		
	2009	2007	percentage point change	2009	2007	percent change
Total households	**94.6%**	**94.3%**	**0.3**	**$29,600**	**$31,300**	**−5.4%**
Non-Hispanic white	96.9	97.3	−0.4	47,700	50,100	−4.8
Nonwhite or Hispanic	89.2	87.3	1.9	8,500	10,200	−16.7

Source: Federal Reserve Board, Surveying the Aftermath of the Storm: Changes in Family Finances from 2007 to 2009, Jesse Bricker, Brian Bucks, Arthur Kennickell, Traci Mach, and Kevin Moore, Finance and Economics Discussion Series, 2011-17, Appendix tables, Internet site http://www.federalreserve.gov/pubs/oss/oss2/2009p/scf2009phome.html; calculations by New Strategist

Table 11.4 Financial Assets of Nonwhite or Hispanic Households, 2007 and 2009

(percent of nonwhite or Hispanic households that own financial assets, and median value of assets for owners, 2007 and 2009, percentage point change in ownership and percent change in value, 2007–09; in 2009 dollars)

	percent owning financial asset			median value of financial asset		
	2009	2007	percentage point change	2009	2007	percent change
Any financial asset	**89.2%**	**87.3%**	**1.9**	**$8,500**	**$10,200**	**−16.7%**
Transaction accounts	84.9	84.7	0.2	1,800	2,100	−14.3
Retirement accounts	42.3	41.5	0.8	26,000	29,500	−11.9
Life insurance (cash value)	20.8	18.1	2.7	5,000	5,200	−3.8
Stocks	9.1	9.7	−0.6	5,500	7,100	−22.5
Savings bonds	8.2	8.1	0.1	500	900	−44.4
Certificates of deposit	7.4	7.7	−0.3	11,300	10,400	8.7
Pooled investment funds (mutual funds)	5.4	5.8	−0.4	20,000	30,800	−35.1
Bonds	0.8	0.4	0.4	25,000	18,300	36.6

Note: Pooled investment funds exclude money market funds and indirectly held mutual funds. They include open-end and closed-end mutual funds, real estate investment trusts, and hedge funds.
Source: Federal Reserve Board, Surveying the Aftermath of the Storm: Changes in Family Finances from 2007 to 2009, Jesse Bricker, Brian Bucks, Arthur Kennickell, Traci Mach, and Kevin Moore, Finance and Economics Discussion Series, 2011-17, Appendix tables, Internet site http://www.federalreserve.gov/pubs/oss/oss2/2009p/scf2009phome.html; calculations by New Strategist

Most Nonwhite Households Own Nonfinancial Assets

Vehicles are the most commonly owned nonfinancial asset.

Most households own nonfinancial assets, with 95 percent of non-Hispanic white households and 86 percent of nonwhite or Hispanic households owning homes, cars, businesses, or other nonfinancial assets. The median value of the nonfinancial assets owned by nonwhite or Hispanic households was $90,200 in 2009, well below the $204,000 median for all households. Between 2007 and 2009, the median value of the nonfinancial assets owned by nonwhite or Hispanic households fell 10 percent, after adjusting for inflation. This decline was nearly identical to the one experienced by non-Hispanic white households.

Vehicles are the most commonly owned nonfinancial asset regardless of race or Hispanic origin. Eighty percent of nonwhite or Hispanic households own a vehicle. The median value of their vehicles plunged between 2007 and 2009, largely because households held on to their aging cars and trucks rather than upgrade during the Great Recession. Fifty-four percent of nonwhites or Hispanics owned a home in 2009. The median value of their homes was $150,000 in 2009—20 percent less than the $186,400 of 2007.

■ Because nonwhite or Hispanic households are less likely than non-Hispanic white households to own a home, their net worth is lower.

The median value of the nonfinancial assets owned by nonwhite households is below average

(median value of nonfinancial assets for total households and nonwhite or Hispanic households, 2009)

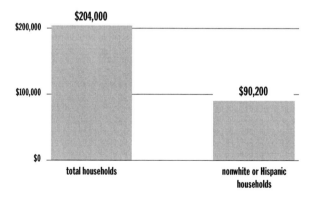

Table 11.5 Ownership and Value of Nonfinancial Assets by Race and Hispanic Origin, 2007 and 2009

(percentage of households that own any nonfinancial asset and median value of nonfinancial assets for owners, by race and Hispanic origin of householder, 2007 and 2009; percentage point change in ownership and percent change in value, 2007–09; in 2009 dollars)

	percent owning any nonfinancial asset			median value of nonfinancial assets		
	2009	2007	percentage point change	2009	2007	percent change
Total households	**92.6%**	**92.7%**	**–0.1**	**$204,000**	**$234,800**	**–13.1%**
Non-Hispanic white	95.4	95.1	0.3	259,800	287,700	–9.7
Nonwhite or Hispanic	86.0	86.9	–0.9	90,200	100,200	–10.0

Source: Federal Reserve Board, Surveying the Aftermath of the Storm: Changes in Family Finances from 2007 to 2009, Jesse Bricker, Brian Bucks, Arthur Kennickell, Traci Mach, and Kevin Moore, Finance and Economics Discussion Series, 2011-17, Appendix tables, Internet site http://www.federalreserve.gov/pubs/oss/oss2/2009p/scf2009phome.html; calculations by New Strategist

Table 11.6 Nonfinancial Assets of Nonwhite or Hispanic Households, 2007 and 2009

(percent of nonwhite or Hispanic households that own nonfinancial assets, and median value of assets for owners, 2007 and 2009, percentage point change in ownership and percent change in value, 2007–09; in 2009 dollars)

	percent owning nonfinancial asset			median value of nonfinancial asset		
	2009	2007	percentage point change	2009	2007	percent change
Any nonfinancial asset	**86.0%**	**86.9%**	**–0.9**	**$90,200**	**$100,200**	**–10.0%**
Vehicles	79.5	82.3	–2.8	9,000	12,400	–27.4
Primary residence	54.0	52.7	1.3	150,000	186,400	–19.5
Other residential property	8.3	9.7	–1.4	130,000	170,900	–23.9
Business equity	7.5	7.8	–0.3	46,700	73,300	–36.3
Nonresidential property	5.2	5.7	–0.5	45,000	67,300	–33.1

Source: Federal Reserve Board, Surveying the Aftermath of the Storm: Changes in Family Finances from 2007 to 2009, Jesse Bricker, Brian Bucks, Arthur Kennickell, Traci Mach, and Kevin Moore, Finance and Economics Discussion Series, 2011-17, Appendix tables, Internet site http://www.federalreserve.gov/pubs/oss/oss2/2009p/scf2009phome.html; calculations by New Strategist

Debt Is Falling among Nonwhite Households

Fewer have credit card debt.

Between 2007 and 2009 median debt for all households climbed to $75,600, an 8 percent increase after adjusting for inflation. The median debt of households headed by nonwhites or Hispanics is lower, at $44,000, and the amount owed declined by 3 percent during those years. Eighty percent of nonwhite or Hispanic households are in debt, slightly above the all-household average.

Credit card debt is the most common type of debt for nonwhite or Hispanic households. Forty-six percent carried a balance on their credit cards, although the median amount owed was just $2,000. Thirty-nine percent of nonwhite or Hispanic households had mortgage debt, owing a median of $120,000. Thirty-two percent had vehicle loans, and 22 percent had education loans. The median amount nonwhite or Hispanic households owe on education loans climbed by an enormous 45 percent between 2007 and 2009, after adjusting for inflation.

■ Because nonwhite families have little wealth, many must take out education loans to go to college.

Nonwhite households saw their education debt increase between 2007 and 2009

(median amount owed for education loans by nonwhite or Hispanic households with education debt, 2007 and 2009; in 2009 dollars)

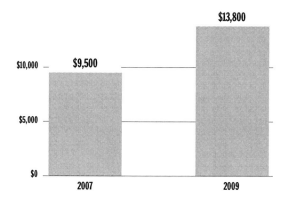

Table 11.7 Debt of Households by Race and Hispanic Origin, 2007 and 2009

(percentage of households with debts and median amount of debt for debtors, by race and Hispanic origin of householder, 2007 and 2009; percentage point change in households with debt and percent change in amount of debt, 2007–09; in 2009 dollars)

	percent with debt			median amount of debt		
	2009	2007	percentage point change	2009	2007	percent change
Total households	**77.5%**	**79.7%**	**−2.2**	**$75,600**	**$70,300**	**7.5%**
Non-Hispanic white	76.5	79.7	−3.2	89,000	82,800	7.5
Nonwhite or Hispanic	79.7	79.6	0.1	44,000	45,300	−2.9

Source: Federal Reserve Board, Surveying the Aftermath of the Storm: Changes in Family Finances from 2007 to 2009, Jesse Bricker, Brian Bucks, Arthur Kennickell, Traci Mach, and Kevin Moore, Finance and Economics Discussion Series, 2011-17, Appendix tables, Internet site http://www.federalreserve.gov/pubs/oss/oss2/2009p/scf2009phome.html; calculations by New Strategist

Table 11.8 Debt of Nonwhite or Hispanic Households, 2007 and 2009

(percentage of households with debts and median amount of debt for debtors, by race and Hispanic origin of householder, 2007 and 2009; percentage point change in households with debt and percent change in amount of debt, 2007–09; in 2009 dollars)

	percent with debt			median amount of debt		
	2009	2007	percentage point change	2009	2007	percent change
Any debt	**79.7%**	**79.6%**	**0.1**	**$44,000**	**$45,300**	**−2.9%**
Credit card balance	45.5	50.3	−4.8	2,000	2,100	−4.8
Mortgage on primary residence	39.3	39.9	−0.6	120,000	119,100	0.8
Vehicle loans	32.1	34.6	−2.5	12,000	10,500	14.3
Education loans	21.9	18.7	3.2	13,800	9,500	45.3
Home equity line of credit loan	6.4	5.4	1.0	30,000	25,900	15.8
Other residential debt	3.9	4.8	−0.9	150,000	103,600	44.8

Source: Federal Reserve Board, Surveying the Aftermath of the Storm: Changes in Family Finances from 2007 to 2009, Jesse Bricker, Brian Bucks, Arthur Kennickell, Traci Mach, and Kevin Moore, Finance and Economics Discussion Series, 2011-17, Appendix tables, Internet site http://www.federalreserve.gov/pubs/oss/oss2/2009p/scf2009phome.html; calculations by New Strategist

Older Blacks Depend on Social Security

Some older blacks are still in the labor force.

Social Security is the major source of income for blacks age 65 or older. Eighty-five percent of older blacks receive Social Security. Among those who do, the median amount received in 2009 was $11,260.

Thirty-one percent of older blacks receive retirement income, and those with retirement income got a median of $11,985 from this source. Twenty-eight percent have pensions, receiving a median of $11,975. Twenty-five percent of blacks aged 65 or older receive interest income, but the median amount received was just $1,499 in 2009. Seventeen percent of older blacks supplement their Social Security and retirement income by working. Their median earnings were $21,025, a larger amount than they receive from any other source.

■ Without Social Security income, many older Americans would be living in poverty.

One in six blacks aged 65 or older has income from earnings

(percent of blacks aged 65 or older with income from selected sources, 2009)

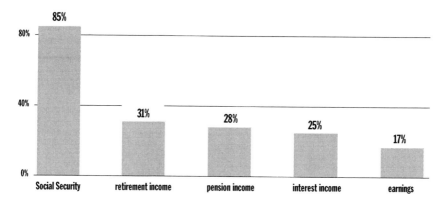

Table 11.9 Sources of Income for Blacks Aged 65 or Older, 2009

(number and percent of blacks aged 65 or older with income from selected sources and median income for those with income, ranked by number receiving income, 2009; people in thousands as of 2010)

	number with income	percent with income	median amount received by those with income
Blacks aged 65 or older with income	**3,214**	**100.0%**	**$14,660**
Social Security	2,744	85.4	11,260
Retirement income	983	30.6	11,985
Pension income	890	27.7	11,975
Interest	802	25.0	1,499
Earnings	550	17.1	21,025
Supplemental Security Income	242	7.5	4,583
Dividends	156	4.9	1,952
Rents, royalties, estates, or trusts	112	3.5	2,146
Survivor's benefits	119	3.7	8,426
Veteran's benefits	96	3.0	9,531

Note: Blacks are those who identify themselves as being black alone and those who identify themselves as being black in combi-nation with other races.
Source: Bureau of the Census, 2010 Current Population Survey, Internet site http://www.census.gov/hhes/www/cpstables/032010/perinc/new08_068.htm; calculations by New Strategist

Glossary

adjusted for inflation Income or a change in income that has been adjusted for the rise in the cost of living, or the consumer price index (CPI-U-RS).

American Community Survey An on-going nationwide survey of 250,000 households per month, providing detailed demographic data at the community level. Designed to replace the census long-form questionnaire, the ACS includes more than 60 questions that formerly appeared on the long form, such as language spoken at home, income, and education. ACS data are available for areas as small as census tracts.

American Housing Survey The AHS collects national and metropolitan-level data on the nation's housing, including apartments, single-family homes, and mobile homes. The nationally representative survey, with a sample of 60,000 homes, is conducted by the Census Bureau for the Department of Housing and Urban Development every other year.

American Indians Include Alaska Natives (Eskimos and Aleuts) unless those groups are shown separately.

American Time Use Survey Under contract with the Bureau of Labor Statistics, the Census Bureau collects ATUS information, revealing how people spend their time. The ATUS sample is drawn from U.S. households completing their final month of interviews for the Current Population Survey. One individual from each selected household is chosen to participate in ATUS. Respondents are interviewed by telephone about their time use during the previous 24 hours. About 40,000 households are included in the sample each year.

Asian Beginning with the 2000 census and in 2003 for government surveys, Asians can identify themselves as being Asian and no other race (called "Asian alone") or as being Asian in combination with one or more other races (called "Asian in combination"). The combination of the two groups is termed "Asian alone or in combination." In this book, the "Asian alone or in combination" population is shown whenever possible.

average hours per day On the time use tables, the average number of hours spent in a 24-hour day (between 4 a.m. on the diary day and 4 a.m. on the interview day) doing a specified activity. Estimates are adjusted for variability in response rates across days of the week. Average hours per day are shown in decimals. To convert decimal portions of an hour into minutes, multiply 60 by the decimal. For example, if the average is 1.2 hours, multiply 60 by 0.2 to get 12 minutes, so the average is 1 hour and 12 minutes. If the average is 0.05 hours, multiply 60 by .05 to get 3 minutes.

If the average is 5.36 hours, multiply 60 by 0.36 to get 21.6, so the average is 5 hours and about 22 minutes.

baby boom U.S. residents born between 1946 and 1964.

baby bust U.S. residents born between 1965 and 1976, also known as Generation X.

Behavioral Risk Factor Surveillance System A collaborative project of the Centers for Disease Control and Prevention and U.S. states and territories. It is an ongoing data collection program designed to measure behavioral risk factors in the adult population aged 18 or older. All 50 states, three territories, and the District of Columbia take part in the survey, making the BRFSS the primary source of information on the health-related behaviors of Americans.

black Beginning with the 2000 census and in 2003 for government surveys, blacks can identify themselves as being black and no other race (called "black alone") or as being black in combination with one or more other races (called "black in combination"). The combination of the two groups is termed "black alone or in combination." In this book, the "black alone or in combination" population is shown whenever possible.

Consumer Expenditure Survey An ongoing study of the day-to-day spending of American households administered by the Bureau of Labor Statistics. The CEX includes an interview survey and a diary survey. The average spending figures shown are the integrated data from both the diary and interview components of the survey. Two separate, nationally representative samples are used for the interview and diary surveys. For the interview survey, about 7,500 consumer units are interviewed on a rotating panel basis each quarter for five consecutive quarters. For the diary survey, 7,500 consumer units keep weekly diaries of spending for two consecutive weeks.

consumer unit *(on spending tables only)* For convenience, the term consumer unit and household are used interchangeably in the Spending chapter of this book, although consumer units are somewhat different from the Census Bureau's households. Consumer units are all related members of a household, or financially independent members of a household. A household may include more than one consumer unit.

Current Population Survey A nationally representative survey of the civilian noninstitutional population aged 15 or older. It is taken monthly by the Census Bureau for the Bureau of Labor Statistics, collecting information from more than 50,000 households on employment and unemployment. In March of each year, the survey includes the Annual Social and Economic Supplement (formerly called the Annual

Demographic Survey), which is the source of most national data on the characteristics of Americans, such as educational attainment, living arrangements, and incomes.

disability The National Health Interview Survey estimates the number of people aged 18 or older who have difficulty in physical functioning, probing whether respondents could perform nine activities by themselves without using special equipment. The categories are walking a quarter mile; standing for two hours; sitting for two hours; walking up ten steps without resting; stooping, bending, kneeling; reaching over one's head; grasping or handling small objects; carrying a ten-pound object; and pushing/pulling a large object. Adults who reported that any of these activities was very difficult or they could not do it at all were defined as having physical difficulties.

dual-earner couple A married couple in which both the husband and wife are in the labor force.

earnings A type of income, earnings is the amount of money a person receives from his or her job. *See also* Income.

employed All civilians who did any work as a paid employee or farmer/self-employed worker, or who worked 15 hours or more as an unpaid farm worker or in a family-owned business, during the reference period. All those who have jobs but who are temporarily absent from their jobs due to illness, bad weather, vacation, labor management dispute, or personal reasons are considered employed.

expenditure The transaction cost including excise and sales taxes of goods and services acquired during the survey period. The full cost of each purchase is recorded even though full payment may not have been made at the date of purchase. Average expenditure figures may be artificially low for infrequently purchased items such as cars because figures are calculated using all consumer units within a demographic segment rather than just purchasers. Expenditure estimates include money spent on gifts for others.

family A group of two or more people (one of whom is the householder) related by birth, marriage, or adoption and living in the same household.

family household A household maintained by a householder who lives with one or more people related to him or her by blood, marriage, or adoption.

female/male householder A woman or man who maintains a household without a spouse present. May head family or nonfamily households.

foreign-born population People who are not U.S. citizens at birth.

full-time employment Thirty-five or more hours of work per week during a majority of the weeks worked.

full-time, year-round Fifty or more weeks of full-time employment during the previous calendar year.

General Social Survey A biennial survey of the attitudes of Americans taken by the University of Chicago's National Opinion Research Center, which conducts the GSS through face-to-face interviews with an independently drawn, representative sample of 1,500 to 3,000 noninstitutionalized people aged 18 or older who live in the United States.

generation X U.S. residents born between 1965 and 1976, also known as the baby-bust generation.

Hispanic Because Hispanic is an ethnic origin rather than a race, Hispanics may be of any race. While most Hispanics are white, there are black, Asian, American Indian, and even Native Hawaiian Hispanics.

household All the persons who occupy a housing unit. A household includes the related family members and all the unrelated persons, if any, such as lodgers, foster children, wards, or employees who share the housing unit. A person living alone is counted as a household. A group of unrelated people who share a housing unit as roommates or unmarried partners is also counted as a household. Households do not include group quarters such as college dormitories, prisons, or nursing homes.

household, race/ethnicity of Households are categorized according to the race or ethnicity of the householder only.

householder The person (or one of the persons) in whose name the housing unit is owned or rented or, if there is no such person, any adult member. With married couples, the householder may be either the husband or wife. The householder is the reference person for the household.

householder, age of Used to categorize households into age groups such as those used in this book. Married couples, for example, are classified according to the age of either the husband or wife, depending on which one identified him or herself as the householder.

housing unit A house, an apartment, a group of rooms, or a single room occupied or intended for occupancy as separate living quarters. Separate living quarters are those in which the occupants do not live and eat with any other persons in the structure and that have direct access from the outside of the building or through a common hall that is used or intended for use by the occupants of another unit or by the general public. The occupants may be a single family, one person living alone, two or more families living together, or any other group of related or unrelated persons who share living arrangements.

Housing Vacancy Survey A supplement to the Current Population Survey, providing quarterly and annual data on rental and homeowner vacancy rates, characteristics of units available for occupancy, and homeownership rates by age, household type, region, state, and metropolitan area. The Current Population Survey sample includes 51,000 occupied housing units and 9,000 vacant units.

housing value The respondent's estimate of how much his or her house and lot would sell for if it were for sale.

iGeneration U.S. residents born in 1995 or later.

immigration The relatively permanent movement (change of residence) of people into the country of reference.

in-migration The relatively permanent movement (change of residence) of people into a subnational geographic entity, such as a region, division, state, metropolitan area, or county.

income Money received in the preceding calendar year by each person aged 15 or older from each of the following sources: (1) earnings from longest job (or self-employment); (2) earnings from jobs other than longest job; (3) unemployment compensation; (4) workers' compensation; (5) Social Security; (6) Supplemental Security income; (7) public assistance; (8) veterans' payments; (9) survivor benefits; (10) disability benefits; (11) retirement pensions; (12) interest; (13) dividends; (14) rents and royalties or estates and trusts; (15) educational assistance; (16) alimony; (17) child support; (18) financial assistance from outside the household, and other periodic income. Income is reported in several ways in this book. Household income is the combined income of all household members. Income of persons is all income accruing to a person from all sources. Earnings are the money a person receives from his or her job.

industry The industry in which a person worked longest in the preceding calendar year.

job tenure The length of time a person has been employed continuously by the same employer.

labor force Includes both the employed and the unemployed (people who are looking for work). People are counted as in the labor force if they were working or looking for work during the reference week in which the Census Bureau fields the Current Population Survey. The labor force tables in this book show the civilian labor force only.

labor force participation rate The percent of the civilian noninstitutional population that is in the civilian labor force, which includes both the employed and the unemployed.

married couples with or without children under age 18 Married couples with or without own children under age 18 living in the same household. Couples without children under age 18 may be parents of grown children who live elsewhere, or they could be childless couples.

median The amount that divides the population or households into two equal portions: one below and one above the median. Medians can be calculated for income, age, and many other characteristics.

median income The amount that divides the income distribution into two equal groups, half having incomes above the median, half having incomes below the median. The medians for households or families are based on all households or families. The median for persons are based on all persons aged 15 or older with income.

metropolitan statistical area A large population nucleus with adjacent communities having a high degree of social and economic integration with the core. The Office of Management and Budget defines the nation's metropolitan statistical areas. In general, they must include a city or urbanized area with 50,000 or more inhabitants and a total population of 100,000 or more. The county (or counties) that contains the largest city is the "central county" (counties), along with any adjacent counties that are socially and economically integrated with the central county (or counties). In New England, MSAs are defined in terms of cities and towns rather than counties.

millennial generation U.S. residents born between 1977 and 1994.

mobility status People are classified according to their mobility status on the basis of a comparison between their place of residence at the time of the March Current Population Survey and their place of residence in March of the previous year. Nonmovers are people living in the same house at the end of the period as at the beginning of the period. Movers are people living in a different house at the end of the period than at the beginning of the period. Movers from abroad are either citizens or aliens whose place of residence is outside the United States at the beginning of the period, that is, in an outlying area under the jurisdiction of the United States or in a foreign country. The mobility status of children is fully allocated from the mother if she is in the household; otherwise it is allocated from the householder.

National Ambulatory Medical Care Survey An annual survey of visits to nonfederally employed office-based physicians who are primarily engaged in direct patient care. Data are collected from physicians rather than patients, with each physician assigned a one-week reporting period. During the week, the physician or office staff record a systematic random sample of visit characteristics.

National Compensation Survey Conducted by he Bureau of Labor Statistics, this survey examines the incidence and detailed provisions of selected employee benefit plans in small, medium, and large private establishments, and state and local governments. Each year BLS economists visit a representative sample of establishments across the country, asking questions about the establishment, its employees, and their benefits.

National Health and Nutrition Examination Survey A continuous survey of a representative sample of the U.S. civilian noninstitutionalized population. Respondents are interviewed at home about their health and nutrition, and the interview is followed up by a physical examination that measures such things as height and weight in mobile examination centers.

National Health Interview Survey A continuing nationwide sample survey of the civilian noninstitutional population of the U.S. conducted by the Census Bureau for the National Center for Health Statistics. In interviews each year, data are collected from more than 100,000 people about their illnesses, injuries, impairments, chronic and acute conditions, activity limitations, and use of health services.

National Hospital Ambulatory Medical Care Survey Sponsored by the National Center for Health Statistics, it is an annual national probability sample survey of visits to emergency departments and outpatient departments at non-Federal, short stay and general hospitals. Hospital staff collect data from patient records.

National Household Education Survey Sponsored by the National Center for Education Statistics, it provides descriptive data on the educational activities of the U.S. population, including after-school care and adult education. The NHES is a system of telephone surveys of a representative sample of 45,000 to 60,000 households in the U.S.

Native Hawaiian and other Pacific Islander The 2000 census identified this group for the first time as a separate racial category from Asians. In most survey data, however, the population is included with Asians.

net migration Net migration is the result of subtracting out-migration from in-migration for an area. Another way to derive net migration is to subtract natural increase (births minus deaths) from total population change in an area.

nonfamily household A household maintained by a householder who lives alone or who lives with people to whom he or she is not related.

nonfamily householder A householder who lives alone or with nonrelatives.

non-Hispanic People who do not identify themselves as Hispanic are classified as non-Hispanic. Non-Hispanics may be of any race.

non-Hispanic white People who identify their race as white alone and who do not indicate an Hispanic origin.

nonmetropolitan area Counties that are not classified as metropolitan areas.

occupation Occupational classification is based on the kind of work a person did at his or her job during the previous calendar year. If a person changed jobs during the year, the data refer to the occupation of the job held the longest during that year.

occupied housing units A housing unit is classified as occupied if a person or group of people is living in it or if the occupants are only temporarily absent—on vacation, example. By definition, the count of occupied housing units is the same as the count of households.

outside principal cities The portion of a metropolitan county or counties that falls outside of the principal city or cities; generally regarded as the suburbs.

own children Sons and daughters, including stepchildren and adopted children, of the householder. The totals include never-married children living away from home in college dormitories.

owner occupied A housing unit is "owner occupied" if the owner lives in the unit, even if it is mortgaged or not fully paid for. A cooperative or condominium unit is "owner occupied" only if the owner lives in it. All other occupied units are classified as "renter occupied."

population versus participant measures On the time use tables, average time spent doing an activity is shown for either the population as a whole (such as all 25-to-34-year-olds) or only for those participating in an activity in the previous 24-hours, or diary day. Data referring to the population as a whole include every respondent, even those who did not engage in the activity on diary day. This type of calculation allows researchers to see how Americans prioritize the entire range of daily activities, but it results in artificially short amounts of time devoted to activities done infrequently (such as volunteering). Data referring to participant time show only the time spent on specific activities by respondents who reported doing the activity on diary day. They more accurately reflect the amount of time people spend doing specific activities when they do them.

part-time employment Less than 35 hours of work per week in a majority of the weeks worked during the year.

percent change The change (either positive or negative) in a measure that is expressed as a proportion of the starting measure. When median income changes from $20,000 to $25,000, for example, this is a 25 percent increase.

percentage point change The change (either positive or negative) in a value which is already expressed as a percentage. When a labor force participation rate changes from 70 percent of 75 percent, for example, this is a 5 percentage point increase.

poverty level The official income threshold below which families and people are classified as living in poverty. The threshold rises each year with inflation and varies depending on family size and age of householder. For more on poverty thresholds, go to Internet site http://www.census. gov/hhes/www/poverty/data/threshld/index.html

primary activity On the time use tables, primary activity is the main activity a respondent was doing at a specified time.

principal cities The largest cities in a metropolitan area are called the principal cities. The balance of a metropolitan area outside the principal cities is regarded as the "suburbs."

proportion or share The value of a part expressed as a percentage of the whole. If there are 4 million people aged 25 and 3 million of them are white, then the white proportion is 75 percent.

race Race is self-reported and can be defined in three ways. The "race alone" population comprises people who identify themselves as only one race. The "race in combination" population comprises people who identify themselves as more than one race, such as white and black. The "race, alone or in combination" population includes both those who identify themselves as one race and those who identify themselves as more than one race.

regions The four major regions and nine census divisions of the United States are the state groupings as shown below:

Northeast:

—New England: Connecticut, Maine, Massachusetts, New Hampshire, Rhode Island, and Vermont
—Middle Atlantic: New Jersey, New York, and Pennsylvania

Midwest:

—East North Central: Illinois, Indiana, Michigan, Ohio, and Wisconsin
—West North Central: Iowa, Kansas, Minnesota, Missouri, Nebraska, North Dakota, and South Dakota

South:

—South Atlantic: Delaware, District of Columbia, Florida, Georgia, Maryland, North Carolina, South Carolina, Virginia, and West Virginia
—East South Central: Alabama, Kentucky, Mississippi, and Tennessee
—West South Central: Arkansas, Louisiana, Oklahoma, and Texas

West:

—Mountain: Arizona, Colorado, Idaho, Montana, Nevada, New Mexico, Utah, and Wyoming
—Pacific: Alaska, California, Hawaii, Oregon, and Washington

renter occupied *See* Owner Occupied.

Retirement Confidence Survey Sponsored by the Employee Benefit Research Institute (EBRI), the American Savings Education Council (ASEC), and Mathew Greenwald & Associates (Greenwald), it is an annual survey of a nationally representative sample of 1,000 people aged 25 or older. Respondents are asked a core set of questions that have been asked since 1996, measuring attitudes and behavior towards retirement. Additional questions are also asked about current retirement issues.

rounding Percentages are rounded to the nearest tenth of a percent; therefore, the percentages in a distribution do not always add exactly to 100.0 percent. The totals, however, are always shown as 100.0. Moreover, individual figures are rounded to the nearest thousand without being adjusted to group totals, which are independently rounded; percentages are based on the unrounded numbers.

self-employment A person is categorized as self-employed if he or she was self-employed in the job held longest during the reference period. Persons who report self-employment from a second job are excluded, but those who report wage-and-salary income from a second job are included. Unpaid workers in family businesses are excluded. Self-employment statistics include only nonagricultural workers and exclude people who work for themselves in incorporated business.

sex ratio The number of men per 100 women.

suburbs *See* Outside principal city.

Survey of Consumer Finances A triennial survey taken by the Federal Reserve Board. It collects data on the assets, debts, and net worth of American households. For the 2007 survey, the Federal Reserve Board interviewed a representative sample of 4,422 households. To capture the effect of the Great Recession on household wealth, the Federal Reserve re-interviewed in 2009 the households that participated in the 2007 survey.

unemployed Unemployed people are those who, during the survey period, had no employment but were available and looking for work. Those who were laid off from their jobs and were waiting to be recalled are also classified as unemployed.

white The "white" racial category includes many Hispanics (who may be of any race) unless the term "non-Hispanic white" is used.

Bibliography

Bureau of Labor Statistics

Internet site http://www.bls.gov

—2009 Consumer Expenditure Surveys, Internet site http://www.bls.gov/cex/

—2009 American Time Use Survey, Internet site http://www.bls.gov/tus/home.htm

—Employee Tenure, Internet site http://www.bls.gov/news.release/tenure.toc.htm

—Labor Force Statistics from the Current Population Survey, Internet site http://www.bls.gov/cps/tables.htm#empstat

—*Monthly Labor Review*, "Labor Force Projections to 2018: Older Workers Staying More Active," November 2009, Internet site http://www.bls.gov/opub/mlr/2009/11/home.htm

Bureau of the Census

Internet site http://www.census.gov/

—2000 Census, *An Overview: The Asian Population 2000,* 2000 Census Briefs, Internet site http://www.census.gov/population/www/cen2000/briefs.htm

—2000 Census, *An Overview: The Black Population 2000,* 2000 Census Briefs, Internet site http://www.census.gov/population/www/cen2000/briefs.htm

—2000 Census, *An Overview: The Hispanic Population 2000,* 2000 Census Briefs, Internet site http://www.census.gov/population/www/cen2000/briefs.htm

—2007, 2008, and 2009 American Community Survey, Internet site http://factfinder.census.gov/servlet/DatasetMainPageServlet?_program=ACS&_submenuId=&_lang=en&_ts=

—2010 Census, *An Overview: Race and Hispanic Origin and the 2010 Census*, 2010 Census Briefs, Internet site http://2010.census.gov/2010census/data/

—2010 Census Factfinder, Internet site http://factfinder2.census.gov/faces/nav/jsf/pages/index.xhtml

—2010 Census, *State Population Distribution and Change: 2000 to 2010*, 2010 Census Briefs, Internet site http://2010.census.gov/2010census/data/

—American Housing Survey for the United States, Internet site http://www.census.gov/hhes/www/housing/ahs/ahs.html

—America's Families and Living Arrangements, 2010 Current Population Survey Annual Social and Economic Supplement, Internet site http://www.census.gov/population/www/socdemo/hh-fam/cps2010.html

—Families and Living Arrangements, Historical Time Series, Current Population Survey Annual Social and Economic Supplements, Internet site http://www.census.gov/population/www/socdemo/hh-fam.html

—Geographic Mobility: 2008 to 2009, Detailed Tables, Current Population Survey Annual Social and Economic Supplement, Internet site http://www.census.gov/population/www/socdemo/migrate/cps2009.html

—Health Insurance, Internet site http://www.census.gov/hhes/www/cpstables/032010/health/toc.htm

—Historical Income Tables, Current Population Survey Annual Social and Economic Supplements, Internet site http://www.census.gov/hhes/www/income/histinc/histinctb.html
—Historical Poverty Tables, Current Population Survey Annual Social and Economic Supplements, Internet site http://www.census.gov/hhes/www/poverty/histpov/histpovtb.html
—Housing Vacancy Surveys, Internet site http://www.census.gov/hhes/www/housing/hvs/hvs.html
—*Income, Poverty, and Health Insurance Coverage in the United States: 2009,* Current Population Report, P60-238, 2010; Internet site http://www.census.gov/hhes/www/income/data/incpovhlth/2009/index.htm
—National Population Estimate*s,* Internet site http://www.census.gov/popest/national/asrh/
—Number, Timing, and Duration of Marriages and Divorces: 2004, Detailed Tables, Internet site http://www.census.gov/population/www/socdemo/marr-div/2004detailed_tables.html
—School Enrollment—Social and Economic Characteristics of Students: October 2009, detailed tables*,* Internet site http://www.census.gov/population/www/socdemo/school/cps2009.html

Centers for Disease Control and Prevention
Internet site http://www.cdc.gov
—Behavioral Risk Factor Surveillance System, Prevalence Data, Internet site http://apps.nccd.cdc.gov/brfss/
—HIV/AIDS, Internet site http://www.cdc.gov/hiv/surveillance/resources/reports/2008report/table2a.htm

Federal Reserve Board
Internet site http://www.federalreserve.gov/pubs/oss/oss2/scfindex.html
—"Surveying the Aftermath of the Storm: Changes in Family Finances from 2007 to 2009," Appendix tables, Internet site http://www.federalreserve.gov/pubs/oss/oss2/2009p/scf2009phome.html

National Center for Education Statistics
Internet site http://nces.ed.gov
—Digest of Education Statistics: 2010, Internet site http://nces.ed.gov/programs/digest/
—Projections of Education Statistics to 2019, Internet site http://nces.ed.gov/programs/projections/projections2019/tables.asp

National Center for Health Statistics
Internet site http://www.cdc.gov/nchs
—*Anthropometric Reference Data for Children and Adults: United States, 2003–2006,* National Health Statistics Reports, Number 10, 2008, Internet site http://www.cdc.gov/nchs/products/pubs/pubd/nhsr/nhsr.htm
—*Births: Preliminary Data for 2009*, National Vital Statistics Reports, Vol. 59, No. 3, 2010, Internet site http://www.cdc.gov/nchs/births.htm
—*Deaths: Preliminary Data for 2009*, National Vital Statistics Reports, Vol. 59, No. 4, 2011, Internet site http://www.cdc.gov/nchs/deaths.htm

—Health, United States, 2010, Internet site http://www.cdc.gov/nchs/hus.htm

—Summary Health Statistics for U.S. Adults: National Health Interview Survey, 2009, Series 10, No. 249, 2010, Internet site http://www.cdc.gov/nchs/nhis.htm

—Summary Health Statistics for U.S. Children: National Health Interview Survey, 2009, Series 10, No. 247, 2010, Internet site http://www.cdc.gov/nchs/nhis.htm

—Summary Health Statistics for the U.S. Population: National Health Interview Survey, 2009, Series 10, No. 248, 2010, Internet site http://www.cdc.gov/nchs/nhis.htm

—United States Life Tables by Hispanic Origin, Vital and Health Statistics, Series 2, No. 152, 2010, Internet site http://www.cdc.gov/nchs/deaths.htm

Survey Documentation and Analysis, Computer-assisted Survey Methods Program, University of California, Berkeley

Internet site http://sda.berkeley.edu/

—General Social Surveys, 1972-2010 Cumulative Data Files, Internet site http://sda .berkeley.edu/cgi-bin/hsda?harcsda+gss10

Index

drinking, 68–69
drugs, prescription
    children taking, 82, 84
    spending on, 247
dual-earner couples, 166, 168

earners, 166–167
earnings
    by educational attainment, 135–137
    by sex, 135–137
    by union representation, 169–170
    in retirement, 282–283
eating and drinking, time spent, 258–271
economy versus environment, 15, 17
education
    loans, 280–281
    spending on, 225, 228, 231, 234, 251
    time spent, 258–271
educational attainment
    by age, 42, 44–46
    by sex, 45–46, 135–137
    comparison with total, 42–43
    earnings by, 135–137
    household income by, 120, 124
    of labor force, 135–137, 162–163
employment as reason for moving, 115
employment status. See Labor force.
entertainment, spending on, 225, 228, 231, 234, 239–240
environment versus economy, 15, 17
euthanasia, attitude toward, 38, 40
evolution, attitude toward, 28–29

families, female-headed. See also Families, male-headed
    and Families, married-couple.
    by age, 187–188
    homeownership of, 97–99
    in poverty, 138, 142–143
    income of, 120–121, 123
    share of total, 178, 186
    with children, 178, 183, 186–188
families, male-headed. See also Families, female-headed
    and Families, married-couple.
    by age, 187–188
    homeownership of, 97–99
    in poverty, 138, 142–143
    income of, 120–121, 123
    share of total, 178, 186
    with children, 178, 186–188
families, married-couple. See also Families, female-
    headed and Families, male-headed.
    by age, 187–188
    dual-earner, 166, 168
    homeownership of, 97–99
    in poverty, 9, 138, 142–143
    income of, 7, 120–121, 123
    share of total, 178, 186
    with children, 178, 183, 186–188
family
    as reason for moving, 115
    as source of news, 36
    income relative to average, 18–19

females. See also Children and Single-person households.
    births, 72–76
    earnings of, 135, 137
    educational attainment, 45–46
    in poverty, 138, 141
    income of, 129, 131, 133–134
    labor force, 146–151, 162, 164–165, 169–170,
        172–174
    life expectancy, 87
    living arrangements, 190
    marital status, 191, 193–195
    population, 203, 206
    school enrollment, 49
    time use of, 258, 261–262, 265–267, 270–271
    weight status, 70–71
finances, satisfaction with, 18, 20
financial products and services, spending on, 225, 228,
    231, 234, 241–242
fireplace, in home, 100, 102
flood zone, percent living in, 105
food preparation and clean–up, time spent, 258–271
food, spending on, 223, 226, 229, 232, 244–246, 252
footwear, spending on, 224, 227, 230, 233, 238
full-time workers
    earnings of, 135–137
    income of, 129–134
    percent of labor force, 130–134, 162, 164
furniture, spending on, 224, 227, 230, 233, 249–250

garage, in housing unit with, 100, 102
gated communities, percent living in, 103–104
gasoline, spending on, 224, 227, 230, 233, 255
gay marriage, attitude toward, 32, 34
geographic mobility
    by age, 113–114
    by type of move, 112, 114
    reason for, 112, 115
    share of total, 112–113
    since age 16, 15–16
gifts for people in other households, spending on, 225,
    228, 231, 234, 243
graduates
    college, 59–64
    high school, 47, 52
groceries, spending on 223, 226, 229, 232, 244–246
grocery store in neighborhood, 107
grooming, time spent, 258–271
gun control, attitude toward, 38–39

happiness, 12–13
happiness of marriage, 12–13
headaches, 82–83
health care
    government's role, 24, 27
    spending on, 224, 227, 230, 233, 247
health care visits, 82, 84
health conditions. See also AIDS.
    of adults, 82–83
    of children, 82, 84
    share of total, 82–84
health insurance
    coverage by age, 77–81
    coverage by type, 77, 79–81

time use of, 258, 260, 262, 264, 266–267, 269, 271
weight status, 70–71
malignant neoplasms. *See* Cancer.
marital history, 191, 195
marital status
births by, 9, 72–73
by age, 191, 193–195
by sex, 191, 193–195
living arrangements of children by parent, 183, 189
share of total, 192
married, 191–195
Medicaid coverage, 77, 81
Medicare coverage, 77, 81
medical care, government's role, 24, 27
medicine, degrees earned, 59, 64
metropolitan areas, population of, 207, 213–220
middle class, 18–19
Midwest. *See* Region.
minimum wage workers, 169–170
mobile homes, percent living in, 101
mobility, geographic
by age, 113–114
by type of move, 112, 114
reason for, 112, 115
share of total, 112–113
since age 16, 15–16
moderate political leanings, 36
mortgage
debt, 280–281
interest, spending on 223, 226, 229, 232, 253
Moslem, 30
mutual funds, as financial asset, 276–277

neighborhood
attitude toward, 109, 111
characteristics, 103–108
problems, 103, 106
reason for choosing, 115
net worth, 274–275
never-married, 191–195
newspapers, as source of news, 35–36
Northeast. *See* Region.

occupation, 152–160
optometry, degrees earned, 64
overweight. *See* Weight status.

park, percent living near, 103–104
part-time workers, 162, 164–165
patio, housing units with, 100, 102
pension income, 282–283
pensions, spending on, 225, 228, 231, 234, 241
personal care, spending on, 225, 228, 231, 234, 251
pets, spending on, 240
pharmacy, degrees earned, 64
podiatry, degrees earned, 64
police protection, attitude toward, 108
political attitudes, 35–37
population
by age, 203–206
by metropolitan area, 207, 213–220
by race and Hispanic origin, 5, 198–202
by region, 6, 207–208

by sex, 203, 206
by state, 6, 207, 209–212
porch, houses with, 100, 102
poverty
by age, 138, 140–141
by sex, 138, 141
families in, 9, 138, 142–143
people in, 9, 138–141
share of total, 138–139
premarital sex, attitude toward, 32–33
prescription drugs
children taking, 82, 84
spending on, 247
private enterprise, attitude toward, 15, 17
projections
of high school graduates, 47, 52
of labor force, 172–174
Protestant, 28, 30
public transportation
access in neighborhood, 103, 107
commuting by, 107, 169, 171
spending on, 224, 227, 230, 233, 256

racial identification, 5, 198–202
radio, as source of news, 36
reading
spending on, 225, 228, 231, 234, 251
time spent, 258–271
region
homeowners by, 94–96
household income by, 120, 125
population by, 6, 207–208
renters by, 94, 96
religious activities, time spent, 10, 258–271
religious beliefs, 28, 30–31
rent, spending on 223, 226, 229, 232, 253
renters
access to public transportation, 103, 107
attitude toward housing unit, 109, 111
attitude toward neighborhood, 109, 111
by age, 92–93
by household type, 99
by region, 94, 96
characteristics of housing, 100–102
characteristics of neighborhood, 103–108
satisfaction with police protection, 103, 108
satisfaction with public schools, 103, 107
satisfaction with shopping, 103, 107
share of total, 92, 94, 96, 99
Republican political party, 35, 37
respiratory disease
as cause of death, 86–87
as health condition, 83
restaurants, spending on 223, 226, 229, 232, 252
retirement
accounts, as financial asset, 276–277
income, 282–283
rooms, number in housing unit, 102

school enrollment. *See also* College enrollment.
by age, 47–49
by sex, 49
by state, 47, 50–51
share of total, 47–48, 50–51